Cambridge on the Charles

Cambridge on the Charles

by

ALAN SEABURG

THOMAS DAHILL

CAROL ROSE

THE ANNE MINIVER PRESS
CAMBRIDGE, MA
2001

Library of Congress Control Number: 2001126131
ISBN: 0-9625794-9-1

Printed in the United States of America
First printing, 2001

This book has been produced on a Macintosh PowerBook G3 using the software applications QuarkXPress and Adobe Photoshop.
Text composed in Minion and Gill Sans.
Print coordination by Daniel J. Griffin, Andover Content Group
Printed by Eagle Offset Printing, Inc., Haverhill, MA.
The paper is Exact Natural Opaque Text.
Binding by Acme Bookbinding, Boston, MA.

Contents

CHAPTER ONE

Cambridge on the Charles   1

CHAPTER TWO

Cambridge the Town   11

CHAPTER THREE

Cambridge the City   31

CHAPTER FOUR

Cambridge Cares for Its Family   65

CHAPTER FIVE

Cambridge Works   95

CHAPTER SIX

Cambridge Educates Its Community   129

CHAPTER SEVEN

Cambridge Educates the World   155

CHAPTER EIGHT

Cambridge Worships   191

List of Illustrations

CHAPTER FOUR

CHAPTER FIVE

CHAPTER SIX

Acknowledgments

Works such as this are not possible without the help and assistance of many people. We are happy to be able to acknowledge our indebtedness to them.

First we thank the hard-working and friendly staffs of the following libraries: the Andover-Harvard Theological Library and especially Donna Maguire, Frances O'Donnell its Curator of Manuscripts and Archives, and Louise Johnson; the Harvard University Library and especially Kenneth E. Carpenter; the Harvard University Archives; the Harvard University Theatre Collection; Radcliffe College; Hilles Library and especially Stephen Love; the Cambridge Public Library; the New York Public Library; the Wellesley, Ma. Free Library; the Ithaca College Library; the Francis A. Countway Library of Medicine; and the Smithsonian Institution Libraries.

Next, and with much pleasure, we thank these individuals who graciously shared their time and talents with us: Joan Wilson Andrews; Ethan Beeler, Supervisory Park Ranger, Bunker Hill Monument; Carolyn and Bob Bell; W. J. Blessington; the Rev. Dr. Janet H. Bowering; Cynthis F. Brown; Evangelist Darnley Brown; Winifred and Robert Campbell; Dr. Ernest and Dr. Beverly Cassara; Cassiopeia; Larry Cohen, Editor-in-Chief, MIT Press; Lorna Condon and Jessica M. Parr, Society for the Preservation of New England Antiquities; Kathryn Downing; Timothy Driscoll; Archie Epps; Elizabeth Falsey; Elvida Fanfa; William B. Finch; Daniel J. Griffin; Maria Grossmann; M. Cherie Haitz, Director, Tartakoff Health Sciences Library; the office staff of Holy Trinity Armenian Apostolic Church; Allan Jones, the Athenaeum Group; Pallas C. Lombardi, Executive Director, Cambridge Arts Council; Dr. Eugene C. McAfee, Allston Burr Senior Tudor, Lowell House; David and Anne Miniver; Suzanne Morgan whose design for our book on the Middlesex Canal, *The Incredible Ditch*, inspired our approach for this book; Captain Oliver; Kit Rawlins, Cambridge Historical Commission; Sammantha the Panther; Connie Scribner; Ann and Bill Thomas; Jacqueline A. Tynes, Cambridge College; Herb Vetter; Donald York, Archivist/Analyst, Cambridge Public Library; the Rev. Lawrence Ward; and Hafthor Yngvason, Director of Public Art, Cambridge Arts Council.

Finally, there were seven individuals who provided special and essential help to the project, They are, in alphabetical order, Roxanne Coombs, Reference Librarian in charge of the Cambridge Room and Exhibit Coordinator, Cambridge Public Library; John Hurley, Director of Information/Archivist, Unitarian Universalist Association, Boston; Gloria J. Korsman, Public Services Librarian, Andover-Havard Theological Library; Daniel J. McCarron, University Printer, Harvard Printing and Publication Services; Charles Sullivan, Executive Director, Cambridge Historical Commission and Editor, Cambridge Historical Society; P. A. M. Taylor, Professor of American History, Emeritus, University of Hull, England; and Conrad Wright, Professor of American Church History, Emeritus, Harvard Divinity School. Somehow just printing their

Roxanne Coombs

Daniel J. McCarron

P. A. M. Taylor

John Hurley

Gloria J. Korsman

Conrad Wright

names and titles did not quite seem adequate to us, and so we include here their photographs. As a result, you can see, that there are real faces—real human beings—attached to the names in our list. (For Sullivan see page 152.)

Every effort has been made to trace the ownership of any copyrighted material used in this book. If any infringements have been inadvertently made, apologies are hereby tendered, and the authors will be happy upon due notification to correct such omissions in future editions of this work. Sincere thanks are due to the following publishers, agents, libraries, societies, or individuals holding copyrights in the selection/illustrations specified, for permission to use them in this book. The Rev. Dr. Janet H. Bowering for the photograph of Kennedy biscuits; the Cambridge Arts Council for four pieces of public art commissioned by the City of Cambridge through the Cambridge Arts Council's Public Art Program; the Cambridge Historical Commission for the photograph of the replica of the hoofprint left by Dawes' horse, and the 1830 and the 1877 maps of Cambridge; the Cambridge Public Library for two prints from the Cambridge Memorial Room ("View of the New Athenaeum" and Bartlett's "View of the Cemetery of Mt. Auburn"); the Community Newspaper Company for the photograph of Carl and Alan Seaburg; David Fichter for his mural "The Potluck"; Harley P. Holden and the Harvard University Archives for the Samuel Farrar perspective view of Christ Church; Claire Moss for the 1896 watercolor of the First Parish by Mary Winlock; the Mount Auburn Hospital for the aerial view of the hospital circa 1940; the Society for the Preservation of New England Antiquities for "Two Churches and Graveyard" by E. S. B.; the National Park Service, Charlestown Navy Yard, for the image from their diorama at the Boston National Historical Park; and Conrad Wright for the reproduction of his hand-colored copy of the drawing by Eliza Susan Quincy of the 1836 procession of Harvard alumni.

We conclude with two comments. The first is a warning Conrad Wright made to us after reading the first draft of the book: "But so far as historical accuracy goes, to be approximately right is not good enough. Mistakes in print spread like viruses, and we never catch up to them. They are the bane of academic historians—who, to be sure, can be as guilty as anyone." Finally, Dr. P. A. M. Taylor, after completing a most extensive bit of proof reading of the entire manuscript, wrote at the end of his list of necessary corrections to the text: "I acknowledge the help of Highland Park whisky in the preparation of this paper."

Alan Seaburg
Thomas Dahill
Carol Rose

For My Brother

Carl and I were born in Medford, Massachusetts, where our mother and father, Eva and Henry, a housewife and an assistant to the vice president for sales of a Boston wholesale coal and coke firm, had settled after their marriage in 1921. Our grandparents were ordinary working people—laundress, housewife, laborer, waiter, and tailor—who had immigrated in the 1880's and the early 1890's to Boston from Sweden, England, and Prince Edward Island.

Both of us were educated in Medford, first in the public schools and then at Tufts University. Here Carl majored in history, music, and religion; I in literature and religion. He received his B.A. in 1945 and his B.D. in 1947; I received mine in 1954 and 1957.

We were both ordained into the Unitarian Universalist ministry. Carl went on to serve churches in North Montpelier, Vermont; East Boston, Massachusetts;Norway, Maine; then, from 1971 until his retirement in 1985, he was Director of Information and Archivist for the Unitarian Universalist Association in Boston. My working life, after serving a Boston church, was as Curator of Manuscripts and Archivist at the Harvard Divinity School. During almost all of these decades we lived in Medford, only a few streets away from one other.

Associated with his ministry were the religious anthologies he edited as well as the hymns he com-

Carl and Alan. *(Courtesy of the Community Newspaper Company.)*

posed, several of which are in the current Unitarian Universalist hymnbook, *Singing the Living Tradition.* One of the hymns, "Be That Guide," was originally written for my ordination. His most familiar, "Rank By Rank Again We Stand," proclaims "Though the path be hard and long, / Still we strive in expectation, / Join we now their ageless song, / One with them in aspiration."

His anthologies, which were immensely popular, include *Great Occasions: Readings for the Celebration of Birth, Coming-of-Age, Marriage, and Death; Celebrating Christmas; The Communion Book; and Celebrating Spring and Easter* (edited with his friend Mark Harris). The latter anthology was finished just before his death in 1998, and I published it for him through my small press. All the proceeds went to the scholarship in his name established by the family at the Meadville/Lombard Theological School in Chicago.

In 1990 he gave the Minns Lectures—published as *Inventing a Ministry*—at Harvard Divinity School. Their focus was the life of his friend, Charles Vickery, who was a gay Unitarian Universalist minister when one did not come out of the closet. He was also a field worker for the Universalist Service Committee, rescuing displaced young people in postwar Germany and later was in charge of volunteer programs for the Unitarian Universalist Service Committee. Carl's point was that we each make our own practical ministry.

The Meadville/Lombard Theological School, a Unitarian Universalist institution, gave Carl in 1991 the honorary Doctor of Divinity degree. It was in recognition of his dedication "to that greater fellowship of liberal religion that unites many people around the globe" and for his anthologies "that continue to be consulted on a daily basis by hundreds of our colleagues and parishioners."

While Carl never married, he did have a strong and effective family and extended family. His attention to them all is exemplified by his more than thirty years of daily care for Aunt Peachie—the matriarch of our family—who lived the last of her life with the pain of arthritis and in blindness. He got her meals, did her washing, and made sure she always had "talking" books at hand. He also opened their house to his friends and visiting ministers which gave her a life far beyond what she could have had alone. Amazingly, she soon

charmed all who came to the house. Here also, for Carl was the family chef, we celebrated birthdays, Thanksgiving, and Christmas.

For Aunt Peachie, however, living with Carl had one problem: his library of 12,000 books, many of them in his study above her chair in the living room. She worried for decades that the house was sinking and that one day the books would suddenly come to visit her. They never did, yet that library was available to all of us and covered many fields of human knowledge, especially Western history, English and French literature, twentieth century American and European poetry, art, modern scientific studies, philosophy, psychology, and, of course, religion. Within these broad categories he had several extensive collections on individuals—John Keats, Andre Gide, John Dewey—and on subjects—Boston history and gender issues—that particularly related to his ongoing writing projects. His was the best and most useful personal library I ever encountered, and just as vital, he had a knack of introducing me to books that made my mind and abilities act more effectively.

Lastly, it was Carl who discovered our "other" home, up a dirt road, next to Roaring Brook and Pulpit Mountain, in Green River, Vermont. Here he had a small log cabin and my family a simple elderly farm house. The summers we all worked and lived here are summers wondrous and sweet, filled with the juice of the blackberries we picked each August to make blackberry slump.

Then there were his books on history. They are what will survive the knowledge of his daily activities and thoughts.

The first was *Boston Observed.* It is a popular and lavishly illustrated history of Boston, dedicated to his immigrant grandparents. Its focus is not the upper classes and a few favored sections of the city, but a literary and broad-gauged approach to the whole of Greater Boston, and its vibrant and colorful inhabitants. Next was the *Merchant Prince of Boston,* a biography of Thomas Handasyd Perkins, which he wrote with Stanley Paterson, his friend since the second grade. Perkins was one of the community's most successful merchants during the antebellum era. His fleet of ships was active in the China and Dutch East Indies trade. He was also an important philanthropist and Federalist leader. This book was the 26th volume in the Harvard University Studies in Business History.

For the 350th anniversary of the founding of Medford in 1980 he and I wrote *Medford on the Mystic.* Published by the Medford Historical Society, it tells the story, with hundreds of contemporary black and white photographs, of our birth city, which was well known for its nineteenth century shipyards and its clipper ships built for the China trade, for its extensive brickyards, and its world-famous Old Medford Rum.

Then came a profusely illustrated history of Nahant, amusingly entitled *Nahant on the Rocks,* where in the last century many wealthy Bostonians maintained summer houses. This he also wrote with Stanley.

Finally there was *The Incredible Ditch,* our bicentennial history of the Middlesex Canal (1793–1852). The canal, in part the idea of Medford business leaders, ran through the town, as it was then, on its way from Charlestown to Middlesex Village (Lowell) and the Merrimack River. It opened up central New Hampshire to trade with Boston and was the most important of the early major transportation canals in the United States.

There was a world of difference between the way we worked together on the Medford book, which was our first effort at a collaboration, and the canal book. For both projects it was Carl who devised the basic structures and theme development. In Medford he assigned me chapters and later would review my work and revise it as necessary. I did not attempt that for his chapters. In the canal book we followed the same approach but now I had become more confident and so criticized his chapters as he did mine. I remember how surprised he reacted when I literally savaged his first draft of chapter one. He put it aside for a month and then re-wrote it—generally along the line of my suggestions. That was just one of the many times I was proud of him.

At the time of his death he was working on eleven additional books including a long poem—for both of us are poets—dealing with the Lewis and Clark overland expedition to the Pacific Ocean. Other projects dealt with the moral folly of capital punishment and a biographical essay on John Keats, one of our favorite poets. Chief among these unfinished volumes was a study of the Tudors of Boston, especially of Frederic Tudor, popularly called the Ice King because he made his fortune by being the first to transport and sell ice from New England ponds and lakes to Havana, the West Indies, India, and the southern coastal regions of North America. Its publication became another collaboration between us for it was left to me to edit the volume and see to its publication by the Massachusetts Historical Society.

In tribute to his life and accomplishments, therefore, this new history of Cambridge, patterned after our history of Medford, is dedicated to my brother. Our lives and actions were intertwined and bound up for 66 years. If I began with the simple admiration of a younger brother for an older brother, we soon became equals. That was one of the wonderful aspects of the relationship. He once joked that while there were ten years between his birth and that of the "twins," for my sister and I were born minutes apart, we were really triplets. He added that it was unfortunate for mother that Nancy and I were so slow in arriving.

But you know, it is not a bad image for the relationship that we were able to build from our individual independence, humor, common endeavors, shared enthusiasms, differences, and gentleness—especially toward each other. Over the years we came to listen and to teach one another, and that was the best part of Carl and Alan.

Alan Seaburg

An early view of Cambridge and the Charles.

CHAPTER ONE

Cambridge on the Charles

Welcome to Cambridge on the Charles River. One of the earliest of the English visitors to this area was William Wood who published *New England's Prospect* in 1634, based on his experience here between 1629 and 1633. His account of Cambridge pointed out its "fair structures," its "handsome" streets, and its "very rich" citizens with their cattle "of all sorts." Of the Charles River he noted that here it is narrow, tidal, and replete with meadows and marshlands. This is a Cambridge on the Charles which we will never experience first hand for almost four hundred years have changed dramatically both the river and the landscape. Charles M. Sullivan of the Cambridge Historical Commission puts it this way: "The present Lower Basin of the Charles River, from Gerry's Landing in Cambridge to the Charles River Dam, presents an entirely man-made appearance; not a single aspect of the scene is natural.... The natural history and human culture of the tidal, working river that was so important to its surrounding communities has entirely disappeared."

What happened is very similar to the starry sky we see at night. As a result of the light bulb, it has become impossible to see the night sky clearly and as distinctly as did either the First People living in this basin or its first immigrants, the Puritans. It is similar also to the fact that now we can have fresh fruit and vegetables year round where previous generations knew them only seasonally; and so the abundant flavor, the first sweet taste of fresh blueberries long absent from the diet, or apples, peas or lettuce, is now sadly just about inaccessible to us. So be it, but what can we know of the early history of the river and of the land upon which the English built their settlement?

The short answer is that far back in geologic time Cambridge was once a part of the African continent. The Atlantic met the old North American continent's steep underwater edge about thirty miles west of our present city limits. Then something remarkable started to take place: the two continents gradually came together about 380 million years ago, eliminating the old Atlantic as it did so, to form a super continent geologists refer to by the Greek word for "all land," Pangaea or Pangea. But that was not the end of the remarkable.

After a while Pangea broke up, but not in the area which it had earlier come together. The result was that Cambridge was shifted from the new African continent to the new North American continent. The Atlantic as we think we know it started to expand again (and still does about an inch per year) some 180 million years before the present time and so once again came to separate the two continents.

The present Cambridge, then, rests upon 600 million year old Pre-Cambrian sedimentary slate-like or argillite rock—sandstone, mudstone, puddingstone (rounded cobbles and pebbles in sand)—and a bit of lava and volcanic ash. This surface was eventually subject to at least a million years of rough handling by ice from the Northern area of the hemisphere moving forward then melting back over the Massachusetts Bay

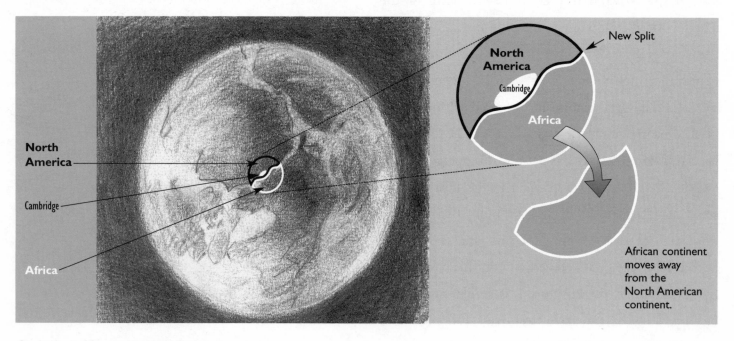

North America

Cambridge

Africa

New Split

North America

Cambridge

Africa

African continent moves away from the North American continent.

Cambridge in Africa and in North America.

region, grinding and crushing to debris everything in its way without mercy. When this process came to its present end about eleven thousand years before our time, it left behind a broad depression we call the Boston Basin.

It also left deposits of sand, gravel, and clay, some of which became the higher lands of the present city. As the ice melted it left bowls of water on the earth's surface; Fresh Pond is such a hollow. The Charles is one of the rivers that drain the Boston Basin.

Nature evolved the sterile work of glaciation into the attractive landscape and the river which greeted the English immigrants of the seventeenth century. Extensive salt marshes and fields ran alongside the river as it flowed through the area we call Cambridge: away from its tidal banks and fine oyster beds were low hills, oak and walnut trees, pines, shrubs and other pleasing plant life, springs, swamps, Alewife Brook and Fresh Pond. Near the bank of the Charles there was also peat which was to prove useful as fuel.

The first living creatures that existed here did so in the sea. Some of the relatives of the earliest inhabitants of our Cambridge can still be viewed—with a magnifying glass: sea fans or bryozoa, for example, are found in the Indiana limestone used to build Widener Library, and on Chestnut Avenue in Mt. Auburn Cemetery it is possible to examine an ammonite, an early relative of the squid family.

The river bears the name of the English monarch Charles I. It runs from Echo Lake in Hopkinton this way and that but never in a straight line, visits several towns and cities along its course to Watertown just above Cambridge, and then by our city to spill its flow into Massachusetts Bay and more or less the Atlantic. The length is about eighty miles, for river mileage varies according to local conditions and a constantly changing environment, rather like some people's age. It was affected by the ocean tides twice a day up as far as Watertown Square. This changed in 1910 when, after years of debate and a temporary dam had been constructed, the Charles River Dam was completed. Then was created by *Homo sapiens* the Charles River Basin we are familiar with today.

That dam was supplemented by a new and better one built by the Army Corps of Engineers between 1974 and 1978. In 1981 the Corps turned its operation over to the Metropolitan District Commission (MDC). Six pumps control the water entering and leaving the Basin, providing a reliable way to manage floods resulting from hurricanes and severe rain storms.

Night and day: that is what the construction of the Charles River Dam and basin has meant to the river's shoreline, to its banks, to the entire natural topography, and later to both the physical and cultural environment of the city. For centuries the salt water and fresh water had met in the river and intermixed, and for centuries at low tide the mud flats and some of the river bottom had appeared regularly. This was the tidal river in its natural state. It had no smell. But as soon as the river was used for human waste it did.

The earliest Cantabrigians.

William Brewster, an ornithologist at Harvard, described this scene as he saw it during the last decades of the nineteenth century. "The tidal reaches of Charles River above the Basin," he wrote, "have changed strikingly in general aspect within my personal recollection. I can remember when they were bordered on both sides, nearly all the way from Cambridgeport to the Watertown Arsenal, by salt or brackish marshes. These must have been practically continuous, originally....

In Cambridgeport the marshes stretched uninterruptedly along the northern shore of the river ... [there was] no obvious defacement or alteration by the hand of man, before 1875. Since then they have been almost completely obliterated...."

The filling in of the Back Bay by 1880 made Boston a far different city but had not eliminated the problems associated with the tidal Charles. Cambridge had also tried to improve the matter by constructing seawalls,

4

Charles Davenport.

by dredging the river, and by putting the mud dug up behind the seawalls. Charles Davenport, who had started in 1832 near today's Central Square to make carriages and railroad cars, began now to buy up quite cheaply the wetlands along the Charles. With others he formed in 1881 the Charles River Embankment Company to build in Cambridge the same kind of homes that then adorned Boston's Back Bay. Davenport was one of the first to have an urban design vision for this Basin, but more importantly, he was the first individual to be in a position to implement his vision. The Charles

River Embankment Company tried to accomplish by private means what the Commonwealth had done in the Back Bay beginning in the 1850s: reclaim the flats, lay out and construct streets and sell house lots. His esplanade actually predated Boston's esplanade; originally, only a seawall separated the Back Bay houses from the water, not a park. Functionally, Cambridge's esplanade was the equivalent of Commonwealth Avenue in Boston.

At this time the agitation of numerous individuals, private and public, who saw the vital need for the river and its shoreline to provide the people an opportunity for better recreation and an enjoyable and healthy landscape, coalesced to create—eventually and after several intermediate steps—in 1919 the Metropolitan District Commission. The mission of the Commission is to plan for the fifty-four cities and towns it represents a shared approach to the larger community's need for good parks, clean water, and a sensible solution to the waste generated by...in the phrase of Honoré de Balzac..."la Comédie Humaine." The key to unlocking the whole matter was, as has been seen, the damming up of the Charles.

Harvard University also made a major contribution to the city throughout the twentieth century as it refined and made more lovely its relationship to the river. One of its graduates, Larz Anderson, gave the Metropolitan Parks Commission, the MDC's predecessor, the money for a new four hundred forty foot long bridge to Harvard's new football stadium on Soldiers

Field, while others gave the University funds to erect the Weld Boathouse in 1907 on the Cambridge side of the Charles. Further donations over a span of several years resulted after 1926 in the land and in the collection of buildings that comprise the Harvard Business School and the John W. Weeks foot bridge. In addition there is its "campus" by the river—President Lowell's Georgian style undergraduate houses. Finally, in the 1970's, Harvard built the Kennedy School of Government. Simultaneously, the many new buildings added to the MIT complex after the Second World War made the lower basin complete. At long last the shoreline of the Charles was beginning to look better than it had for decades.

The bathers.

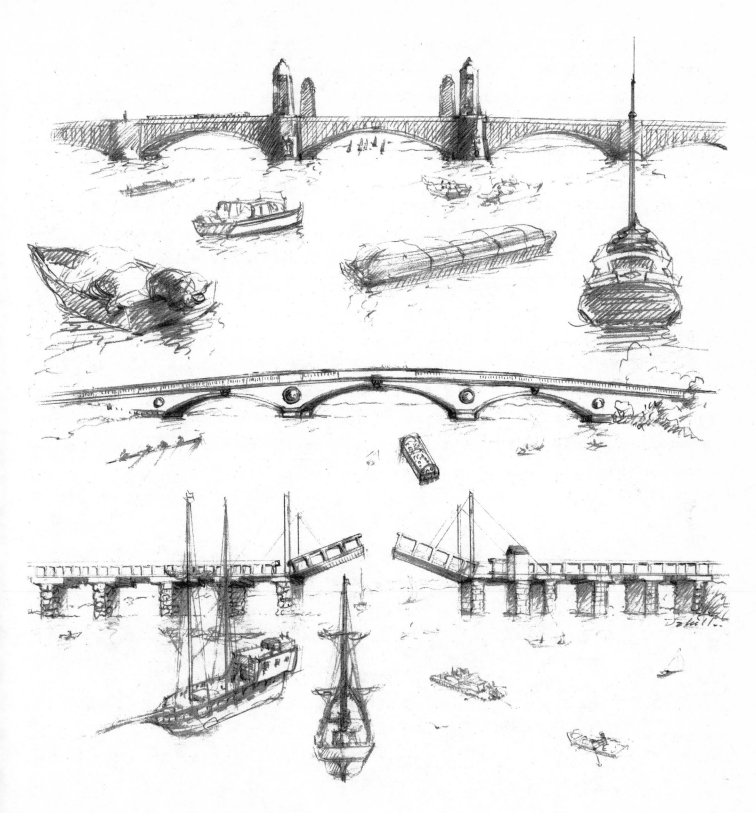

The bridges: the Longfellow, the Weeks, the Great Bridge.

This was, however, just the start of a series of improvements which still continue. Thus in 1963 the Leagues of Woman Voters in the communities beside the river formed a group to study its needs, called the Charles River Valley Group; two years later was born The Charles River Watershed Association. A new Charles River dam, pumping station, three locks, and provision for the passage of fish, was built. Finally, in 1981 a sewage treatment plant was opened at Prison Point in Charlestown. A further improvement has been the attempt to clean up the entire Charles, resulting from an infusion of state and federal grant money especially in the 1970's.

If perfection has not been reached—and it has not been—the river, its banks and shoreline, though radically transformed from the days of the First People and the first British immigrants, has begun again to welcome people in a variety of good ways. Now there is Magazine Beach with its pool; there is the Paul Dudley White Bikepath; there are sail boats, power boats, canoes, row boats, school and university crews with their racing shells all enjoying the river; there are those who can go again to the river to fish; there is the annual Head-of-the-Charles Regatta; and there is an excellent chance that one day those dwelling in Cambridge can again swim in their river.

If private and if public authorities, and if just plain citizens, continue to care for their natural environment, it may well be that this generation and those of the new twenty-first century will discover that they can live in harmony and enjoyment with a river and shoreline as pleasing, as lovely, and as satisfying as that known by the peoples of the seventeenth and previous centuries.

Charles River canoe.

FURTHER READING

BREWSTER, WILLIAM. *The Birds of the Cambridge Region of Massachusetts*. Cambridge, MA: Published by the Club, 1906.

EHRENFRIED, GEORGE. "This Old Land of Cambridge." Adapted from a lecture presented at the Mt. Auburn Branch of the Cambridge Public Library. Cambridge Conservation Commission, April 1991.

ELIOT, CHARLES W. 2ND. "The Charles River Basin," *Cambridge Historical Society Proceedings*, 39 (1961–1963) 23–38.

EMMET, ALAN. *Cambridge, Massachusetts: The Changing of a Landscape*. Department of Landscape Architecture, Harvard University, 1978.

HALL, MAX. *The Charles: The People's River*. Boston: Godine, 1986.

MCADOW, RON. *The Charles River: Exploring Nature and History on Foot and by Canoe*. Marlborough, MA: Bliss, 1992.

MARCHIONE, WILLIAM P. *The Charles: A River Transformed*. Dover, NH: Arcadia, 1998.

SANDERS, STEWART. *An Alewife Area Ecology Guide*. ed. J. M. Connor. Cambridge, MA: Mystic River Watershed Association, 1994.

TOUGIAS, MICHAEL. *Exploring the Hidden Charles: A Guide to Outdoor Activities on Boston's Celebrated River*. Boston: Appalachian Mountain Club Books, 1997.

WILKIE, RICHARD W. AND JACK TAGER, EDS. *Historical Atlas of Massachusetts*. Amherst: University of Massachusetts Press, 1991.

WOOD, WILLIAM. *New England's Prospect*. Ed. by Alden T. Vaughan. Amherst: University of Massachusetts, 1977.

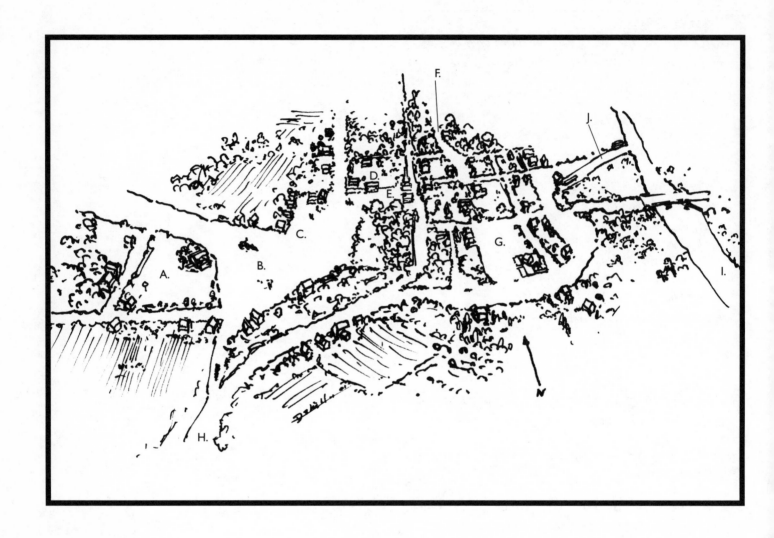

Seventeenth century Cambridge (after a hand drawn map.): (A.) The Square, (B.) The Common, (C.) The Pound, (D.) The Coledge (College), (E.) The Town House, (F.) The Way to the Neck, (G.) The Market Place, (H.) The Way to Watertown, (I.) Cambridge River, and (J.) The Creek.

CHAPTER TWO

Cambridge the Town

People had been living in the great bay of Massachusetts for centuries and, therefore, when the Pilgrims and then the other colonists arrived in the seventeenth century, they were immigrants to an area with a settled and well defined culture and society. Unfortunately for the resident inhabitants, the newcomers came with a differing set of religious beliefs and political ideas which were supported by a more effective military arsenal than they possessed. As a result, the immigrants, dramatically assisted by the European diseases earlier visitors to these shore had brought with them which killed many of the local people, eventually assumed the rule once possessed by these "First People" of the Bay.

After the Pilgrims founded Plymouth in 1620, the English invasion of coastal Massachusetts occurred rapidly. The most important of the new communities in this decade was Salem (1626): its leadership role, however, was eclipsed when the Massachusetts Bay Company founded Boston on the hilly wooded peninsula where the river to be called the Charles flows into a natural harbor. One hundred years later Boston and its port had 40 wharves, a dozen shipyards, about thirteen thousand inhabitants, and was the largest and most significant of all the British centers established in North America.

Before Boston was started, the colonists had founded Charlestown, Watertown and other towns, as well as Newtowne, which was their first capital. It was in Newtowne that they launched their school of higher learning in 1636. Two years later they gave the town its current name Cambridge, which was after the university from which many of the Puritans had graduated from in England. As the town grew it developed three rather separate sections: Old Cambridge—although this term did not come into use until the 1820s—with its farms, large estates, and the college; Cambridgeport on the northwest bank of the river; and East Cambridge at Lechmere's Point with its swamps and lowlands which were largely not good ground for farming but which in time were to become the town's chief industrial center and after 1916 also the home of the Massachusetts Institute of Technology. Cambridge became a city in 1846.

THE EARLY YEARS

The original plan of the colonists was to make Newtowne their provincial capital, and as a result, several leaders of the colony had agreed to build homes there. In the end only three did: Thomas Dudley, Simon Bradstreet, and the Governor of the colony, John Winthrop (whose house was partially destroyed in a storm and so was never completed.) Nevertheless, the town grew, and by 1631 it could boast of ten dwelling

places and four years later of eighty-six, and while it never became the capital of the colony it did become in 1643 the governmental seat for its county (Middlesex).

This was the way the town appeared about forty years after it had been established. There was the Charles, then marsh land, then the town, then the Burying Ground, then the common grazing land which extended as far as the present Linnaean Street, and around all this the "Pallysadoe"—stakes, willows, and a trench that had been constructed to keep their cattle from roaming and wolves from the cattle. The lanes and streets of the town ran approximately north and south; between these and the common was Watch House Hill (about where the center of Harvard Square is today.) By now Newtowne also had beside the large houses of Dudley, Haynes and Thomas Hooker numerous smaller and plainer houses along with their cow-yards, a meeting house with a bell, a parsonage, a college, a public grammar school, a courthouse and jail, a town spring, and on a creek from the river a wharf and ferry landing. Abiel Holmes provides this census for the town in 1647: there were 135 persons living in 90 houses, 208 cows, 131 oxen, 229 young cattle, 20 horses, 37 sheep, 62 swine, and 58 goats. While his census is helpful in establishing a quick overview of the town, it does contain an error when it seems to show the average household as little more than one person. Of course the persons counted in the census may not have included children, servants, slaves, or women.

When the Great Bridge between the town and

Boston was opened in 1662, it facilitated the journey from the one to the other. Nevertheless, it was 8 miles across the bridge and by way of Roxbury to the neck. Beyond the town and going through the common and then the trees and underbrush was the highway or trail—and it was still the quickest way—to Charlestown; a second highway by the town spring led to Watertown. The area towards Cambridgeport and East Cambridge at this stage was largely uninhabited marshes, meadows, and forest.

The boundaries of the town during its early history were far more extensive than are those of the present city. If it started small with but Thomas Graves' one hundred acres, it soon included many hundreds more; indeed, by the 1640's it was some thirty miles long and stretched northwest from the Charles to Bedford and Billerica. Beside these two communities, Cambridge consisted of much if not all of today's Lexington, Arlington, Newton, Brighton, as well as sections of Belmont and Winchester. As settlers moved into these

Original Cambridge superimposed on today's comsat photograph.

13

areas, however, and gradually developed their own sense of community with their own parish church, the familiar map of Massachusetts as we know it emerged.

The Massachusetts Bay Company was set up as a trading company, run by its stockholders. The charter was drafted on the expectation that the headquarters would be in England. When the settlers took the charter with them, it became the governing instrument of the colony, though not ideally phrased for the purpose. One of the problems was the franchise was restricted to the stockholders, until the decision was made to enlarge it. As a practical way of defining a larger constituency, the franchise was given to persons in full church communion. So that "restriction" was a pragmatic enlargement, not an ideological statement. There are instances, not so uncommon as to be unusual, for persons admitted to full communion not to apply to be made freemen of the colony.

While Oliver Cromwell ruled the homeland as a Puritan state those in Massachusetts had pretty much of a free hand to govern as they saw fit, but when Charles II and royal government were returned to power, things changed. In 1684 the charter was revoked and Sir Edmund Andros was sent over as their governor and in the following century the hated Church of England secured a foothold in Boston itself. Things were never to be the same. It was, then, within this mosaic that local government in Cambridge operated.

When local individual matters became pressing in the various scattered communities of the colony, the inhabitants of each of the towns started to hold regular meetings to deal with them. Cambridge began to do so in 1632 and before very long its local government had evolved into a Board of Selectmen, a Town Surveyor, and a Constable who were charged with the responsibility of carrying out the town's business within the rules and regulations laid out by the general town meetings and the Massachusetts Bay Company.

Initially their functions were very simple ones such as granting land and house-lots, laying out roads, and supporting the poor; gradually the scope of their tasks and duties were to become more complex. It is important to remember that the right to vote during this period rested at first with church members, although at a relatively early date all the inhabitants could vote in local affairs.

What were these early Cambridge folk like and how did they make their living? For most of them their lives were marked by hard work and plain living, rather like the rough-hewn boards that were used to build their dwellings. The majority of the males were involved in farming and cattle raising which included doing their own carpentry and blacksmithing; it was the males also who were the ministers and teachers at the college; the wives and other women folk tended to the children, cooked the meals, made the clothing, weaved, sewed, planted and harvested both the herb and kitchen gardens, and cared for the sick, for contagious diseases were as familiar as the seasons. So was the death of infants and mothers giving birth. Children had their

A young man haying.

games, dolls, hoops and balls, but infant mortality was high for too many of them; however, if they survived to be twenty, their life expectancy was much improved: if they were males it was sixty-six, and if they were females it was fifty-six.

The heart and soul of this early Cambridge town was its Puritan religion. It was a religion without frills: the churches were plain and without the adornments of stained glass windows or statues, lavish high alters or liturgies, fancy Christmas celebrations with expensive gifts, candles, rich food or wild wicked dancing about May poles. What it did have, what it did insist upon, was a church consisting of those whom God had elected to everlasting life, God's visible saints in other words, who were admitted to the Lord's Table and whose children had the right of baptism. Such a church was bound and united by its covenant. Further, for the Puritans God was both sovereign and judge, and those that sinned their God condemned. It was a serious religion seriously taken, and because of Adam's sin individual Puritans watched their thoughts and actions with a hard responsibility.

The first church was formed in 1632 and the first settled ministers in the town were Thomas Hooker and Samuel Stone, and when they came they brought their own congregation with them. Hooker had been preaching in the vicinity of Braintree, England, but William Laud, Bishop of London, and his supporters there, upset with his views, had driven him to Holland. This persecution decided some of his congregation to flee too, but they opted not for Holland but for Massachusetts Bay. Once settled at Mount Wollaston, now Braintree, they invited Hooker to take charge of their church. He agreed but when he reached Boston in 1633 he found they had all moved to Cambridge (which caused its population to jump to five hundred). Hooker and his company did not remain long in Cambridge, however, and once again but for the last time, they moved to Hartford, Connecticut.

There remained now but eleven families who had attended services at Hooker's church after that organization had left town, but that was enough to start afresh which occurred in February, 1636. That fall the Reverend Thomas Shepard, who had just arrived from England, again with his own congregation, was settled at Cambridge as the minister of this new church. He served with great success until his untimely death at 43 in 1649. He was succeeded by Jonathan Mitchell. While it is easy to presume that in a Puritan community all its people must be church members, this was clearly not the case in Cambridge. In the 1660's, for example, only three-fourths of the households in the town contained church members. But that was more than enough for the Puritan church to wield its power in matters religious.

In 1650 the original meetinghouse was replaced by a new one set where the Watch House Hill had previously been located. This structure stood for more than fifty years and was not replaced until 1706. Mitchell's term and those of his two successors were not of long dura-

Reverend Thomas Shepard. (Dahill conceptualization)

tion; indeed, it was only during the long and faithful pastorate of William Brattle (1696–1716/7) that the congregation finally enjoyed the fruits of a peaceful and satisfying ministry.

David Hall in a study of seventeenth-century church and society in Cambridge was able to identify at least six basic "values" descriptive of the life its residents thought fair and reasonable. First, every person or household was entitled to a share of the community's resources (its land, waterways, trees); second, if an individual's share seemed "inadequate," the communi-ty could and did act to address the matter; third, the community felt it essential to "the process of social reproduction" to maintain both minister and school teacher; fourth, the rights of the community carried more weight than the rights of individuals; fifth, "that the generality of households" had the right and duty to decide how the town's resources were distributed; and sixth, that distribution was made "in proportion to household wealth and farm stock." These values illumi-nate clearly the social and political structure which guided those living in early Puritan Cambridge.

THE WAY TO INDEPENDENCE

At the start of the eighteen century the people of Cambridge, now about a thousand, faced different challenges and opportunities than did those of the founding generations. Their town had been well established beside the Charles and the necessary local institutions of government, church, school, and even a college, had been created. Furthermore, the good idea of toleration of other views had begun to take root through the work of their minister William Brattle and other leaders, through the election in 1707 of the liberal John Leverett (The Great Leverett) as president of the college, and through the vote of the Province in 1691 abolishing the requirement of church membership as a necessary prerequisite for the privilege of casting a ballot. Clearly the theocratic experiment in Massachusetts was now in a process of fraying and fading, and the new century was to eventually see Cambridge and the other towns engaged in a very different kind of experiment.

What did the town look like during the first half of this century? The college and the area about it remained its center and by 1750 its outlines, while filled-in with additional houses, buildings, and the rough, dusty, often muddy roads, really didn't look too different than it had in 1700 or even a hundred years earlier. Clearly Cambridge continued to be a small if now thriving and more comfortable farming and college community, and its eastern end was still largely remote and undeveloped. After Spencer Phips bought Graves' Neck to build his own far more elaborate estate he soon thought better of the plan and went on to secure land in a better social location: the area around the college. Land holdings fared better in Cambridgeport, and the Inmans were satisfied with the land they had purchased back of the present city hall.

What changed the climate of the town in the first half of the eighteenth century was the arrival, mostly from the West Indies, of "the Tories," those who accepted royal rule as the right rule for the colonies, who, while never more than ten percent of the population, established in Cambridge a more luxurious way of living than had previously existed. With them came their beautiful estates, fancy furniture and other doodads, pretty dresses and manners, servants and a swirl of social activities and balls heretofore unknown to the first English settlers on this side of the Charles. In time they even brought their own religion, the Church of England, and a little more than fifteen years before the start of the American Revolution erected Christ Church almost in the center of the old town.

These Tories—the Vassals, Inmans, Phipses, Lechmeres to name but a few—earned their living in the port of Boston and their money came out of their service to the king and their mother country, from their mercantile interest and shipping houses, their plantations in the West Indies, and their immoral trading (and possession for their own use as servants and coachmen) of human beings. In a census of 1754 Cambridge is listed as having 56 such individuals legally owned by others. These sources created the funds they used to build in addition to their Boston residences their sumptuous Cambridge estates, just west of the town on the road to Watertown, adorned with mansion houses, lovely lawns, blooming flower gardens, fruit trees, as well as unusual varieties of trees and shrubs from Europe. As they were mostly Tories, eventually this road came quite logically to be called Tory Row.

They chose Cambridge because of its nearness to their Boston offices, its attractive country setting near the Charles, and the fact that the community that made up Tory Row were either related through their families, or by marriage, or as close personal friends. "Never had I chanced upon any such agreeable situation," observed the Baroness de Riedesel in 1777. "Seven families, who were connected by relationship, or lived in great intimacy, had here farms, gardens, and splendid mansions, and not far off orchards; and the buildings were at a quarter of a mile distant from each other. The owners had been in the habit of assembling every afternoon in one or another of these houses, and of diverting themselves with music or dancing, and lived in affluence, in good humour, and without care ..."

If ten percent of the population lived extremely well for several decades of the eighteenth century, the remaining ninety percent, which now included, besides farmers and teachers at the college, tailors, blacksmiths, carpenters, tanners, lawyers and various other tradesmen, for the most part were not so badly off themselves. Certainly they lived in more comfortable dwellings and with more security than did the first inhabitants. Of course, there were several outbreaks of smallpox, one of influenza, and the earthquake of 1744, but such catastrophes were part of the norm in those days.

As for other kinds of community excitement, there was the annual July graduation exercises of the college at their meetinghouse, the building of a new court house in 1707 and a larger replacement for it in 1757, as well as the construction of a new meetinghouse in 1706 and yet again in 1756—the town's third and fourth meetinghouses. In addition there was in 1755 the public hanging at the execution place on the common just south of today's Linnaean Street of two "negroes" for poisoning their "master" (fortunately the last such grotesque public display in the town) and the great fire at the college on the night of 1764 when Harvard Hall burned to the ground. The real excitement of the century, however, was simmering in their thinking and conversation with their neighbors, near and far, and was to lead eventually to revolution.

There is a real question if there had to be a bloody revolution for the colonists to gain their independence from Britain. Her rule and administration of the colonies during the seventeenth century and the early decades of the eighteenth had been rather lenient and laws had often been half-heartedly enforced. In truth, the existing arrangement had benefited both Britain and the colonists. If British administration had not grown more harsh and less flexible during the 1760's it is conceivable that independence could have evolved naturally as it has in other areas controlled by the British government. A series of actions taken by His Majesty's government beginning in 1763, however, resulted in hard stands developing on both sides that effectively blocked the growth of any peaceful resolution of their differing views.

The underlying struggle was really the question and nature of the authority, especially as they related to tax matters, vested in the royal governors appointed by the Crown and the powers held by the representatives elected by the colonists to their individual Assemblies. As regards taxation, the sticking point was not the trade taxes levied by Parliament as much as the taxes required to be paid by the colonists without their approval and consent that went directly into the Royal coffers for support of the home budget. This led directly to the fighting slogan "no taxation without representation."

A series of Acts of Parliament beginning in 1763 banning land settlement beyond the Allegheny Mountains, forbidding the colonies from issuing their own legal-tender, restricting colonial trade in sugar and the imposition of duty on that item, the requirement that they underwrite the cost of the soldiers stationed in North America, and finally the infamous Stamp Act forcing them to purchase stamps for newspapers, play-

ing cards, marriage licenses, and other legal documents, clearly resulted in such actions as the Boston Massacre, the Boston Tea Party, the gathering of the First Continental Congress, and the battles at Lexington and Concord.

THE REVOLUTION IN CAMBRIDGE

It was husky thirty year old William Dawes riding from Boston as fast as he could who just before dawn on the 19th of April 1775 alerted the people of Cambridge that the British were on the march to Lexington and Concord. A group of citizens, black and white, and some of the college students, went off to Concord to help their comrades defend themselves and their military supplies; others helped to tear out the wooden planks on the Great Bridge between Boston and the town when they learned that some of the troops were approaching from that direction. Later, during the fighting that took place when the British were returning to Boston under heavy American musket fire, six Cambridge men were to lose their lives.

After the start of hostilities hundreds of volunteers from all over New England, by May about sixteen thousand of them, flocked to Cambridge ready and prepared for battle with the redcoats; they were housed in the various buildings of the college, in the mansions along Tory Row (whose owners had wisely fled the scene), in Christ Church, and in today's Central Square where General Israel "Old Put" Putnam camped with his men from Connecticut.

They waited for the British to make a move but nothing much happened until June 17th when Gage and his men advanced against Charlestown and the American fortifications on nearby Breed's Hill in what is now known as the Battle of Bunker Hill. They took the victory but at great cost.

Meanwhile, George Washington, who had been appointed by the Continental Congress meeting in Philadelphia as the Commander-in-Chief of the Continental Army, made his way from the Congress to Cambridge to assume charge of this hastily gathered untrained "army"; he did so most simply on July 3rd in Wadsworth House, the home of the president of Harvard. Sadly the appealing romantic myth that he did so under an American elm near Garden and Mason Streets is just that: a myth.

What he accomplished in the next year was amazing: he had to organize his forces, to keep the British locked up in Boston, to secure gun power and cannon for his fortifications, and finally to chase the redcoats from Boston. They, and many of their Tory companions, evacuated the town on March 17, 1776, almost a year after the first shots had been fired in Lexington.

No longer needed locally, Washington and his troops departed for New York leaving behind them a mess—dwelling places devastated by the volunteers who had bunked in them and woods badly damaged because of

WILLIAM DAWES
REPLICA OF HOOFPRINT LEFT
BY HIS HORSE AT
CAMBRIDGE COMMON
MIDNIGHT APRIL 18 = 19, 1775

the need for firewood to keep warm during the bitter winter weather. If the citizens of Cambridge were glad to be rid of the Redcoats, and they were, many of them were just as glad to see the last of their own army. This did not mean, however, that they had lost their zeal and commitment for freedom and the birth of their special nation.

The remaining events of the contest and struggle for independence occurred elsewhere except for an odd little Cambridge footnote when, rather unwillingly, the town quartered for about a year General Burgoyne and the soldiers who had been defeated and captured with him at Saratoga, New York. It having been decided by those in authority to ship them back to England with a pledge not to become engaged again in this war, they were directed to Cambridge until they could be sent home. When this did not occur, they were eventually moved elsewhere. Cambridge was glad to see another army leave the town.

The colonists finally achieved their goal of independence as a result of Cornwallis' surrender at Yorktown and the victory of their ally France over the British in the West Indies; this led to peace negotiations which produced the Treaty of Paris which formally ended the hostilities between the parties. Congress on January 14, 1784, ratified this treaty, and now the patriots had to construct their democratic republic. This proved to be no easy assignment for them as witness the fact that it took them more than eighty years to abolish slavery throughout the new union and almost a century and a half to allow women the right to vote.

Massachusetts, as a result of the American Revolution, had to draft a new state constitution. It did so in 1779 at a constitutional convention held in Cambridge and presided over by John Adams, who had a large part in its composition. The constitution was adopted in 1780 and, although it has been amended over 100 times, it remains the oldest governing constitution in the world. Many of its features were later to influence the shape and content of the Federal constitution.

THE NEW REPUBLIC

What was the situation in Cambridge and what were its future prospects at the start of this new republican venture? First, it's fair to suggest that no one in the town was aware of how dramatically it would grow, especially in the areas to be called Cambridgeport and East Cambridge; nor did anyone suspect that in less than seventy-five years it would no longer be a town but rather a city. Yet that is exactly what happened, and these two developments were to highlight the first decades of Cambridge's history in the new republic. On the surface, however, when the fighting ceased Cambridge seemed much as before, and there was little reason to think life would be much different than it had been. But that appearance, of course, was deceptive.

At the close of the Revolution the town had a little more than sixteen hundred residents; as the nineteenth century approached, its population had increased by only another five hundred persons. Even ten years into the new century it had not changed greatly; but by 1840 it had increased almost three fold to eight thousand four hundred and nine, and five years later it was over twelve thousand. What was as remarkable as this population explosion was the fact that the newcomers were not flocking to Old Cambridge but to the hitherto lightly settled and developed areas of Cambridgeport and East Cambridge.

One might well ask, "What was going on?" With peace between Britain and her former American colonies came a period of economic growth for the new nation, and Cambridge shared in this boom along with the other towns. Further, on the local scene the great mansions and land holdings of Cambridge's pre-revolutionary affluent citizens who, because they had been Tories had been forced to flee the town, had been seized as public property. The state now began to sell them. Their new owners were not interested in living in the town as were the previous ones but only had their eye on the money they could make from their new land purchases. The possibilities of doing just this were greatly increased through a series of bridges now built between Boston and Cambridge. In 1793 the West Boston Bridge (on the site of today's Longfellow Bridge) was opened; next came in 1809 the Canal (Craigie) Bridge; then in 1810 the River Street Bridge; and finally in 1824 the Western Avenue Bridge. Suddenly the local land speculators were playing with a new deck of cards.

As land became more valuable especially in Cambridgeport and East Cambridge where it was held by but a few individuals, and as a direct result of the bridges bringing the "hub of the universe" closer to Cambridge, more people began to be interested in settling in Cambridge. Therefore, house and store lots were laid out and sold. In December 1793 a grocery store opened in what is now Kendall Square and in the following year a tavern was built next to it. Before long there were several such businesses as well as a number of homes. Soon the idea of Cambridgeport as a "port" was in the air. Marshes were drained and filled with gravel, canals were dug, wharves constructed, and brick houses built. In January 1805 Congress designated Cambridgeport as an official port of entry—although only as part of the port of Boston—and this resulted in attracting even more tradesmen and home owners. Today's Massachusetts Avenue and Broadway, Hampshire and Main Streets were becoming realities. Another result of this growth was the need for schools in this part of the town; and also for churches.

The economic boom, however, as such periods of prosperity often do, now went into a tailspin; it was helped in this direction when President Jefferson issued his trade embargo of 1807 forbidding commerce with foreign countries, especially with Britain and France. The new nation and Britain eventually went to war in 1812 over the rights of neutrals on the world's oceans, and this was not a war that enhanced New England trade and businesses. All this meant that Cambridge's newly certified port never got an opportunity to develop and become a port; and so the local land speculators were soon on the run as lot prices sank. But some people's problems and adversity can lead to opportunities for another's dreams and hopes of finding great financial rewards. So it proved in this situation for Mr. Andrew Craigie.

Craigie and his wife were living at this time in what is now known as the Longfellow House and he was very

Andrew Craigie.

much aware of the exciting developments in the town as regards land speculation and that here was to be found ready money for a smart investor. Therefore, beginning in 1795 he started to buy land from Lechmere's Point through to Inman Square—usually however not in his own name. In this manner he was able to acquire more than three hundred acres at a low price. Then he arranged to have a wooden bridge 2,796 feet long and 40 feet wide built (where today's Museum of Science stands) connecting Boston to guess where: Lechmere's Point.

He was not always this skillful or lucky. For some time the town had been considering the laying out of a major new road to start at "Elmwood" which might follow either of two differing routes: it could start at Brattle and Mason Streets which would have brought it almost straight as an arrow to Craigie's Bridge and Lechmere Point or it could go from the present Brattle Square to Cambridgeport and its West Boston Bridge. Craigie obviously favored the first way and those in Cambrideport the latter. After heated debate and twice changing its collective mind, the town finally favored the Cambridgeport route and the road now called Mount Auburn Street was constructed.

Andrew Craigie and his Lechmere Point Corporation bounced right back. He had his desired road (Cambridge Street) laid out which tied Old Cambridge into his bridge at his expense and then talked the town into accepting it. Meanwhile, the sale of his East Cambridge land plots were languishing and he pondered what could be done to make them sell briskly; and he came up with an ingenious solution which favored his business interest.

He had his Lechmere Point Corporation donate to Middlesex County and its Court of Sessions land and also the necessary construction funds for, as we would now say, a state-of-the-art courthouse and jail in East Cambridge. Previously the courthouse had been near the college. The town objected to this plan as did the land speculators of Cambridgeport but to no avail. By 1816 the courthouse which had been built on Third

The 1896 Registery of Deeds and Probate Court, East Cambridge.

Street was ready and was immediately put into use. Amazingly enough, the Lechmere Point Corporation also saw an immediate increase in its land sales.

In the almost four decades since the end of the Revolution a great change had begun to shape the town anew. Up to now, Cambridge had been for many the area around the college, for here was where most of its inhabitants had dwelled and made their living, gone to school and church, and some of the lucky ones to the college and some of those not so fortunate saw the inside of the courthouse. And much more. But now the Cambridge that had been largely undeveloped wilderness and marsh was coming into its own. As a result, there was a period of struggle, competition, and rivalry between the three sections of the town.

Cambridge has sometimes been described as three separate villages or towns at this point in its history, but it was really still the one town, its size of course cut and trimmed over the years from what it had back in the 1630's, but still the one community working hard to come to terms with its growing pains.

It was within this general context then that two

cultural developments occurred that each in their own way altered the religious and social complexion of the town.

The first concerned the First Parish and the First Church which had been established by the Puritans as the "gathered church" of the town—defined by one minister as a "congregation of the faithful called and gathered out of the world by the preaching of the gospel." This company, which consisted of God's Elect, of God's community of Saints in Cambridge, had been for years the only religious institution in the town until the building of Christ Church in 1761. Even then it continued to serve and to represent most of the inhabitants' religious needs and views. But as change is a fact of the universe and life, so it is of human institutions, and slowly it percolated its way through seventeenth and eighteenth century religious life and thinking so that by the early decades of the nineteenth century many of the churches of the standing order in Massachusetts were in conflict in regard to basic religious ideas. The debate was between the Orthodox, those who held to earlier beliefs, and the Liberal Christians, those who expressed a differing interpretation of the shared basic theological questions.

The result was the separation of the Congregational churches of Massachusetts into two divisions, Unitarian and Congregational. In Cambridge the Unitarians were in the majority in the Parish, and they took control of that organization and the meeting house, for the Parish held the title to that structure, while the majority of the members of the Church along with Abiel Holmes, the minister at the time of the breakup, held to doctrinal orthodox ideas and left the meeting house, most reluctantly however for they felt that they were rightly the church of Puritan days. They immediately organized a religious society—The Shepard Congregational Society—and claimed to be the continuing Church. (But legally they were not.)

So the religious unity that had been typical (to some degree) in the religious situation in the towns of the Massachusetts Bay had run its course never to return. A new era of religious pluralism had emerged. In 1834 by popular referendum the voters of Massachusetts made this certain when they passed the eleventh amendment to their state constitution guaranteeing everyone legal religious freedom. As Cambridge's representative in the legislature at that time, the Reverend Thomas Whittemore, put it: "no civil government has a right to compel the citizens to support any system of religion whatsoever."

The second turning point in the history of Cambridge at this period was the building of a town hall in 1832 in Cambridgeport. The choice of this location was quite a logical one: it was central to everyone. Previously town meetings had been held in Old Cambridge in the meeting house and then the court house but it had been clear for some time that larger quarters were necessary. The new Town House as it was called consisted of a large room with two smaller ones at the back of the structure. When Cambridge became

Reverend Lucius Paige.

a city; it continued to be used by the Mayor and the Aldermen until it was destroyed by fire in 1853.

The location of the town offices outside of Old Cambridge, when linked with Andrew Craigie's sleight of hand courthouse ploy, greatly helped to unify the community as one community. As the historian of Cambridge, Lucius Paige, some years later sagely observed, the "sources of mutual jealousy had disappeared, and time had at least partially healed the wounds occasioned by events which were beyond remedy. The new villages had become sufficiently strong to protect their own interests and to secure for themselves a fair and equitable proportion of public conveniences. At the same time, no one section was able to control or oppose the two others; and it does not appear that any desire to do so was cherished...all had a common pride in the reputation of the whole town, and desired the prosperity of all its institutions."

Finally, what was it like to be living in this Cambridge during this period? What was life like for the average citizen? It certainly was different than it had been a hundred years earlier, and while there was still some farming done in Cambridge, the community no longer could be considered a farm town. The college remained as an important factor for the community, but its impact was limited pretty much to Old Cambridge.

The newer inhabitants, still mostly Yankees, now worked as artisans, tradesmen, gardeners, servants, liverymen, and those domiciled in Cambridgeport often worked in Boston; East Cambridge also had folks crossing into the Hub but had people employed in local businesses and on-the-spot industries producing among other goods glass, brushes, furniture, and soap. As farmers regularly drove their cattle and hogs through to Boston, taverns sprang up and prospered as did those in parts of the town such as in North Cambridge near its slaughterhouse and cattle market.

The dwellings in Old Cambridge because of the age of their construction were not in good repair; in addition many had been turned into stores or tenements.

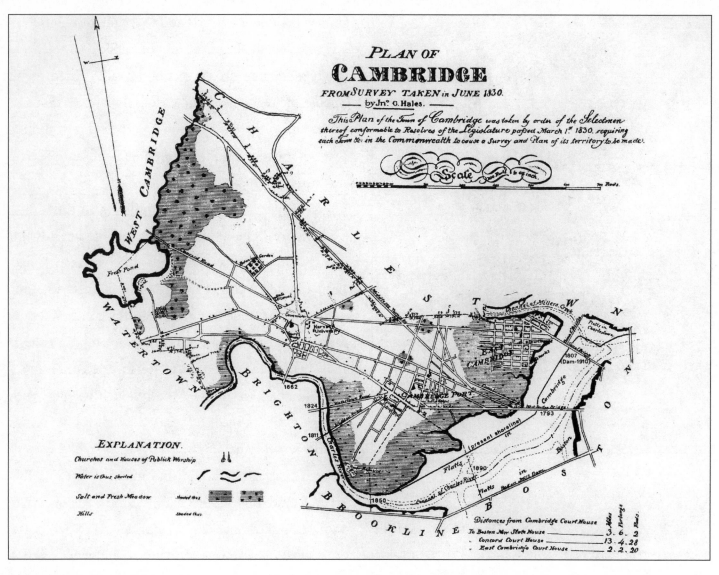

The Hales Survey Map of 1830. *(Courtesy of the Cambridge Historical Commission)*

The buildings in the other section of town were newer and better, and families often lived in either single or two family houses. Without electricity and gas, lighting remained poor and people got their water for washing and drinking from wells, and outhouses and cesspools were the rule. Yet there remained for the inhabitants lots of pleasant activities to take part in and there were still marshlands and woodland to enjoy walking in and wildflowers to gather.

Cambridge was now on the eve of moving from being a town to being a city although no one quite knew that this was going to happen and that it did probably surprised most of the citizens. So what happened? How did it all come about?

FURTHER READING

ARCHER, RICHARD. "New England Mosaic: A Demographic Analysis for the Seventeenth Century." *William and Mary Quarterly,* 47 (Oct. 1990) 477–502.

BEALE, JOSEPH H. "The History of Local Government in Cambridge," *Cambridge Historical Society Proceedings,* 22 (1932–1933) 17–28.

BINFORD, HENRY C. *The First Suburbs: Residential Communities on the Boston Periphery 1815–1860.* Chicago: University of Chicago, 1985.

BURTON, JOHN D. *Puritan Town and Gown: Harvard College and Cambridge, Massachusetts, 1636–1800.* Thesis (Ph.D.), College of William and Mary, 1996.

CHIDSEY, DONALD BARR. *The Siege of Boston.* New York: Crown, 1966.

ELIOT, SAMUEL A. *A History of Cambridge, Massachusetts 1630–1913.* Cambridge, MA: Cambridge Tribune, 1913.

HALL, DAVID. "Church and Society in Seventeenth-Century Cambridge, Massachusetts: An Experimental History." Lecture delivered at Millerville University, PA, November 4, 1998.

HOLMES, ABIEL. *The History of Cambridge.* Boston: Hall, 1801.

LILLIE, RUPERT B. "The Gardens and Homes of the Loyalists," *Cambridge Historical Society Proceedings,* 26 (1940) 49–62.

MCMANIS, DOUGLAS R. *Colonial New England: A Historical Geography.* NY: Oxford, 1975.

MORISON, SAMUEL ELIOT. *The Puritan Pronaos.* NY: New York University Press, 1936.

PAIGE, LUCIUS R. *History of Cambridge, Massachusetts. 1630–1877.* Boston: Houghton, 1877. *Supplement and Index.* Mary Isabella Gozzaldi. 1930.

RIEDESEL, FRIEDERIKE CHARLOTTE LUISE. *Letters and Memoirs Relating to the War of American Independence.* New York: Carvill, 1827.

SUTTON, S. B. *Cambridge Reconsidered: 3 1/2 Centuries on the Charles.* Cambridge, MA: MIT, 1976.

WRIGHT, CONRAD. *Harvard and the First Parish: A 350th-Anniversary Retrospective.* Cambridge, MA: No publisher listed, 1987.

Immigrants sailing to America.

CHAPTER THREE

Cambridge
the
City

"To the Honorable Senate and House of Representatives of the Commonwealth of Massachusetts. The undersigned inhabitants of the westerly part of Cambridge, being that part of the town usually called Old Cambridge, respectfully ... pray that the town of Cambridge may be divided ..." This petition which came from a group of Old Cambridge citizens (among the petitioners were such prominent professors at the Law School as Joseph Story and Simon Greenleaf, leading businessmen such as Jacob Bates and George Coolidge, and the physician Dr. Benjamin Waterhouse) was dated December 15, 1842, and surprised most of the town.

The desire to divide the town was a mix of several factors. Some people in Old Cambridge, for example, felt that the town was spending too much money and that fiscal restraint was essential for the proper economic health of the older community. Along with this group were various real estate promoters and other entrepreneurs who, seeking increased profits for their business endeavors, felt that their golden egg lay more around the College and the northern edge of the town rather than in Cambridgeport, East Cambridge, and some kind of business partnership with Boston and its merchants. Then there were those who felt dissatisfaction with the limits and imperfections in local government which seemed clearly revealed in the vote to enclose the Common, the creation of major town roadways, and the location of the town hall. Finally, many people in Old Cambridge felt a growing fear of the newer (different) people moving into the community. Clearly some of the motivation behind the petition was boldly expressed in a political handbill put out eight years later which asked the question: "Will you permit the clique of Harvard College and Old Cambridge, after their attempts to be set off from the town, to elect all the officers of the city from their own section, and rule with aristocratic sway the municipal affairs of the people?"

The General Court postponed taking any action on the request until it next met, by which time the original petitioners had sent another one. While it still asked that the town be divided, it now asked that their part of the division have the name Old Cambridge. The General Court inquired of the town its opinion and at the town meeting of January 22, 1844, the town said no thank you to both petitions.

At the March town meeting that same year, there began a long struggle by some residents to restructure town government. While this never happened, it did result in a request from several citizens in January 1846 that the Selectmen appoint a committee to look into the possibility of asking the General Court for a City Charter. Meanwhile, a third petition came from some in Old Cambridge to set their section off from the rest of the town. This request and idea was overwhelmingly defeated (246 to 50) at the following town meeting.

Some of those who had wanted to break up the town, of course reserving for themselves the name Cambridge or Old Cambridge, opposed the petition for a City Charter. Once again they were defeated in town meeting, 645 to 224, with support in favor of becoming a city coming from all sections of the town, and so Cambridge became a city. During 1855 two more attempts to divide the city were made but both of them went nowhere.

Many of those living in and about the College who left written remembrances saw their old town quite differently than it actually was—one might say they saw it with rose colored memories and phrases. For James Russell Lowell it was a lovely simple country, nay English, village; Charles Eliot Norton as well felt that Old Cambridge—by which he meant Cambridge although he realized that there was more to it than Old Cambridge—was just "a country village, distinguished from other similar villages mainly by the existence of the College." Thomas Wentworth Higginson was more aware of the "Port chucks" and the "outlying settlements of East Cambridge" because he had to ride through them to get to Boston. He remembered better, and with more descriptive language, that "the children of Cambridge"—by which he also meant those of Old Cambridge—"had the increased enjoyment of life that comes from country living."

These recollection, however, no matter how charming and delightful reading they might be, are not a true photograph or description of the town during the decades before it became a city. The historical reality was more diverse, more colorful, more exciting, and much more challenging. No wonder that the clear majority of its citizens refused on every occasion to split up their community.

THE NEW CITY GOVERNMENT

The new charter had created a Mayor, a Board of six Aldermen elected at large, and a Common Council of twenty elected by wards, to replace the former selectmen. The Mayor represented the former Chair of the Selectman and the other Aldermen the Selectmen; the Common Council took the place of the former Town Meeting. Under this plan it was the City Council which was charged with making the laws, raising money, appointing the clerk and treasurer, and other such matters such as the laying out of streets. This arrangement worked until the voters revised the charter in 1891 to allow the city's chief business to be carried out by the Mayor in consultation with a Board of Aldermen (now with eleven members) and a Common Council (now with twenty-two members.) This proved an effective change. It was not until 1916 that the city moved to the Plan B form of government which continued the post of a strong Mayor but merged the Aldermen and Common Council into one body with fifteen members (who for the first time received a salary for their serv-

Tower of East Cambridge Faces, sculptured by James Tyler, and located in Canal Park.

ice.) The major change to the charter in the twentieth century was not made until 1940 when the city adopted its present form of Plan E government.

Henry C. Binford in his excellent study of Boston's pre-civil war suburbs, especially Cambridge and its neighbor Somerville, feels that this transformation from town to city was really, at least initially, a kind of half-hearted adventure. "In both places," he concluded, "leading citizens assumed that local government would still be government by a small elite of stewards ... The new Cambridge city council was viewed as a limited and structured substitute for the town meeting. Throughout the 1840s, men of standing—almost all Whigs, except for the Democratic elite in East Cambridge—controlled the council's membership by means of ward caucuses, which nominated slates. In reconstructing their governments, suburban residents thought they were keeping the best of the old, while bending to new conditions ... Yet their New Model governments were fragile creations based on assumptions that were true in 1840 but would not remain so for long."

The cost of doing city business the first year was forty thousand dollars, but as more and more people came to live in Cambridge, and as new industries located or were started here, the need arose for not only the older community services but for numerous newer ones. Meeting these social demands resulted in increased fiscal budgets and higher taxes (much to the annoyance of some.)

The new City Council conducted its business in the town house built in 1832 on Harvard Street, corner of Norfolk, until it was destroyed by fire twenty-one years later. It was replaced with a new one on Main and Pleasant Streets which continued in use until the present structure was erected in 1889 on Main Street, soon renamed Massachusetts Avenue, close to Central Square.

The city hall was a gift from Frederick Rindge who had earlier given the city a main library and a Manual Training School. Rindge, the son of a wealthy Cambridge businessman, had grown up in East Cambridge but now lived for reasons of health in California. He made his several important gifts to the city and its citizens in appreciation of that Cambridge childhood. It was here that his father's wealth had been obtained; some of that money he believed should be returned to the community. On the 7,047 pound bell in the new city hall tower was placed this simple poem:

Cheerfully I ring the hour
From my home within the tower;
But I would a lesson teach,—
Even bells men's hearts may reach.

THE LESSON
Keep the ballot free and pure,—
Thus the rights of all secure;
Public wrong finds antidote
When each voter casts his vote.

Frederick H. Rindge.

THE NEW IMMIGRANTS

They came, the new immigrants to Cambridge, across the Atlantic as had the Puritans, and they settled first in Boston as had many of the Puritans. Then some migrated into East Cambridge and later throughout the community to feed the city's growing industries and tenement housing.

Who were these new immigrants? They were the Irish, and they were largely from the rural areas of that beautiful country and were driven from their homeland by the terrible Irish famine of 1845–1854. Mostly they were landless, or nearly so, agricultural laborers and cottiers who had worked plots actually owned by well-to-do families who never hesitated to get rid of those behind in their rent payments.

The famine that gave the workers of Ireland such hardship was caused by a blight to the potato crop not known before in the British Isles. And growing potatoes was the chief product of Ireland's small and fragmented agriculture system. Ironically, the blight struck North America first and then traveled to Europe.

It reached Ireland in September 1845 and destroyed just about completely the potatoes remaining to be harvested. The same havoc occurred again in 1846 and 1848. In 1847 and 1849–1852, the potato crop also suffered partial failure. During these bitter years over one million people died from starvation and its related diseases. While the British government had tried to help the victims of the resulting famine, its assistance was slow in coming and inadequate; as a result over a million persons emigrated in search of a better life. In 1997 a monument to their memory—especially those who died—was placed on the Cambridge Common; its inscription reads in part, "Never again should a people starve in a world of plenty."

Fortunately for those wishing to come to America, the means of doing so on passenger ships had been developed during the end of the preceding century and greatly improved during the first three decades of the nineteenth-century. But if there was a way of getting to various American ports, the trip was anything but pleasant. Oliver MacDonagh, in an essay entitled "The Irish Famine Emigration to the United States," described the typical forty-day voyage this way: "There was little more than two square feet of clear space for each passenger.... There was little or perhaps no ventilation except through the open hatchways.... There was no sanitary system whatsoever on most vessels.... Filth, and with it dangerous bacteria, accumulated on the floors. The wooden berth, in layers little more than two feet high, and only six square feet in area, bedded at least four people—often more." Furthermore, passengers were required to bring their own food and if they ran out that was just too bad. Their drinking water on the other hand was provided by the ships' owners; however it usually proved to be brackish, even muddy. During the voyage most everyone experienced several days of seasickness. And when they arrived, the New World did not greet them with open arms and friendship. What helped them to survive the trip and their new homeland was their Roman Catholic faith, the fact that they were a communal and literate people, and that they had long been accustomed to meager diets and poor living conditions.

It is important to remember too, that there had been much Irish migration before the Famine, that the movement went on, on a big scale, for decades afterwards. Steamships reduced the hazards of the crossing, though without ending discomfort. But the immigrants were different, and came from a different Ireland. They came from a reformed agriculture, were more certain to speak English; and above all they had many earlier migrants to help their adjustment. Further, their Church was now firmly established in the social structure of the Cambridge community.

Two sets of simple statistics explain what now took place in Cambridge. In 1820 there were three hundred eighty-two people living in East Cambridge; by 1850 there were almost four thousand, half of whom had been born in a foreign country. This figure is especially revealing when one realizes that on the voting list for the entire town in 1822 only four names out of the total of 481 vaguely suggest that those individuals might not be of Protestant Anglo-Saxon descent.

Business and industrial firms in Cambridge increased from ninety-four in 1845 to 578 in 1885; this translated to 1269 jobs in 1845 and 14,258 jobs forty-five years later. What were these jobs? They were of various types: harvesting ice, making bricks, toiling in the tanneries, glass and soap works. The wage paid for the labor was low and the workers were mostly the new immigrants. They were the ones who provided the cheap human resources for the new factories springing up in the city—except in the Old Cambridge area. There the Irish provided the inexpensive nannies and servants for those involved with the College. Derogated as Paddy, and often characterized as drunks, many of the poorest Irish lived in what can best be called huts alongside the Charles. Yet even Old Cambridge had its share of employment opportunities beyond nannies

The home of the poet Henry Longfellow.

A worker's cottages, North Cambridge

and servants. There were job opportunities at the gas works, the street railway, the Riverside and University presses and other commercial printers, and numerous blacksmiths and carriage makers.

An illustrative example of the conflict that arose in the city during the last decades of the century between the new Irish and older Yankee immigrants is captured by the words "temperance" and "alcohol." In Massachusetts a serious Temperance Movement began in the 1850's. For its advocates temperance really meant teetotalism, and for them it was a moral crusade (similar in many ways to the anti-abortion movement of the late twentieth century.) Its first supporters in the city—the Protestant clergy and a number of Old Cambridge citizens—chiefly related the growth of saloons and the resultant increase of public drunkenness and barroom brawls with the new laboring classes, those who earned their underpaid living through their brawn and sweat. In other words, not Yankees but the new immigrants. Here was the seedbed of the vile vice.

After 1881 when state government allowed each community to determine if it would permit saloons to exist within its own borders, agitation to ban bars in Cambridge commenced seriously. After a six year struggle, the citizens finally voted in 1886 for a "No-License" law which effectively made the city "dry" until 1933 when the Prohibition amendment to the United States Constitution was repealed. The passage of "No-License" in Cambridge succeeded when Catholic church leaders came to support the proposition.

The citizens always remained divided on the issue and the illegal sale and availability of "demon rum" was always a menace or opportunity, despite the best efforts of the police to root it out. Furthermore, if anyone wanted a lawful drink all they had to do was cross a bridge into Boston where Temperance was not King. The condition of those who were poor, ill paid, and discriminated against were improved not so much through "No-License" as the temperance leaders were wont to proclaim as through their own efforts, their own determination, and the rise of the American labor movement.

As the city was doing little to assist the new immigrants at this time, they turned for help and caring to their religious faith, Roman Catholicism. Their cry in their Cambridge wilderness did not go unheard or unanswered. Their Church offered them charity, help in locating jobs, adult classes in English grammar and in elementary math skills. Clearly the struggle of the early Irish in their new homeland was hard and harsh, but they persisted and survived and have become as important to the Cambridge mixture as has been the College formed long ago in the seventeenth century.

The British and the Irish were only the first two waves of immigrants to the land of the "First People." After the bloody conflict of the cruel American Civil War, Canadians of French, Irish and Scottish backgrounds began to arrive along with Portuguese from the North End of Boston as well as some Germans,

Italians, and Swedes. The religious faith of most of these continued to be Roman Catholicism. Blacks now started to move north and some resettled in Cambridge; they were not the first African Americans in Cambridge, however, as there was one at the college in the mid 17th century. The Loyalist had been slave holders who, when they had fled to Canada after the start of the Revolution, often took their slaves with them. Now the descendants of some of them made up the new immigrants from the Maritime Provinces. But the Tories also left some of their slaves behind, and their descendants can be traced into the 20th century.

When the American economy fell on hard times in the 1870s there was a temporary halt to immigration, but by the 1880s it had started again with newcomers from Scandinavia, France, Germany, and Spain. Then as the economic situation in Ireland in 1880 turned sour once more, a second group of immigrants came, more than half of them single women. By this time the first wave of Irish immigrants had begun to move up in the social and wage scale. With the growth of Cambridge as a center for printing and publishing along with jobs in the Cambridge Gas Company and the Boston Elevated Railroad, they were able to develop the skills of compositors, electrotypers, pressmen, machinists. Some became shopkeepers. These hard working immigrants of the nineteenth century deserve to be remembered with pride for the life of each one enriched the community known as the City of Cambridge.

THE TRANSPORTATION REVOLUTION

The chief contributions of the nineteenth century as we have seen were the arrival of the Irish and other immigrants, along with the growth in many areas of the city of a vital and significant industrial and commercial base thereby strengthening its economic lifeline. But there was a third ingredient continuing into the next century: the revolution in transportation.

Earlier generations had to be content to travel either by using their own locomotion or by employing the assistance of boats, horses, carriages, and wagons. Most people's travel was irregular and occasional. Now with every nook and cranny of the city filling up, being utilized for business, educational, religious, and dwelling purposes, there were not only more people to move around, there was a greater need for efficient and comfortable means of travel. Also the new need to travel involved distance and regularity. In time the trains, the horse car, the trolley, the subway, and the automobile solved this problem; and in doing so dramatically transformed the history not only of Cambridge but the whole way we have come to understand and visualize the city.

As the Civil War approached, Cambridge, with about 20,000 citizens, was served by six bridges across the Charles to Boston, Brookline, and Brighton. For six years in the 1860's the Harvard Branch Railroad with its station near the present Harvard Law School offered

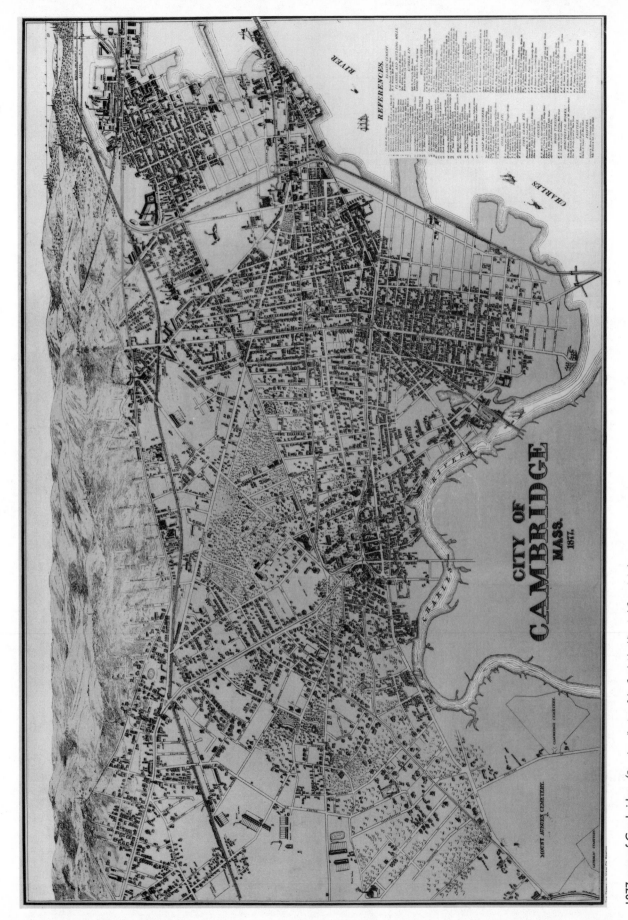

1877 map of Cambridge. (Form the collection of the Cambridge Historical Commission)

41

Modes of traveling.

very limited train service to Boston. The Fitchburg Railroad whose trains passed through Porter Square (as does the T today) carried freight and passengers to Boston. The chief transportation system, however, was still the Cambridge Stage Company with its horses, omnibuses (when it snowed they replaced the wheels with runners), and four well traveled routes into Boston.

Change quietly arrived in 1853 when several citizens incorporated the Cambridge Railroad. This was the first street railway in the city and in New England, and it was also one of the earliest on the planet. It took three years for the railway to become operational, and the formation of a second corporation, the Union Railway Company, to secure enough funds to buy the horses, cars, and other equipment needed to run it.

The Omnibus and view of the New Cambridge Athenaeum from *Gleason's* 1851. *(Courtesy of the Cambridge Public Library)*

Trial trips were made in March, 1856, and by the start of June cars were traveling regularly about every seven and a half minutes during the day between Mount Auburn, Harvard Square, Cambridgeport, East Cambridge and across the river into Boston via the West Boston Bridge. Service was also provided to Porter Square; later extensions connected the city to Watertown Square and Arlington Center. During the Civil War a line was put through along Garden Street and Concord Avenue.

The new street railway was a success from its first day and additional cars and horses had to be secured immediately. *The Cambridge Chronicle* described the cars as "spacious" and able to sit twenty-four, and the same number could easily stand in the aisle. "They are also well ventilated; and being lighted by large glass, afford a much better view of the beautiful scenery from our bridges and the other parts of the city than can be obtained in any other close carriage which we have ever seen on our streets." The three mile trip to Boston took but twenty-five minutes and the fare was only eight cents. It should be pointed out too that from the beginning commuters took to reading newspapers as they traveled to and from their business in Boston.

During the next forty years ridership on the cars continued to grow and other companies were interested in getting a share of the business. One, the Charles River Railway, actually got launched but was absorbed in 1886 by the old Union Railroad which was later merged into the West End Street Railway which eventually was to emerge as the major street car system for the entire Greater Boston area. From the start, all the cars of the West End system were colored according to the district they traveled, and it cannot be a surprise to anyone that the color of all the Cambridge lines was crimson.

Some of the woes of today's transportation system were also problems that afflicted the horse cars. Chief of these was the overcrowding during rush hours. As an observer in 1862 noted, "It has not been uncommon to see a car go out with the people crowding upon it like bees about the entrance of a hive." Another declared, "when I rode out in a Cambridge horse-car, I never once had a seat; never."

In 1889 the horse cars were replaced by electric powered cars, first on the West End's Brookline and Allston route and then in Cambridge. Within a few years the new cars supplanted the horse cars, everywhere. If they were more efficient and faster than the horse cars they were also heavier vehicles, required poles and wires, and were very noisy. This was the complaint of those living in the posh houses on Brattle Street, and those complaints resulted in public transportation being moved from that street to Mt. Auburn Street. The trolley cars were a visible and colorful ingredient of Cambridge life for almost three quarters of a century. Then, in 1958, those that remained were discontinued in favor of the bus and the trackless trolley.

Along with the introduction of the electric cars came the Boston subway system which is still the area's major

The first T Dome, 1910.

means of rapid public transit. The Tremont Street subway, the first subway in America, opened in Boston in 1897. That same year saw the West End Street Railway absorbed by the Boston Elevated Railway, which had two years earlier taken over the franchise of its rival, the Meigs Elevated Railway Company. (Josiah V. Meigs had constructed his short "unusual" experimental steam-propelled monorail line in East Cambridge in the 1880s but it never amounted to anything because it was sabotaged by established railway interests.) These mergers were to give the area an integrated subway and surface line system which today is known popularly as the T.

The subway to Cambridge required a bridge to cross the Charles; this was completed in 1907. However, another five years were to pass before the train line became operational because while the Boston Elevated Railway had legislative permission from the late 1890s to build all the way to Harvard Square there was growing opposition to this in the city. In the end, the Boston Elevated Railway had to appeal again to the legislature for authorization to proceed. The subway, which required that a tunnel be dug for the cars to pass under the land surface of the two cities, covered 3.20 miles, cost almost twelve million dollars, and was finally opened on Saturday March 23, 1912. According to Brian Cudahy's history of Boston's subways, "Mrs. Mary Collett, of Revere Street, Cambridge, after standing in line at Harvard Square since 3:00 A.M., purchased the first ticket." The first man to ride the new line was "William Dwyer, a Cambridge physician routinely on his way home after making an emergency night call, who became curious about the people and the noise in Harvard Square." The first train to Park Street Under—as it was then called—consisted of four cars with William Miles as motorman and 286 passengers; it left Harvard at 5:24 and eight minutes later entered the Park Street station. For a number of years just beyond the Harvard Square stop was Stadium Station which allowed those attending Harvard football games direct access to the stadium.

There were two other vehicles that characterized the transportation revolution: the bicycle, lowly to some, romantic to others, and that almost unbelievable four-wheeled monster the automobile along with its two-wheeled cousin the roaring motorbike. (We do not forget roller skates, roller blades, skateboards, tricycles, electric powered wheelchairs, scooters, go-carts, and

John 'Muggsie' Kelly who died May 18, 1982 in an accident while building the New Havard Square T station.

that old childhood favorite the Radio Flyer wagon.) The bicycle made its appearance early in the nineteenth century but it was not until near the close of the century that its development had reached a practical stage for everyday use as a means of public transport. In America for much of the twentieth century its most popular use was for recreation and as a kind of pre-car for young folks; however, as people have come to show more awareness for the environment, it is growing as a vehicle of choice for local travel. Indeed, the city has started to provide bike lanes on certain streets and to reformulate the rules governing their public use especially on sidewalks.

As for automobiles, they need no documentation in the life of any twentieth century community except to say that once Henry Ford introduced the assembly-line technology for producing them in 1914, they increased in popularity, use, size, and expense. With their adoption by the public came a host of related problems: speeding, road rage, accidents, tickets, the boot, parking spaces, garages, insurance, and a bedrock of legal matters. Furthermore, the impact of the automobile is twofold, for Cambridge has to deal with both the cars owned by its residents as well as the cars that travel through the city to other locations or are driven to Cambridge by people who work here but live elsewhere. For a glimpse, and that's all it would be, of Cambridge as it was before this transportation revolution, one would have to go out walking its byways after a mighty blizzard such as that of 1979.

PLAN E

The city adopted its present form of government in 1940 although the new Plan E amendment to the Charter did not begin to operate until January 1942. Under Plan E the city administration is run by a City Manager appointed by the City Council and serving at its pleasure, rather than by an elected Mayor. The City Council and the School Committee are elected by the citizens by a voting process called Proportional Representation (or PR) which is a voting system set up so that those elected to office do so proportionate to their support among the citizens who care enough about their government to vote in any given election. Under the system practiced in Cambridge—called the single transferable vote process—voters mark their ballots by numbers rather than by X's. If the voter's first choice fails of election their vote moves to their next choices in the order of preference which they have selected. The end result is that each voter elects just one member of the Council and of the School Committee.

The philosophy behind PR is that it enables in the fairest way possible for as many different and representative viewpoints of the city's multi-cultural and historical mix to participate in governing the city. If Plan E and PR voting have not worked perfectly for the last sixty years, and it has not—witness for example the sometimes biannual farce of the Council trying to elect the city's ceremonial Mayor—it has proven an effective way to allow the real complexity of people and concerns that is Cambridge to be heard and seen.

Cambridge has had its share of ups and downs trying to conduct its local government efficiently and economically. Plan E came in during one of the downs, during a period marked by accusations of graft and corruption, of town and gown bickering, of struggles between various elected officials, of intense debates regarding the role of government itself as well as the duties it should perform.

The process by which Cambridge adopted Plan E was not a smooth one and not without its comical moments either. Here Plan E originated as a good Government measure promoted by West Cambridge reformers. The first time the question appeared before the voters, in 1938, it was turned down after a savage, often nasty, campaign for which both sides shared responsibility. At one point during this campaign this headline appeared in *The New York Times:* "VOTE TO SECEDE FROM HARVARD IS TAKEN BY CAMBRIDGE CITY COUNCIL." Sometimes perhaps both Harvard and the city wish that had come to pass, but fortunately for the community as a whole, it was merely rhetoric.

The 1940 campaign was more "civilized" even if the opponents worked just as hard to present the issues as they saw them to the public. What helped the reformers was a combination of a sharp tax increase and the indictment of the Mayor, John W. Lyons, for soliciting bribes during the construction of the Rindge Manual Training School. When the ballots were counted the tally showed that Cambridge had voted in Plan E and PR by a clear majority with support for the change coming from the entire community. Colonel John B. Atkinson was chosen as the first City Manager; he served with great success for the next decade and was ably succeeded by John J. Curry who guided the affairs of the city for the next thirteen years.

Not every individual appointed to be the City Manager served as long as the first two occupants, but it would be unrealistic to expect anything different. For some, the position must have seemed to be nothing but a revolving door. The Manager, to be effective, along with all those who are on the city payroll, needs to consult constantly with both the City Council and the School Committee as well as with the city's two major political organizations, the Cambridge Alliance and the Cambridge Civic Association. (Initially the groups were the Cambridge Civic Association and those not endorsed by them called the Independents and later the Alliance for Change.)

These two major associations/alliances (there are smaller ones too) because of their different philosophical approaches did not and do not often share the same answers as to how the city should solve some of its basic problems. Basically, the Alliance, which got started in 1993, stresses the need for "moderate" solutions to city problems. Further, it supports safe neighborhoods, responsible government, and good relations with the city's business community. The Civic Association seeks out "progressive" individuals to endorse at election time; as a "good government" organization, it expects its recommended slate for office to be honest and thoughtful, and to work to see that all people in the community share alike in the benefits of Cambridge living.

Beside these two political groups, there have been from time to time free newspapers devoted to the interests and needs of particular sections of the city or devoted to specialized community issues. For example,

Citizens debating politics before City Hall.

serving East Cambridge is the *East Cambridge News* and serving North and West Cambridge is *Northwest Cambridge News,* an outgrowth of the *North Cambridge News.* The stated purpose of the latter is "to provide for the community, a place where issues important to Cambridge residents can be fully debated and discussed." *EFZ Community Voice,* the newspaper put out by the Cambridge EvictionFree Zone, is representative of publications addressing matters of concern to the entire community.

In addition to broadly based community groups there are specialized neighborhood organizations with their newsletters and publications, such as *The Whistler* which focuses on the activities and concerns of the Agassiz neighborhood, and the *M-C News* which covers events important to the Mid-Cambridge Neighborhood Association and the Longfellow Neighborhood Council.

So Cambridge government can be lively. Yet it is only through a process of debate and then of trying and attempting, sometimes in unity and sometime not, that a community reaches answers. In so doing it creates its own biography. Apropos of this, and always worth remembering, are these words taught to Edward A. Crane, a member of the City Council from 1939 to 1971 except for his service to his country during the Second World War, by the philosopher Ernest Hocking: "Incorporate yourself into reality by aligning yourself with the existing institutions and bending them to your way of thinking."

REINVIGORATING CAMBRIDGE

This overflight of Cambridge's history as a town and a city has focused on local activities, people, and events. But no place, no community, exists just on this one level. It forms a part of a larger community and place and is always beset and benefited by the issues which dominated the larger living of each generation. Immigration and the transportation revolution that has so shaped the present Cambridge are both larger developments that have changed many cities and towns. This has been especially true for Americans whenever their country has had to ask them to answer the call to defend their ideals of democracy, liberty, and justice for all.

These engagements have been many and have involved disputes with the First peoples, the British, America's own Civil War, two world wars, as well as struggles in North Korea and Vietnam. In the last part of the twentieth century some citizens also participated for their country in peace keeping assignments throughout the world for the new international organization, the United Nations. If some served far from Cambridge, others served in different ways at home, ways that included alternative forms of military service. These engagements demanded courage from all and for some their very lives. If all of these engagements were not considered just by every citizen of Cambridge, and some were honestly protested as unjust, that does not take away from the courage and service of anyone.

John J. Shea, U.S.N., who grew up in North Cambridge and attended its St. John the Evangelist Church and who was reported as missing in action in 1942 while serving aboard the U.S.S. *Wasp,* wrote to his young son Jackie before his death these thoughts: "You know we have a big country, and we have ideals as to how people should live and enjoy the rights of it, and how each is born with equal rights to life, freedom and the pursuit of happiness…Because there are people and countries who want to change our nation, its ideals, form of government and way of life, we must leave our homes and families to fight." His words express the ideas which have motivated generations of Cambridge men and women.

The character of the city's business and industry radically changed after the Second World War. The roots for this lay in two events: the first was the move in 1916 of MIT to Cambridge and the second was the new technology required by the war which transformed the Institute's curriculum, research, and

Those who served their community and country.

experimentation. This influence soon impacted Cambridge and some of the other neighboring communities clear to Rt. 128 which itself was on the verge of its own unique development. Christopher Rand, who had first known this area in 1948, described in his book on Cambridge what he found when he returned to it in 1962 this way: "... at once I found changes afoot. I saw new defense plants that had shot up in Cambridge and its environs, attracted by the scientists of M.I.T.... Soon I decided that I had found a renaissance ... It has its patrons, its Medici, in the faceless U.S. government and the great impersonal foundations ... it has a bent for research, as opposed to teaching, and for group research at that; its savants are usually banded in teams, working on complex projects that cut across the old academic disciplines. These teams are sometimes housed in defense plants—making missiles, say, or warning-nets—and sometimes in new institutions called centers, which have sprouted from the universities themselves ... they are run by leaders of a new type: by academic entrepreneurs, who are men of affairs as well as learning—who know how to raise money, and put an organization together, and get results in the outside world."

If the ring round about Greater Boston, Rt. 128, became the outer symbol of the new R & D (research and development), its heart and brain was centered clearly in Cambridge. For Cambridge with Harvard and MIT had the institutional links, the trained personnel, and the ideas which late twentieth-century industry needed. Indeed what has happened in the American Cambridge has also happened in the English Cambridge.

M. P. Conzen and G. R. Lewis in their study of the Boston area after the Second World War described what took place, and still is occurring, this way: "As traditional industries moved out ... a close alliance began to grow between manufacturing interests and the leading universities of the metropolis to forge new production based on advanced technology." The result was that the "electronic industry" became the "major component of the Greater Boston economy. This time the investment came not from accumulated commercial capital, but from the assembled intellectual capital of institutions like Harvard University and the Massachusetts Institute of Technology." Furthermore, they pointed out "the pace of scientific research has built into electrical engineering a high degree of technological obsolescence, thus ensuring that the national market would constantly absorb sustained production of ever-new items."

So concerns long associated with the city which specialized in glass and brick making, in boiler works, soap factories and steel foundries, were supplanted by a very different kind of industrialization, global in scope, and employing the insight of sophisticated engineering, the new technology of electronics and computers with their demand for ever newer software. Thus Cambridge moved into the Age of Polaroid, Arthur D. Little, the Electronic Corporation of America, Abt Associates,

Bolt, Beranek and Newman, and Draper Laboratory. The new concerns—they bear such familiar names as MITRE, Sylvania, The Radio Corporation of America, Raytheon, and Avco—were started on shoe-string financing; many were started in the lofts of East Cambridge, often having been spun off from the laboratories of MIT; all required a new breed of worker, and so the nature of the new work force changed from a heavy dependence on brawn and laboring tasks to one requiring brains and imagination. In a short span of time then blue collar workers were replaced by scientists and engineers.

Rand's use of the word "renaissance" for what had taken place is probably in one sense a misuse of what the term stands for in the cultural history of western civilization. But in another sense, the last five decades of Cambridge in the twentieth century when understood with the French root of renaissance—renaître—in mind have proven to be on many levels a period when the city's industry and business was liteally born again.

The first woman ever to serve the city as its mayor was Barbara Ackermann. She was later to reflect thoughtfully upon her political and civic service during the 1960's and the 1970's in a book entitled *You the Mayor?* Here she captured the passion, the commitment, and the concept of government that motivated all those who ran for public office and all those who were elected to public office in Cambridge during the last decades of the twentieth century. "The city," she declared, "is an extended family, with all a family's angers and affections. To keep it safe and clean and out of debt, to help its young grow into full citizenship, this is the tremendous task of local government and its employees, police officers and street sweepers, teachers and budget analysts and all. It's a householder's job. The dishes we washed this morning are dirty again tonight. The paint job we think of as new is beginning to peel. And it's a deadly serious job."

So it is. But the year by year and decade by decade accomplishments of local government in any city or town, which are sometimes negative and sometimes positive, have never come to pass without an explosion of passion and emotion, debate and compromise, luck and good timing. It was not by chance that the long time Councillor Al Vellucci advised the inexperienced new Councillor Ackermann "to read Machiavelli, whose Prince adds political skill to inherent power," for a part of the genius of democracy is that one feels one can do it better. And the second part of that genius, and maybe its most significant aspect, is in this observation of a Cambridge police officer: "Listen, let me tell you something; people are very quick to say what we should do, very slow to help …"

Cambridge throughout these decades was run, as has been indicated, by the Plan E form of government which, while it had been put in place by the voters in 1940 in an effort to weed out political corruption, was really endorsed by them as a way to ensure for their beloved community a better and fairer means of taking care of all the members of the extended family. While there were attempts in the 1970's to get rid of it, the voters always refused to do so.

Plan E in Cambridge was made even more effective when the community understood the legacy that came out of citizen involvement during the 1960's. In that struggle two themes predominated: the need to gain for all Americans their constitutionally guaranteed civil rights and the need to make the Federal government review and revise its war policy in Vietnam. The citizen success in both these endeavors led to a realization that residents could do more than simply vote for city councilors and school committee members every two years and work on just single issues, usually ones of protest, but that they could, through active local organizations and educational efforts, be a regular ongoing part of community problem solving.

So during the next decades, a number of area groups were formed, as needed. Examples are the East Cambridge Planning Team, Mid-Cambridge Neighborhood Association, the Longfellow Neighborhood Council, the Agassiz Neighborhood Council, the Harvard Square Defense Fund, the Save Central Square Association, and the Central Square Neighborhood Coalition. These citizen efforts eventually grew to be 31 neighborhood groups spread throughout the city's 14 organized neighborhoods. But no one currently living in the city will be surprised by this development, for as Jennifer Peck observed in a 1998 profile on the city for the *Boston Globe* this is the place "where civic activism is alive and well."

This kind of citizen participation is now welcomed by city officials, and the various bodies of the government itself now regularly issue freely distributed informational publications such as the newsletter of the Cambridge Council on Aging, the seasonal Resource Guide with translation assistance available in Portuguese, Creole, and Spanish put out by the Department of Human Service Programs, and *From the Source*, the newsletter of the Cambridge Water Department Source Protection Program. By the end of the twentieth century, then, the goal of government has become the more the merrier in dealing with the problems of living together in diversity of backgrounds, experiences, and ideals.

After the Second World War there proved to be for Cambridge as for all American cities and towns several major new challenges, none of which could be solved as easily as earlier community concerns. One of these—rather prosaically and deceptively termed The Inner Belt—threatened the very existence of the city as a viable human place in which to dwell.

The Inner Belt and Southwest Expressway proposals were part of a national transportation plan that was one of the country's responses to the problems facing its large urban centers. In the case of Greater Boston and Cambridge, the Inner Belt was the theory of highway planners and had behind its thrust the wisdom

Beat the Belt, wall painting by Bernard LaCasse, 1980.

and financial assistance of the Federal government along with the approval of many influential state leaders, business groups, the *Boston Globe* and the *Herald Traveler.*

It was first suggested in 1948 by the Massachusetts Department of Public Works but went nowhere until Congress in the sweeping new highway bill of 1956 agreed to assume almost all the cost of bringing it into reality. There followed a number of years of heated local discussion as to its exact route; the proposed eight-lane highway would affect the communities of Roxbury, the Fenway, Brookline, Medford, Somerville, Charlestown and Cambridge. It seemed for a while that nothing could prevent The Inner Belt and the Southwest Expressway from being constructed.

In Cambridge the 1962 version of the plan would have cut the city in half, and if Route 2 had been extended along the Somerville border of the city, further destruction to the community would have resulted. Indeed, The Inner Belt called for demolishing about 5 percent of the city—in other words some 1,300 structures which its citizens without Brattle Street incomes called their homes and their neighborhoods. These citizens as a later study indicated were "typical working-class families—the husband employed at a nearby candy factory, book bindery or electronics plant, the wife full time at home or working part time also at a factory, as a sales clerk or as a nurse or nurse's aide … Almost half the residents have lived here more than ten years; over a third have lived here more than 20 years. Most are pleased with their home and neighborhood and like the schools and the convenience to transportation and shopping … Most of their social life is spent at home, with nearby friends and, most characteristically, with relatives." In short, they were a vital part of the mosaic that is Cambridge and they were not wrong to fear the coming of The Inner Belt.

That it did not was due to an alliance of local leaders and hardworking citizens from all economic, ethnic, and racial backgrounds. Their slogan was simple: "Cambridge is a city, not a highway." The fascinating and complicated story of how they and other citizens from all parts of Greater Boston forced those with the power behind the project to reconsider the whole proposal and eventually to kill most of it is ably recounted in the book *Rites of Way* by Alan Lupo, Frank Colcord, and Edmund P. Fowler, and in briefer fashion in the sociological study "Dagger in the Heart of Town" conducted by Gordon Fellman, Barbara Brandt, and Roger Rosenblatt.

Some of the local leaders in this struggle that present and future dwellers in Cambridge should be especially grateful to are Ansti Benfield, Bill Ackerly, Father Paul McManus and their group Save Our Cities; the city's assistant city manager Justin Gray; two MIT graduates, Tunney Lee and Fred Salvucci; James Morey, who con-

vinced the American Friends Service Committee to provide a grant which helped fund the Greater Boston movement against The Inner Belt; Boston Mayor Kevin White and his young executive assistant Barney Frank; and finally the then Governor, Francis Sargent, who had both the wisdom and the courage to change—finally—his mind on The Inner Belt concept and announce in 1970, "I have decided to reverse the transportation policy of the Commonwealth of Massachusetts."

So, in the end, the ordinary people of Cambridge and the other communities of Greater Boston, by pooling their efforts and learning how to made democracy function better, by working together to influence government, had made their cities not a place to drive cars through but a place in which to live.

A third very important concern of these decades can be summed up by two words: Rent Control. It became the city's law in 1970 and remained in place until 1995 when a referendum was put on the state ballot by opponents to the idea. The referendum was narrowly approved, 51–49 percent, in that autumn's state election by Massachusetts voters and effectively eliminated the practice of controlling rents in Cambridge, Boston, Brookline and several other communities.

Among those who strongly supported getting rid of rent control were landlords of large apartment complexes who insisted that rents needed to be fair and directly related to the market in order for them to have enough income to be able to maintain them in good

Some Cambridge Landlords.

repair. Also opposing rent control were small home owners who felt, as indeed did the large apartment owners too, that with rent control the city was subsidizing some citizens (including a few who had incomes that should have made them unallowable for a rent controlled apartment) and so robbing them of money that rightly was theirs.

The underlying argument against rent control was three-fold and can be summarized easily. 1) Rent control was a device to meet an emergency situation and was never intended to be a solution to a chronic social problem. 2) A chronic social problem, such as a tenant to social and income diversity, which is a matter of common concern, should be addressed in a way that the burden is shared, not imposed on one group (i.e. landlords.) 3) People would not oppose rent control if its proponents would agree to consider modifications to the existing plan.

The philosophy behind rent control in the city, although many did not see it this way which does not invalidate their rejection of the idea, was to try to maintain Cambridge's historic mixture of individual and family income levels. One of the keys to understanding the town and then the city's history is caught by one word: immigrants. Except for the First People, every other large grouping of individuals came to Cambridge from another original homeland—including the Puritans. It has been therefore a place where traditionally there has been affordable room for newcomers to the country called the United States of America. As the drift and disparity of incomes between workers dramatically increased over the decades, and especially over the last one hundred and fifty years, rent control was seen and was employed as a device which could allow Cambridge to continue to be a home for new immigrants as well as its older residents and for people at all the various economic and social levels that make up American society.

Although Cambridge voters by a clear majority remained in 1995 in favor of rent control as a valuable and positive tool for keeping their city truly attractive for both its older and less affluent citizens as well as providing an option to those who might like to live here, the state referendum phased it out but in a way that offered some protection for a limited period of time for some of those who might need it. The truth or falsity of arguments for and against it, and those opposed insist that its removal will permit a proper

economic incentive for improvements to the dwellings which residents inhabit, will now be measured during the next generational time span of the community.

The 1995 election did not cause the debate and discussion about the city's population and economic mixture to end. Both sides still felt strongly that their arguments for and against were still valid. It is of course too early to know who was right and what changes no rent control will bring to the city although some hints are emerging. A *Boston Globe* article in 1998 which examined its early influence in the Craigie Circle cul-de-sac of Cambridge noted:

> "Today, three years later, Craigie Circle is changing, but more gradually and less dramatically than some had predicated. Rents have surged when units have become vacant, but for those who have chosen to stay in their apartments, increases have been smaller but steady … The fabric of the neighborhood is changing as well. Life in Craigie Circle, once marked by stability and a sense of permanence, is in transition … At least 17 of the 82 units in the two apartment buildings changed hands between 1996 and 1997, and before the calendar turned to 1998, four of those newcomers had already moved on."

The article went on to point out that rents increased by 40 percent for those who had not moved after the

Some of those affected by the loss of Rent Control.

defeat of rent control and by 85 percent for those who moved into the vacated flats.

A 1997 *New York Times* article indicates that the end of rent control resulted in "about 800 new luxury rental units" and a city that "is buzzing with renovation activity" and a flood of new residents. One of these living near Kendall Square wrote to *The Cambridge Tab* concerning the new cinema there saying "that at maximum 15 percent of the audience at the theater at any given time is from this neighborhood. Clearly the Kendall Theater panders to yuppies who do not live in East Cambridge and while this is not a bad thing in itself it does not mean that the neighborhood is being 'revitalized.'" As the twentieth century comes to an end one of the Cambridge questions for the next century is this: Will the city retain its historic population character or will the community become homogeneous?

Also, as the century closed, a new and quite revolutionary development emerged. This development, the product of both cultural evolution and current technology, can be reduced to one word—Cyberspace. This concept includes familiarity with networked computers and the global network of computers, the Net and the World Wide Web, on-line libraries and bookstores, ATM banking, and food and all kinds of other shopping from home through a series of Websites, E-mail, the fax, the cellular phone.

The historical question that can be drawn from this is simple: what impact will this new challenge and

Central Square Municipal Parking Lot 5 wall mural *The Potluck* by David Fichter.

opportunity have on the future shape and quality of Cambridge living? Thomas J. Campanella, a graduate student in the Department of Urban Studies and Planning at MIT puts it this way: "The 'Net is an ethereal info-skein hovering above the bump and grind of the material landscape, an invisible meta-landscape of the mind. It has opened fast new channels of communication which, for the most part, have no spatial component. Information is increasingly untethered by the architectural or urbanistic anchors associated with society's manifold institutions … Digital technology now permits once exclusively urban functions to break free entirely of the city's gravitational pull." The question remains then: how will the world of Cyberspace impact the city of Cambridge, the community of Cambridge?

Pearl Street Parking Garage wall mural *Crossroads*, 1986, by Daniel Galvez.

Will it be as Marshall McLuhan thought? Will cities like New York and Los Angeles and by implication Cambridge "disappear like the dinosaur ... dissolve like a fading shot in a movie." Or will it be more as William J. Mitchell and Oliver Strimpel suggest in *Beyond Calculation: The Next 50 Years of Computing*: "The general decentralization of activity that seems likely to follow from the shift to cyberspace will enhance, rather than diminish, the importance of those urban centers that have genuine cultural significance."

Certainly Cambridge has the components that contribute to the concept "genuine cultural significance." It has an abundance of excellent colleges and universities, it has more than 200 software companies, it has a literate, compassionate, and diverse population, and as this history has shown as a town/city it has always been open to fascination and helpful change. In popular slang we can say that Cambridge's next century should be a blast, a ball, brilliant, awesome.

This broad historical survey of the first century and a half of Cambridge the City dramatically reveals the fact that Cambridge and the great City of New York share the same striking working image. Indeed, except for the matter of the size of their population, they are almost as similar as identical twins. That shared image was expressed by a former mayor of New York City, David Dinkins, in this way when he called his city a "gorgeous mosaic." It seems appropriate then to end with this image for truly the community and the culture of Cambridge is a gorgeous mosaic.

FURTHER READING

ACKERMANN, BARBARA. *You the Mayor?: The Education of a City Politician*. Dover, MA: Auburn House, 1989.

ADAMS, FREDERICK J. *Cambridge Fifty Years From Now*. Cambridge, MA: Cambridge Planning Board, 1946.

BEALE, JOSEPH H. "The History of Local Government in Cambridge," *Cambridge Historical Society Proceedings*, 22 (1932–1933) 17–28.

BINFORD, HENRY C. *The First Suburbs: Residential Communities on the Boston Periphery 1815–1860*. Chicago: University of Chicago, 1985.

"Cambridge & the Chronicle's 150th," *The Cambridge Chronicle*, (Special commemorative issue 1996) 80.

The Cambridge Book. Cambridge, MA: Cambridge Civic Association, 1966.

[Cambridge Chronicle, Cambridge, MA] *Seventy-fifth Anniversary*. Cambridge, MA, October 8, 1921, 60.

"Cambridge 150th Anniversary," *The Cambridge Chronicle*, Official Celebration Guide, (September 5, 1996) 30.

Cambridge, MA. *The First Three Centuries*. Progress Report of the City of Cambridge, Massachusetts including the Annual Report for the Centennial Year, 1946.

Cambridge, MA. *The Rindge Gifts to the City of Cambridge, Massachusetts*. Cambridge, MA: City Council, 1891.

CAMPANELLA, THOMAS J. "Of Cyberspace and the City," *harvard.net.news*, 1 (May 27, 1998) 13–14.

CLARKE, BRADLEY H. *Rapid Transit Boston*. Cambridge, MA: Boston Street Railway Association, 1971.

CONZEN, MICHAEL P. AND GEORGE K. LEWIS, "Boston: A Geographical Portrait," in Adams, John S. (Ed), *Contemporary*

Metropolitan America 1 Cities of the Nation's Historic Metropolitan Core. Cambridge, MA: Ballinger Publishing Company, 1976.

CRANE, EDWARD A. "Observations on Cambridge City Government under Plan E," *Cambridge Historical Society Proceedings,* 44 (1976–1979) 87–103.

CUDAHY, BRIAN J. *Change at Park Street Under: The Story of Boston's Subways.* Brattleboro, VT: Stephen Greene Press, 1972.

DIESENHOUSE, SUSAN. "Housing Investment Surges in Cambridge," *New York Times,* December 14, 1997, 51.

ELIOT, SAMUEL A. *A History of Cambridge, Massachusetts 1630–1913.* Cambridge, MA: Cambridge Tribune, 1913.

FELLMAN, GORDON WITH BARBARA BRANDT. *The Deceived Majority: Politics and Protest in Middle America.* New Brunswick, NJ: Transaction Books, 1973.

FELLMAN, GORDON; BRANDT, BARBARA; AND ROGER ROSENBLATT, "Dagger in the Heart of Town: Mass. Planners and Cambridge Workers," in Marx, Gary T. (Ed), *Muckraking Sociology: Research as Social Criticism.* New Brunswick, NJ: Transaction Books, 1972.

GILMAN, ARTHUR., ED. *The Cambridge of Eighteen Hundred and Ninety-six.* Cambridge, MA: Citizens' Trade Association, 1896.

GOODE, DAVID R. *The Quota Question.* Thesis for the Master of Arts in Urban and Environmental Policy, Tufts University, 1994.

HANFORD, GEORGE H. *A Tale of Three Cities in One: Cambridge, 150 Years Later.* Cambridge, MA: Cambridge Historical Society, 1996.

LUPO, ALAN, COLCORD, FRANK AND FOWLER, EDMUND P. *Rites of Way: the Politics of Transportation in Boston and the U.S. City.* Boston: Little, Brown, 1971.

MACDONAGH, OLIVER. "The Irish Famine Emigration to the United States," *Perspectives in American History,* 10 (1976) 357–446.

PAIGE, LUCIUS R. *History of Cambridge, Massachusetts. 1630-1877.* Boston: Houghton, 1877. *Supplement and Index.* Mary Isabella Gozzaldi. 1930.

PECK, JENNIFER. "Cambridge—Where Civic Activism Is Alive And Well," *The Boston Globe* (July 25, 1998) E1.

PENNINGTON, RICHARD. *A Bibliography of Cambridge Government Documents and Related Material Found in the Cambridge Public Library and the Littauer Library.* Unpublished. 78 pages. Cambridge, 1977.

RAND, CHRISTOPHER. *Cambridge, U.S.A.: Hub of a New World.* NY: Oxford, 1964.

SUTTON, S. B. *Cambridge Reconsidered: 3 1/2 Centuries on the Charles.* Cambridge, Ma.: MIT, 1976.

TAYLOR, PHILIP. *The Distant Magnet: European Emigration to the U.S.A.* New York: Harper & Row, 1971.

WOODS, ROBERT A. AND ALBERT J. KENNEDY. *The Zone of Emergence: Observations of the Lower Middle and Upper Middle Working Class Communities of Boston, 1905–1914.* Second Edition. Cambridge, Ma.: M.I.T., 1969.

Cambridge Cares.

CHAPTER FOUR

FIRE PROTECTION

FIRE! FIRE! Fearful words. 9-1-1 9-1-1 Hopeful numbers. The doors of the nearest fire station slide open, men and women take to the poles, pull on their boots and helmets, jump into the polished shiny red trucks, Aerial Tower One, Rescue One, and it's off, it's a go. As one of the members of the department explains it, "We like to help people. Fire fighters in general are a helpful bunch."

That's the way it all started. Neighbors helping neighbors when they heard the call Fire! Fire! Buckets of water passing hand-to-hand up one line from the water source and then back again by a second line. Sometimes, too, buildings on either side of the fire would be torn down to stop the flames from spreading. It was that simple—and primitive—but that was all that was available to the first English immigrants. As Cambridge flourished, as fire fighting methods developed a more sophisticated technology, the simple became more complex and so in 1793 the town organized a Fire Society. Twenty-nine years later, Cambridge was empowered by the state legislature to establish today's Fire Department; Luther Brooks became its first chief, called at that time the chief engineer.

The new department soon had at its disposal four engines for pumping water by hand and one ladder truck that was pulled by the men to the site of the fire. The main method of putting out fires, however,

Cambridge Cares for Its Family

remained the "bucket brigade" (the volunteer fire companies) with the water coming from the nearest available source.

When Cambridge became a city in 1846 there were six official engine houses and companies scattered throughout the community. They were assisted by an additional three companies, also made up of volunteers who were often residents and business employees in their immediate locality. A partial list of their equipment at this time included an engine for pumping water, a hose carriage with twenty-five feet of suction hose, two pipes, a blunderbuss, six buckets, three axes, and a crowbar. The department's staff was composed of eight regularly salaried fire fighters and the volunteers who helped them.

Change, as in every aspect of life, is also the way in fire fighting. These came fairly rapidly during the last 150 years; among the more significant ones were the replacement of hand pumping engines by steam engines (1862), the use of horses for pulling fire equipment (the last horses were retired in 1921), the introduction of flexible hose, electric street fire alarm boxes (first used on September 22, 1869 and it proved to be a false alarm), fire reservoirs (wooden constructions placed underground and fed by rain water through pipes connected to the roof drains of nearby buildings), fire hydrants (there are now more than 1750), motorized fire and ladder trucks (1914), computers, the Uniform Fire Incident Reporting System for managing fire data, air compressor systems, apparatus

for delivering effective streams of water at high elevations, foam pumpers to extinguish flammable liquids, mobile radio sets, oxygen tanks and masks. It is indeed an amazing list of improvements over the old hand bucket.

The placement and location of the city's fire stations/fire houses has varied according to community needs and financial resources which is clearly the way it should be. The 1840s sites included Church Street, Main Street at the corner of Windsor, Pioneer Street, Cambridge Street between Third and Fourth Streets, and the junction of Western Avenue and River Streets. These first fire houses were wooden structures, but they were soon replaced by brick ones. Today's headquarters of the department, Fire House No. 1, sits on the corner of Cambridge and Quincy Streets near Memorial Hall.

Visiting fire houses has always been special for young people and some elders too; usually the magic experience is never forgotten. "Any fire station with its handsome horses and usually a Dalmatian mascot was always exciting," wrote Dan Huntington Fenn some seventy years after his first visit to a Cambridge fire station. "The Firemen showed us how to slide down the brass pole without either burning our hands or landing too hard on our heels. Best of all was when they opened the doors to the horse stalls directly behind the engine and the horses came trotting out to take their places on either side of the pole and directly under the harness, which could be dropped down a foot or so on their

Young visitors at the Firehouse.

backs by pulling a rope and releasing it from the ceiling from which it was suspended. Tighten one or two buckles, and the apparatus was on its way to the fire."

Having said all this but one question remains: What's it like today being a Cambridge fire fighter? Well, it means basically two things: fighting fires and routine maintenance chores. The latter involves such activities as washing floors at station houses, keeping trucks cleaned, polished, ready for the next run, and making sure that fire hoses after a fire are laid out to dry. As for fighting a fire, this is the way one fire person described that part of the job: "Every fire you go to, I think everyone feels really scared. When we go into a building we don't know what we are going to find. We don't know where the wires are. We have no idea what is inside. We go inside like blind men because it is so dark and there is so much smoke. Every fire I go to I don't take lightly." FIRE! FIRE! 9-1-1 9-1-1

POLICE PROTECTION

The town's first constable, Edmund Lockwood, was not elected by its citizens but rather appointed by the Great and General Court of the Commonwealth in May, 1632. He was also given the responsibility with "Mr. Spencer" to confer with the Court along with representatives from the other towns about the "raiseing of a publique stocke." Two years later James Olmstead was the first constable elected by a vote of the town. From the start this office was regarded by the citizens as both an important and honorable one. In 1660 the town opened its first jail and thus was law and order established in Cambridge. As the town's first historian, the Rev. Abiel Holmes, put it, the purpose of laws for the community was "to repress idleness and vice, and to encourage industry and economy."

Serious crimes, however, were not a basic part of the history of Cambridge the town, and in 1845 on the eve of the citizens voting for cityhood, the number of constables had increased to only three, one for each of the three sections of the town. This does not mean that the inhabitants of the town lived without rules and regulations. That was never the Puritan (or their descendants') way.

So law and order ruled that a citizen was required to keep "the street clear from wood and all other things against his own ground," to "help in any business" necessary to the welfare of the town, to keep cocks, hens, and turkeys, out of their neighbor's garden, and to cast out after a month "any stranger" entertained in their home if the "congregation" desires it. Those who failed these legal requirements were subject to appropriate fines or some other kind of just retribution.

What is interesting about this society having all these rules and laws, basically the work of their clergy and legislators, is that largely they were not that necessary for as Roger Thompson pointed out in his 1986 study of Middlesex County (*Sex in Middlesex: Popular Mores in a Massachusetts County, 1649-1699*) it was a community where "there was no great gulf between rich and poor; everyone had food, clothing, shelter, and a recognized place in the social hierarchy." As a result, "tolerance, mutual regard, affection, and prudent common sense all played their part in reducing tensions and nipping criminality in the bud." He concluded based on the evidence he studied that the people living here in the 17th century "far from being a brutal, suspicious, intolerant, and bigoted crew…were concerned, considerate, and cooperative. Consensus and common sense helped to make it a law-abiding place."

When Cambridge decided to organize itself as a city it also restructured its philosophy concerning police protection, although the first mayor, it has been said, thought that if everyone kept a dog that would be all the police protection the city would need. Nevertheless, citing the increasing value of property and the steadily growing population, a police force was created by the new city government. It consisted of seven constables, seven watchmen, and one night policemen. By 1871 it had grown to 50, by 1896 to 94, by 1946, a hundred years after its establishment, to 229, by 1987 to 269, and by the end of the century to 309.

The first police force had no uniforms; they did have, however, most distinctive helmets or as they was popularly called "nail kegs." Actually, they were just high hats made from blue cloth placed over stiff shells. The "watch" also had no patrol wagons or signal system. This meant that when an arrest was made, it usually drew a crowd of interested folks, sometimes as many as one hundred, who regularly followed the officer and the culprit to the lock-up. That trip could be made in three ways: sometimes the two just walked to the jail, sometimes the officer dumped the law breaker into a wheelbarrow and pushed him there, and sometimes he hoisted the man onto his back and carried him there. With them went some of the crowd shouting jests.

Even though the police force was now larger crime still remained low. One of the chief problems the force had to deal with, especially on the Sabbath when males were showing off their "trotters," concerned speeding on the public way. So in 1850, for example, there were 29 individuals arrested for allowing their horses to speed in the city. Another problem was public drunkenness, and in that same year 28 persons were arrested for this crime. By 1920 that figure had risen to 1423. Both still remain serious concerns for contemporary Cambridge.

A constable brings a miscreant to the lockup.

The trend in police service over the last 150 years has been clearly the appointment of more trained staff, better and more useful equipment, and lots more areas of responsibility such as that related to the automobile. One of the significant developments over this time span has been the role of the police not only to apprehend criminals but to try and prevent crimes from ever happening. That is the idea behind Cambridge's Crime Protection Department.

The key word in this work is "education" and there are lots of ways for accomplishing this responsibility. The most obvious is having police officers visit schools to talk about personal safety and such issues as drugs and alcohol abuse. In 1986 the officers began using a fancy and attractive "child safety robot" to better catch youngster's attention. The robot was able on command to move forward or backward, move its arms, flash its eyes, and spin around. In its belly was a VCR monitor; it was also equipped with a audio system. Another education tool, although we tend not to think of it that way, is the department's ability to control and monitor automobile and pedestrian traffic flow by computers. In 1943 this task was accomplished through the Frequency Modulation System whereas today it's handled by an on-line system. Still other education-type tools would be the teaching of self-defense techniques to women to protect them against rape, the stationing of police during the summer at the city's parks and playgrounds to try and eliminate crimes from occurring there, and the development of a citizen's web page to keep them informed about possible criminal problems they might encounter.

A second important response to law and order has been the gradual expansion of the work of the police department into divisions of special responsibilities. So there came to be within the generalized department individuals especially assigned to deal with such specialized tasks as criminal investigations, the search for missing persons, the needs and problems of juveniles and young people in general, traffic matters, crime prevention, and the keeping of accurate records.

Finally, as with the Fire Department, the decades since the 1840's have seen an increase of sophisticated tools available to deal with law and order. A classic example would be the replacement of taking prisoners to the station in wheel barrels or on one's back by the automobile and the patrol wagon. Other examples would be establishing a police laboratory and a police radio room, finger printing of suspects and criminals, motorcycles, the use of parking meters (by 1950 Cambridge had 1200), the introduction in police cars of interactive laptops, and the automation of billing, collecting, and payroll functions. Not to be overlooked is the ability of the police today to work cooperatively with those in neighboring cities, the state, and the federal government, in all law and order matters.

Obviously, the size of the city today and the easy way that law breakers can now transport themselves to attractive crime scenes mandates that larger financial and human resources be a part of the city's realistic attempts to control this problem. Two statistics can reflect the size of the problem: in 1946 there were 886 motor vehicle accidents in Cambridge, in 1980 4,489; and in 1946 there were 850 major crimes in the city while in 1980 there were 8,130 such crimes. Even Robert B. Parker's detective, I think, would be impressed with the daily task facing the police.

The heart-beat of its operations is located in its headquarters at Central Square. This four-story building which was constructed in 1932, also houses the Election Commission. For both departments it has clearly done its duty to the city and its citizens and needs to be retired.

Finally, no historical overflight of law and order in the city can disregard the fact that from time to time the community has had to be critical of some aspects of how it has performed it tasks. People need to remember, however, that society has often used its police forces in somewhat arbitrary ways that have necessarily brought its men and women under strong criticism, some of which is just but certainly some of which is unjust.

When police are directed by the ruling authorities to maintain law and order during such special events as labor, peace, race, and other demonstrations and protests, it very often puts the police force in a no-win position and into situations where mistakes are easily made. Clearly they and society as a whole cannot ignore the ramifications of errors of judgment or the abuse of power even when made honestly during the confusion of maintaining civil order. Indeed no organizations, be they religious, educational, social, or political, can overlook their failures and the resultant consequences.

That's why the Cambridge police monitor their own actions and staff and it is also why the city created in 1984 a Police Review and Advisory Board. The responsibility of this Board is "to ensure that citizen complaints against members of the Cambridge Police Department are met with in a timely, thoughtful, and decisive way, and that determinations are handled through unbiased investigations." It is vital to remember when pondering the actions of any individual, group, or organizations, that we *Homo sapiens* are a far from perfect species. Our saving grace is that sometimes we do educate ourselves and do attempt to clean up our act. As important as that fact is, it does little, however, to ease the pain of those who are the victims of unfair, even cruel, actions.

A most thorough survey of the police department was made at the close of the 1970's by the International Association of Chiefs of Police. It examined how the department was then functioning and made numerous suggestions of how it might better accomplish its work. Especially it noted the need for more minorities and women in police service. The report also took note of how the Cambridge community "perceived" its police department. In short it found that "the majority of individuals interviewed indicated general satisfaction in specific areas with the level of police service." It also found that a goodly number of citizens saw "a need for improvement in particular areas such as training, increased contact between the police and the public, and continuity in beat assignment." Lastly, while there appeared to be "no antagonism" between citizens and the department, there were also "areas of citizen discontent" which the police had to recognize and had to

Frederick Arthur Robinson, the first African American police officer in Cambridge.

GOOD CLEAN WATER

When the First People and the first immigrants wished for clear cool water, they had almost under their noses, so to speak, springs, the Menotomy River, Swamp Creek, Squaw Creek, Sachem Brook, and very soon well water—which had to be pumped by hand. The first well dug was in 1642 in today's Harvard Square. As the new British community grew larger the town had to create a committee to make some rules regarding the use of this water supply, and so after 1700 the Charles River near the Watertown line was the only place farmers could water their cattle and fishing was restricted to the Menotomy River and a weir was put across it. A town dump was also placed here.

These arrangements worked well for over one hundred years until the rapid population growth of the nineteenth century and the need for a reliable supply of water for putting out fires put too heavy a strain on them. So in 1837 a water works charter was given to the Cambridgeport Aqueduct Company to supply the water needs of the Port which up to then had been met by a 103-foot dug well. The new water flowed from springs in nearby Somerville through wooden pipes; a second company, the Cambridge Water Works, was created in 1852 and permitted to draw its water from Fresh Pond. In 1861 it bought out the first company and four years later it was taken over by the City. Since then providing water has been a public responsibility.

address by adopting "policies and strategies which correspond more closely to the needs of these groups."

Law and order as it has been since Puritan Cambridge is still one of the necessary components of this organized community, imperfect as it will probably always be. Nevertheless, it is there to be of help, and if it is a long way to Tipperary, as the old popular song declared, it is also a long way from "nail kegs" and wheelbarrows to the more reliable telephone and POLICE POLICE 9-1-1 9-1-1

Fire hydrants.

When the City assumed this new role, its initial resources included the waters of Fresh Pond, its engine house and about 200 acres of land about them both, a reservoir on the Fayerweather estate, and, finally, a most primitive system for getting water to Old Cambridge as well as the rest of the city. The reservoir was immediately rebuilt and a second one constructed nearby. As the City's population steadily increased—it was 60,000 in 1887 and almost 88,000 ten years later—Cambridge purchased land in Waltham and Weston for a storage basin, and when the state ceded its rights to Fresh Pond to the city, it assumed complete control of the waters available from that source. Later it acquired the land adjacent to the pond which belonged to Belmont and cleared from it all the structures that existed, especially the ice houses which had proven to be a source of water pollution. In due time a lovely park area was developed at Fresh Pond.

In 1923 a purification or filter plant was built here that included space for administrative offices, a laboratory, engine pumps, and facilities that enabled the department to treat the water as needed with appropriate chemicals. Seventy-seven years later it was replaced by a more modern facility. A few years after the first plant was constructed a new electric pumping station and larger more adequate water mains were added. By 1932 water meters had also been placed in all Cambridge homes and buildings; today there are more than thirteen thousand of them.

Further improvements were made after the Second World War. The most significant was a new agreement with the Metropolitan District Commission (since 1984 with the Massachusetts Water Resources Authority) fully connecting Cambridge to its regional system; this allowed the city during emergencies (large fires or during drought periods) to supplement its own water resources with those of the MWRA.

Today the city's water basically comes from Lincoln, Lexington, Waltham and Weston and its two reservoirs—Hobbs Brook and Stony Brook. The first reservoir collects and stores water which is then sent to Stony Brook which is a part of the Charles River Basin complex. From here it flows via an underground pipe through Waltham and Watertown to Fresh Pond where it is treated and pumped to the finished reservoir (Payson Park in Belmont.) The last leg of its journey to homes and buildings is by gravity to the city's water distribution system and its 180 miles of water mains.

Although Cambridge's population growth seems to have leveled off and become stable, the need will always be there to upgrade equipment and replace that which is no longer efficient. In other words, providing Cambridge with a good clean clear water supply is an ongoing municipal responsibility.

COOKING WITH GAS

When manufactured gas first came to the city it was used exclusively for light—in other words, as a source of artificial light to see and read by during the hours of darkness. Such a form of providing light arrived in Cambridge 46 years after it was first used in London (1807) and a generation after it had appeared in Boston. Before gas light, households and business establishments had to get their illumination when the sun set by using open fires, candles, and lamps burning whale oil.

The Cambridge Gas Light Company was formed by several gentlemen in 1852; its first plant was located outside of Harvard Square near the Charles so that the coal it needed to burn to produce manufactured gas could easily be brought over the water to the plant. That took a year to build so that gas did not begin to flow until 1853. By the conclusion of the Civil War the company served 164 houses and firms and operated over 400 street lights throughout the community.

The spread of gas light in the city slowed in the 1870s for several reasons: the economic depression which occurred during that decade, the growing use of kerosene which proved to be safer and more efficient as an alternative to gas light, and the emergence of electricity for lighting purposes. Indeed until the light bulb came along, the kerosene lamp was the most popular artificial light in daily use.

Cambridge Gas & Electric plant next to Magazine Beach.

In spite of these business concerns, the company realized that it was presently using all the gas it could manufacture at its plant and that if it was going to be able to expand its service base it needed to replace that plant with one that could generate more gas. This was done, and the new plant which was located in Kendall Square was formally opened in 1873.

At the same time management also began to investigate the desirability of cooking by gas, although in the early 1880s Cambridge could boast of only two gas stoves in the entire city. Gradually, then, the business of the Cambridge Gas Light Company shifted from lighting to cooking, hot water systems, and eventually to heating homes and business establishments. By the 1950's the company no longer was making its gas from coal but had switched to using the much cheaper natural gas—a mixture of gases from deposits of petroleum—which arrived locally through an amazing national series of pipelines thousands of miles from Cambridge. The Cambridge company continued in operation until Commonwealth Gas, a Massachusetts corporation and wholly-owned subsidiary of Commonwealth Energy System, acquired it on December 31, 1971.

LET THERE BE ELECTRICITY

While Cambridge had gas lights as earlier as 1853, it did not have its first electric lights until 1886, some 33 years later. The first practical use of electric light had taken place in England in 1878 thanks to the work of Sir Joseph Wilson and in America in 1879 thanks to Thomas Alva Edison. Indeed it was Edison who really made electricity possible when he also developed the lines and equipment which enabled power to be communicated between plants and customers.

Twelve months after the formation of the Cambridge Electric Light Company, it was providing power for 77 street lights, 7 commercial arcs, and 847 incandescent lamps; the electricity was supplied from its small plant near the West Boston Bridge. Electric lights proved so popular, however, that within a couple of years the company had erected a new plant at Western Avenue and Memorial Drive.

Soon the company was engaged in negotiations with the West End Street Railway about the possibility of using electricity as the power source for public transportation. Studies showed that this was a real option, and by 1889 electric cars had replaced horse cars on the Harvard Square to Bowdoin Square line. The electricity was supplied via street poles and trolley wires.

The engines and related equipment needed to supply the growing business of the company soon required more space than the second plant was able to provide, and so the company built on the same site a larger and more modern power station which is still in use. For many years the coal that fueled the process of making electricity was delivered to the company's nearby wharf on the Broad Canal.

At about this time Cambridge Electric entered into an agreement with Boston Edison which allowed it to purchase additional electricity as needed. This arrangement worked well during the first half of the twentieth century but then as the demand for electricity steadily increased—beside providing light, electricity was eventually to be used for cooking, radios, heating houses and flats, air conditioning, TVs, computers, CDs, and a host of other new inventions—a second plant was made operational in the Kendall Square area. When atomic energy began to be investigated as a power source for electricity, Cambridge Electric joined with other companies to develop America's first successful atomic energy plant at Rowe in Western Massachusetts. When it went on line this source was utilized until Rowe was shut down in 1993.

If electricity radically re-oriented the way the community spent its evenings and made easier the repetitive humdrum labor-intensive everyday tasks that needed to be done to exist, it also changed the environment of the night sky and the way Cambridge saw the twinkling stars. As with the Charles, we do not know the starry sky of the First People and the first immigrants, for light pollution has effectively driven from our sight the dark sky and has made the visible stars but faint representatives of those enjoyed by previous generations.

WHAT HAPPENS WHEN YOU DON'T EAT AN APPLE A DAY: HOSPITALS

The American Civil War had a dramatic effect on the nation's health care. When that war commenced, such care in America was almost non-existent; by the end of the war the experience gained by the medical services on both sides of that conflict had provided the foundation of our present system for taking care of those who are sick. The Cambridge story reflects closely the growth of health care that took place in the other states during the post-Civil War decades including the establishment of early hospitals "as a product of Protestant patronage and stewardship of the poor." One of the results of the changes occurring was the shift of caring for the sick at home to, as the title of Charles E. Rosenberg's study on the rise of the hospital system puts it, "the care of strangers."

Mount Auburn Hospital

In 1824 when Emily Elizabeth Parsons was born there were no hospitals in Cambridge; when she died fifty-six years later Cambridge Hospital (since 1947 Mount Auburn Hospital) had been founded "for the purpose" as its charter says "of maintaining a Hospital in the City of Cambridge for sick and disabled persons." It came directly out of her work as a nurse, first during the Civil War, then in the city, and from her car-

ing for all who needed such services. Emily understood illness for during her childhood she was its victim on many occasions. Indeed, for most of her lifetime, she suffered with limited eyesight, poor hearing, and lameness.

When the Civil War was over, Emily returned home and started a private campaign to remedy the community's lack of a place where those who were sick and in need of medical assistance but had very limited incomes could come and be helped without having to worry about paying for their care. For the next six years she worked to achieve this goal. She collected donations from her friends (it probably helped that her father was a Professor at the Harvard Law School), and in 1867 she rented a small house for a hospital, but after a year her funds ran out and it had to be closed.

If this was a setback it did not extinguish her work, and in December 1869 she opened a second hospital for women and children on Prospect Street that during the next couple of years had 122 admissions. Her patients, as she was to report in 1871, were "hard working, industrious women, who earn their own support, and, when they have families, supplying either wholly or in part their needs also; but when sick or disabled, they can neither support themselves, nor be properly cared for in their homes."

To start and run a hospital, however, was more than one woman could do, so several men with high social and civic views became the hospital's trustees and saw to its incorporation in 1871. Emily now focused her

Emily Parsons.

efforts on her job as its matron-in-charge. This administrative change did not bring longevity to the institution, however, and a year later the trustees were forced to close its doors. They remained shut for fourteen years until appropriate funding was secured for its re-establishment in 1886.

By then the present site of Mount Auburn, nine and a half acres by the Charles, and the first building were in place. In part they were realized as a result of a generous legacy from Isaac Fay and from the efforts of the Women's Aid Association of the Hospital which had been founded in 1885. The center of the building was devoted to administration activities while its two single story wings served as wards for the patients, one being for men and one for women. The basic therapeutics centered on diet, warmth, cleanliness, and ventilation. Primitive it may have been but it was an important advancement in the medical services available to the community. Sadly, Emily, who had died in 1880, did not see her hope for Cambridge fully realized.

During Cambridge's first two and a half centuries people who were ill were cared for at home. There they had their babies and even their operations. In the eighteenth century when it became common for people to be treated for protection against smallpox by having an inoculation, the town government and the College worked together to promote this practice; later, when Harvard's Medical School was started in Cambridge (before it moved to Boston) they also worked together to establish a hospital that would be associated with it, but lack of funding prevented this from becoming a reality.

Those that were poor were assisted by the town at its Poor House; they were also provided with the services of a doctor. The earliest patients at Mount Auburn Hospital continued to be the poor, for those financially able to do so elected to be cared for at home by their families and servants or to utilize when a doctor recommended it, one of the Boston hospitals. Indeed, it was not until the 1900's that hospital care for everyone became the normal practice although even then, for many families as it had been for generations, the working philosophy left it up to a mother

The Cooper-Frost-Austin House, the oldest "complete" house in Cambridge. The right half was built about 1690; the left half about 1720.

The Hooper-Lee-Nichols House, 159 Brattle Street, headquarters of the Cambridge Historical Society.

Plate 1

The home of the poet
Henry Longfellow.

Cambridge Center for Adult
Education, the former Brattle House, built in 1727.

Plate 2

Wadsworth House, built in
1726.

The Inman Estate, built in
1766.

Plate 3

Some Cambridge birds near William Brewster's Observatory.

Plate 4   Charles River canoe.

An early view of Cambridge and the Charles.

Fresh Pond: yesterday and today.

Radcliffe students studying, 1879.

Plate 5

Harvard University. Eliza Susan Quincy's drawing of the September 1836 procession of Harvard alumni leaving the First Parish Meeting House and walking to the Pavilion. *(Courtesy of Dr. Conrad Wright)*

Two Churches and Graveyard, **watercolor by E. S. B.** *(Courtesy of the Society for the Preservation of New England Antiquities, Photograph by N. L. Stebbins)*

Like Sentinel and Nun, they keep their vigil on the green;
One seems to guard, & one to weep, the dead who lie between.

Plate 6

The First Parish in 1896, watercolor by Mary Winlock, daughter of Joseph Winlock, Director of Harvard College Observatory, 1866–1875.

Plate 7

Blessed Sacrament Church.

1761 - 1986

CHRIST CHURCH CAMBRIDGE

Christ Church Tile.

Plate 8   *Forest Pond at Mount Auburn,* engraved by William H. Bartlett, 1839. *(Courtesy of the Cambridge Public Library)*

employing folklore and home remedies to be both nurse and doctor.

The medical staff of the new hospital consisted of eight "visiting" physicians and two house ones who were as today younger doctors just learning the rudiments of their profession. Between its opening and the end of the century, it treated more than 3,000 persons. The cost of their care was covered by income from the hospital's investments and by gifts from the community. A surgical building was opened in 1898 and the first operation there was performed by Dr. Edmund H. Stevens who was assisted by Dr. John T. G. Nichols. It is a rather nice fact that Nichols had known and worked with Emily Parsons at the start of her efforts to establish a hospital for the community.

The work and usefulness of the hospital gradually increased, especially as the practice of medicine became more scientific and therefore more reliable. In 1907 the hospital trustees decided to open a training school for nurses, thus fulfilling a need for society in general and for the hospital's staffing in particular. At its start the new professional program was for 26 months which was later expanded to two and a half years and finally to three years and was for women between the ages of 21-35. The students lived in their own Nurses' Home (enlarged and renovated in 1918 and in 1929) and followed a set curriculum which consisted of lectures, recitations, demonstrations, and, of course, exams. Instruction was also given "at the bedside of patients, by the visiting physicians and surgeons." In 1915 the school had 52 students, in 1949 97, and by 1953 152. It proved to be for 86 years a vital part of Mount Auburn's mission to the community, but then when its educational work had by and large been shifted into the curriculums of local colleges, it became less significant, and so in 1978 the trustees closed it.

As the population of the city was constantly rising— by the 1930's it had climbed to about 120,000—the demands on the hardworking hospital also rose. Clearly the space and services available in the first set of buildings were no longer adequate. So the trustees began, as they always had to do, a lengthy process of asking for more private community funding to construct additional buildings, and further, to keep the equipment up-to-date and the staff the best that was available. The long-needed addition was finally built in 1913 which doubled the hospital's bed capacity. Soon an obstetrical program was started, and in 1915 a building was opened for the Out-Patient and Social Services Departments. The final building expansions before the Great Depression were begun in 1929 and included space for a children's department, one for private patients, and a substantial addition to the quarters for the student nurses which was not completely finished until 1938.

If the 1930's proved lean financial years for the hospital, they did not affect the needs of its growing constituency. Clearly by the 1940's and the war years the hospital was no longer just a community-based operation but had come to be a "metropolitan"-based

Mt. Auburn Hospital from the air, ca. 1940.

hospital. That fact along with the ever increasing advancements in medical technology and treatment demanded a complete overhaul of hospital space and services.

Indeed, as early as 1939 the trustees had in hand architects, and drawings for such improvements, but it was not until 1958, after a successful funding campaign had been mounted in 1956, that construction began on a new building, then called the South Building. Other renovations were also made, and then in 1973 a new Central Building was erected along with the creation of a parking garage and a Doctor's Office Building. At this period certain older structures no longer serviceable were demolished and so was created the present hospital campus.

At the close of the twentieth century Mount Auburn Hospital had a medical staff of over 500 (this includes full-time and visiting medics), a support staff of 1600, treated more than 11,000 patients a year and more than 255,000 out-patients. It continued its long affiliation with the Harvard Medical School and was one of the founding hospitals of the CareGroup system of Eastern Massachusetts. Its services to its clients are comprehensive, state-of-the-art, and of high quality. At its centennial in 1986 its president could truly say "I cannot help but observe that community support has been and still is the life force that is Mount Auburn Hospital." Nurse Emily Parsons would still be proud of her Cambridge neighbors.

Cambridge Hospital

In the 1911 city election the community authorized the creation of a city-owned and-run hospital, and the next year a Board of Trustees was appointed by the mayor to realize this determination of the citizens. In 1914 land was acquired, construction begun, and on June 1, 1917, the forty-five bed facility opened its doors. Shortly thereafter the hospital started a school for the training of nurses whose first class graduated in 1920.

Clearly the hospital served a public need, for almost immediately a wing (1922) was added to the original building, and eight years later a second wing with additional operating rooms and a children's ward was built along with a new facility for the student nurses. Space was now available to accommodate two hundred patients. Cahill House, the hospital's then new maternity unit, was opened just before World War II.

During the 1960's the hospital became involved in a series of innovative programs which included care for homebound elders, teen parents, non-English speaking immigrants, and the homeless. One of the most important programs was the concept of neighborhood health clinics, and one of the most ardent supporters of the clinics was Estelle Paris, a nurse practitioner for years at the Riverside Clinic and later chair of the Cambridge Health Policy Board. According to Dr. Hilary Worthen, an Inman Square internist, "Estelle is the mother of primary care in Cambridge," and so when the hospital received in 1993 the Foster G. McGaw Prize, which is given to only one American hospital a year in recognition of its health care programs it took the $75,000 donation and with matching funds from the city created the Estelle Paris Scholarship to be used to further education by citizens in health-related areas.

In addition to the clinics, the hospital started Multi-Disciplinary AIDS programs, Healthcare for the Homeless, Midwifery Services, a Child Care Center and a Teen Health Center, House Calls for the elderly, and Linguistic Mental Health Teams. A further significant precedent for the hospital was taken in 1997 when an agreement was reached between the Cambridge Public Health Commission, CareGroup, Inc., and Partners Healthcare System for the latter two groups not to develop or purchase "primary care medical practices" in Cambridge or surrounding cities and towns without discussions and approval from the Cambridge Public Health Commission. In a nutshell, what this did was to curb the ruthless competition in the health market and to promote a sense of collaboration among providers which in the end benefits the consumer.

Supporting these endeavors required extensive renovations and expansion projects to the hospital's plant. These came about after thorough discussions about the needed alterations with nearby residents both in Cambridge and in Somerville. Also taking part in the meetings which led to the final revised plans were the Mid-Cambridge Neighborhood Association, the City of Somerville, and the Somerville Ten Taxpayers group. Once again the involvement of citizens from the local community proved the most desirable way of conducting the city's business.

So as the twentieth century came to a close there was much construction activity at the Cambridge Hospital: it included among other projects a new Outpatient Building and the turning of the first floor of the main building into a new Emergency Department with 16 treatment rooms and an area for fast emergency care.

At the start of the new century Cambridge Hospital remained a city run institution affiliated with the Harvard Medical School and administered by a governing board of representative citizens. Its mission and multi-community oriented programs continued to be, as it was when its doors first opened, excellent health care for all the people of Cambridge. As Jack Barry, regional director of the American Hospital Association, said in 1993, Cambridge Hospital is a "model" for the national health reform America needs so desperately.

Youville Hospital and Rehabilitation Center

Youville which was originally known as the Hospital of the Holy Ghost was opened in 1895 by the Rev. Thomas F. Scully of St. Mary's Church and the "Grey Nuns," or as they are officially called, the Sisters of Charity of Montreal. The order was named for their foundress, St. Marguerite d'Youville, who was canonized by her Church in 1990. In 1970 to honor her they changed the name of their Cambridge Hospital to Youville. The term 'hospital' is especially appropriate to Youville as it comes from the Latin word meaning "a house or institution for guests"; the religious tie is also appropriate for the first hospitals were started in India by the Buddhists 2,200 years before our time.

Its first building was a small cottage with 24 beds; that number was tripled when its main five-story building was opened three years later. Over time additional wings were put up, and in 1969 the main building was remodelled and its fifth floor expanded. The most recent addition to the Youville campus was the opening in 1998 of Youville House, its 95 unit assisted living residence.

Meanwhile, the Sisters had opened a School of Practical Nursing in 1927 which proved of such value that they built for its teaching programs in 1965 a separate eight-story structure. It also served as the dormitory for the School which now offers both full-time and part-time nursing programs.

Today Youville functions as a hospital and as an out-patient rehabilitation center and is still operated by the Grey Nuns as a part of their multi-institutional health care organization, the Covenant Health System. It had revised its mission back in 1946 to include rehabilitation services as well as its hospitalization care.

SERVICES FOR THE EXTENDED FAMILY

The concept of the extended family—yours, that of your immediate neighborhood, and then of the local, national, and world community—is a wonderful one. Also one that has proven essential for the well-being of *Homo sapiens* everywhere. In Cambridge it has always had its role and duty to play in the social living of both the town and the city. A sense of care and concern was embedded in the theology of the Puritan church and from that period on, for better and for worse, it has been a part of the religious and civic structure of the community.

At first it was the church that saw to the needs of the poor and the homeless; however, in 1663 the town also took up that responsibility. Their policy for the next one hundred years was to place indigents in authorized private homes.

In 1779 the Town Meeting moved to set up a home for those of the Cambridge community who needed shelter, and thus was born in the governmental structure a program for General Relief, or as it is now termed, Public Welfare. The refuge created has had over the decades several structures and several names: "the Poor's House," the "almshouse," the Home for the Aged and Infirm or City Infirmary, and after 1974, Neville Manor to honor a former Mayor, Michael J. Neville.

The concept of the extended family involves more than just society's collective duty for the public welfare of its citizens. It includes many other vital community concerns. One of these is the fact that citizens owe certain rights to the men and women who have met the challenges of defending and protecting our liberties and freedoms. In America the idea of such benefits for military veterans reaches back to the Civil War. First there were the war allowances paid to the families of those who had died during the fighting; next came federal and state pensions for veterans, especially those who were disabled. The Soldiers' Relief Act of 1888 extended that coverage to widows of veterans. Since then these benefits have been expanded and improved in countless ways.

As Cambridge grew in population after the Civil War and the living of its citizens became more complicated, there was a need to be more caring rather than less concerned. So, for example, in 1892 the city moved to create a system of public recreational spaces; in 1913 it started to give aid to dependent children; in 1924 it began giving assistance to "citizens sixty-five years or older"; and in 1980 the Department of Human Services was formed and charged with "creating and coordinating services which enhance the quality of life for Cambridge citizens".

That department has come to provide many needed services such as helping those from other world areas learn without charge English as a second language, sponsoring a variety of activities for young people (dance and drama, athletic and leisure classes would be a few examples), funding a multi-service center for the homeless, running a handicapped van, and supplying surplus food to those with inadequate incomes. Two of its more recent concerns are its Commission on the Status of Women and that on Nuclear Disarmament and Peace Education.

Closely related to these matters is the issue of public housing. How to assist those who need a helping hand by their neighbors has always been an essential part of community living. It is the meaning behind Scrooge's cruel response to charity: "Are there no prisons? ... And the Union workhouses? Are they still in operation? ... The Treadmill and the Poor Law are in full vigor, then?" Cambridge's ways of handling this problem were similar to those practiced by other towns and cities.

Today's programs are multi-faceted, managed by several departments and consist of a broad range of services which include those for children, individuals with disabilities, teen centers, fuel assistance, learning centers, and senior centers, in addition to the more traditional ones. These public efforts are of course enlarged by private efforts—especially those provided by the religious community.

Nowhere in Cambridge in the nineteenth century was the religious component of social aid more pressing than the challenges facing the emerging Catholic Church. Its task was two fold. First, it had to recruit priests and build a network of churches to meet the spiritual needs of the new parishioners. At the same time it had to relieve the poverty, the inadequate living conditions, the limited working opportunities, and the hostile prejudice its communicants lived with.

The Church responded both on the diocese level and on the individual community level. On the former, the Church moved to establish hospitals, orphanages, and groups which would meet the collective needs of its people. On the latter, local churches provided the leadership. So in Cambridge educational societies such as St. John's Literary Institute and St. Paul's Lyceum were founded. St. John's was started in 1854 in East Cambridge and focused on the basic immediate needs of the immigrants: how to read and write in English, how to do simple math. As it expanded it had its own circulating library and began offering along with St. Paul's Lyceum in the Harvard Square area "a broad range of activities including lectures, debates, sacred music concerts, poetry readings, children's plays, banquets and dances."

In 1912 the Columbus Day Nursery came into being thanks to the Knights of Columbus (Cambridge Council 74) to care for the non-school age children of working mothers. In North Cambridge at St. John's in 1894 a representative from the Home for Destitute Catholic Children came regularly to church with children needing adoption.

St. John's also had its local St. Vincent de Paul Society. The national St. Vincent de Paul Society was a religious as well as a charitable organization. The founder stressed the spiritual development of members. In this country this included monthly mass, annual retreats and nocturnal adoration of the Sacrament. Charity meant households visited by pairs of S.V.P., then members' discussion and decision. Plus special works, Sunday-school teaching during Archbishop Williams' reign, reception of female immigrants, and care of delinquent boys. At St. John's, the Society during the Depression helped to relieve the distress of many North Cambridge Catholic families.

In the twentieth century one of the most significant tasks facing the extended family of Cambridge was providing good housing for all its citizens. If the attempts to do so did not always reach perfection, the attempts were still honestly made—and could be made as many times as it might be necessary to get it right for each age and period.

The sustained effort began for Cambridge and the country during the 1930's when the Roosevelt administration strongly supported the concept of and the building of public housing as a means of providing working families and those in need with decent places in which to dwell. It did so in several ways but especially through the National Housing Act of 1934, the establishment of the Public Works Administration as well as of the Federal Housing Administration, and the Wagner-Steagall Act of 1937 which provided Federal funds to the states and their local subdivision for construction of low-income housing.

Cambridge's first two public housing projects—Newtowne in 1937 and Washington Elms in 1940—were built after the Massachusetts legislature authorized local communities to do so. Creation of the first project involved the destruction of almost two hundred structures in a fourteen block area. At first many of the units went to victims of the Depression; later the flats were occupied by the many defense workers attracted during the war to jobs in the various factories of the city; and then they became the temporary homes of those who were trying to make do with an inadequate income and of the elderly on fixed income. All of the structures that were built are supervised by the Cambridge Housing Authority, an independent agency with five members, one of whom is appointed by the Governor and the others by the city manager.

After the Second World War when the attention of Americans returned to domestic needs, the Congress passed the Housing Act of 1949 "to remedy the serious housing shortage" facing the country and to eliminate "substandard and other inadequate housing through the clearance of slums and blighted areas." Its purpose was "a decent home and a suitable living environment for every American family." As a direct result of this act, Cambridge constructed another low rent housing project, this one a high-rise building named for FDR. Naming it Roosevelt Towers was completely appropriate for it was that president who both understood the need for public housing and got Congress to make it one of the country's priorities.

Roosevelt wrote in 1937 that "through the Public Works Administration the Federal Government has carried the fight directly to the slum. Today families taken from substandard housing are living happy, healthful lives in our first public housing projects, Atlanta's Techwood development, which replaced eleven blocks of noisome slum with good housing at low rents ... If indeed, the deeper purpose of democratic government is to assist as many of its citizens as possible, especially those who need it the most, then we have a great opportunity lying ahead in the specific field of housing." That was the intent, that was the hope behind all public housing projects, but sadly not always the reality which has been too often scarred by inadequate funding which resulted in poor construction, poor administration, the coming of wide spread use of illegal drugs, shoddy repairs, hallways and stairwells smelling of urine and more, older residents fearful to go out at night, and in time racism. In other words, all the afflictions and too little of the joys that go with being the species *Homo sapiens*.

As a result, during the 1980's and the 1990's, with the help and advice of the tenants involved who had become tired of the conditions in which they were living, with a reconstituted and revitalized administrative board, and with funding from the Executive Office of Communities and Development, Roosevelt Towers was gutted and made new. Washington Elms and Jefferson Park with money allocated by the Department of Housing and Urban Development were also modernized.

At its fiftieth birthday in 1985 the Cambridge Housing Authority could claim that it was currently providing "housing for approximately 10,000 individuals, nearly 11% of the population" of the city and that its program made provision through tenant councils, a tenant Senate, and a number of tenant-staff panels for the participation of all its residents in the decisions which governed their individual and family living in what we term public housing. If this program has never been perfect, if it has from time to time flaws and unmet needs, and if the voice of the community is never fully of one accord on its philosophy and practice, yet the need to be concerned for the welfare of all the members of the community is an essential part of the ways of all those who have lived here by the Charles.

Those involved in and those committed to the idea of Cambridge as an extended family are not limited just to religious groups and governmental agencies. The community supports a host of organizations whose mission is to improve the social and practical needs of its people. A random listing would include the

YMCA, the Cambridge Haitian Services Collaborative, the Margaret Fuller Neighborhood House, Concilio Hispano, Hospice of Cambridge, Cambridge Cares About Aids, Massachusetts Alliance of Portuguese Speakers, Windsor House, Cambridge Community Center, the Pop Warner Football Program, the Women's Center, and Eldercorps. Fortunately, the list

Beverly B. Cassara from Cambridge Senior Volunteer Clearinghouse, at the June 2000 World's Fair in Central Square, explaining how the group matches seniors interested in volunteering with appropriate Cambridge agencies seeking to utilize their skills.

over the centuries includes many other organizations, and as long as the community sees the faces of its neighbors and always hear their voices Cambridge will be an extended family.

"DOWN GENTLY DOWN": BURIAL PLACES

Reader,
Death Is A Debt To Nature Due;
As I Have Paid It So Must You.
Tombstone, Old Burying Ground

There is no question that those who die remain warm and lovely in our hearts and memories; the only question is where to place their sacred bodily remains. The first Cambridge cemetery was located north of today's Ash and Brattle streets and began to be used in 1634-35. Within a year, however, this burial place was closed and the one now between the First Parish meeting house and Christ Church became the town's second official cemetery. In 1735 it was enclosed with a stone wall later to be replaced with a wooden fence and then in 1893 by the present iron one. The City Council had in 1885 put the proper care of this special place with a Board of Cemetery Commissioners who had trees and shrubs planted and the grave markers strengthened. In the early decades of the twentieth-century, however, it was in a condition of general disrepair and the grass between the headstones was often set on fire by cigarettes carelessly cast over its iron fence. Thanks to the concern of a citizen's committee and the city's Plant and Garden Club as well as timely funding from the Economic Recovery Administration it was spruced up and restored in the 1930's. In 1952 it was again cleaned up by the city.

While it was closed to further interments in the 1840s there is still with the permission of the city an occasional burial. For example, the ashes of Dr. Samuel McChord Crothers, minister of the First Parish from 1894 until his death in 1927, and those of his wife, are buried just outside of his study window at the First Parish.

By 1811 the town had need of a second burial place, and so almost three acres on Broadway and Norfolk Streets (now Sennott Park) was purchased and set aside for the rapidly developing Cambridgeport and East Cambridge sections of the community. About forty years later a new city cemetery was established on Coolidge Avenue next to the Mount Auburn Cemetery, and the Broadway one was closed in 1865. After those who had been interred there had been removed to other burial places, the City made it into a public park.

The Coolidge Avenue cemetery was eventually expanded to sixty-six acres from its original twenty-five, and in 1892 an iron fence was erected to replace the previous wooden one. Lots and grave sites continue to be sold and more than five hundred individuals are buried here each year. The city supports a vigorous maintenance program which includes repairing monuments, restoring grave sites, videotaping headstones, and the planting of trees and shrubs.

Mount Auburn Cemetery

On September 24, 1831 two thousand persons listened to an address by Judge Joseph Story at the consecration of the new Mount Auburn Cemetery. (It needs to be pointed out that the cemetery is actually in Watertown, except for a small area at the corner of Coolidge Avenue and Mt. Auburn Street.) In his remarks Judge Story said, "It is to the living mourner--to the parent, weeping over his dear dead child—to the husband, dwelling in his own solitary desolation—to the widow, whose heart is broken by untimely sorrow ... that the repositories of the dead bring home thoughts full of admonition, of instruction, and slowly, but surely, of consolation also." Now widely known as America's first English landscape garden cemetery and one whose design was influenced and inspired by the Père Lachaise Cemetery (1804) in Paris, at its founding the idea that a burial place could also be a place of natural beauty was a novel one in this country.

The cemetery which is nonsectarian started with 72 acres; in 1896 it had increased to 136 acres and today it consists of 170 acres. Originally it was a part of Simon Stone's farm and called Stone's Woods; in 1825 it was purchased by George Watson Brimmer, a Boston merchant who wanted to preserve its trees and natural setting "for some public or appropriate use" (although he also planned to build his house there.) This was never done, and when he and his friends came to real-

Like Sentinel and Nun, they keep their vigil on the green;
One seems to guard, & one to weep, the dead who lie between.

Two Churches and Graveyard, watercolor by E. S. B. *(Courtesy of the Society for the Preservation of New England Antiquities, Photograph by N. L. Stebbins)*

Forest Pond at Mount Auburn, engraved by William H. Bartlett, 1839. *(Courtesy of the Cambridge Public Library)*

ize that it would make a perfect location for a cemetery based on the philosophy and design behind English and French garden cemeteries, he readily sold the land, at a loss, to the Massachusetts Horticultural Society who had agreed to purchase it and sponsor such a cemetery.

In 1831 the state legislature gave the Society permission to use it as a cemetery and after several studies Alexander Wadsworth, a civil engineer, was commissioned to survey the land and lay out basic plots. The General Court four years later authorized the establishment of the Mount Auburn Corporation, a non-profit incorporated organization run by trustees, to oversee its affairs.

The first person buried here was a child from Roxbury. By 1896 the cemetery had 30,861 interments and one hundred years later more than seventy-seven thousand. It is the last resting place of some of America's most famous individuals: poets and actors, scientists and clergy persons, doctors and reformers, historians and painters.

Mount Auburn is also justly famous for its attractive natural environment. It has over two thousand trees and many of its European bushes and black oaks were planted more than a hundred years ago. It has hundreds of different flowering shrubs and many rare foreign trees. The grounds, hills and dells, are accessible by ten miles of roads and by many pathways. There are two chapels, a crematorium, a greenhouse, and a nursery.

After 165 years of public service it has assets of over seventeen million dollars. It continues as an active cemetery and each year performs almost a thousand cremations and more than six hundred burials. The management of the cemetery continues to develop space for future interments and carefully supervises the proper cultivation of landscape and environment. It remains still a wonderful place to view hundreds of different birds in the spring migrating season. In addition, it offers through the Friends of Mount Auburn regular interpretive programs for the public about its "trees, history, monuments, and notable residents" and carries on an extensive restorative and preservation program for the tombstones, monuments, and buildings under its care.

North Cambridge Catholic Cemetery

In 1846 the second Catholic Bishop in Boston, Bishop Joseph Fenwick, arranged for the establishment in North Cambridge of a cemetery to serve the needs of the small but rapidly growing Catholic population of the Boston diocese. He did so because the law of his Church required that its members be buried in consecrated ground, and although the newly opened Mount Auburn Cemetery had provided a section for Catholics which had been duly consecrated, there was a clear need for a Catholic cemetery outside of Boston to serve newly developed parishes.

Due to the anti-Catholic prejudice which was so prevalent at this time, the Church could not purchase the land which was next to Hubbell's Brickyard directly; therefore, it was bought through a "straw" who then graciously gave it to the Church. As a twentieth century Catholic historian noted it was "a cemetery next to a brickyard, near a swamp, along a railroad, for the dead of an outcast group."

In its early years the lots sold for six dollars (at Mount Auburn they were selling for sixty dollars); in addition, the cemetery maintained a Pauper's grave and lots for the youngsters at the Catholic Orphanage in nearby Somerville. The North Cambridge Catholic cemetery soon became the final resting place for many of the Irish, Italian, French, and Portuguese laborers and their families who had immigrated to this area during the nineteenth and early twentieth centuries. Also buried here were many communicants of St. John the Evangelist Church, but it was never that parish's cemetery. Today the cemetery is run by the Diocesan Cemetery Office in Malden.

Into gentleness may our loved ones go.

FURTHER READING

AMES, JAMES B. "The Founding of the Mount Auburn Hospital," *Cambridge Historical Society Proceedings,* 39 (1961–1963) 39–49.

Cambridge, Ma. *The First Three Centuries.* Progress Report of the City of Cambridge, Massachusetts including the *Annual Report* for the Centennial Year, 1946.

Cambridge Electric Light Company. "Historical Sketches." N.P. 1960.

Davis, John F. "The Life Story of Cambridge Water," *Cambridge Historical Society Proceedings,* 41 (1967–1969) 7–15.

DE AMESTI, FELIX. *Reintegrating Public Housing Projects: Projects with the City, Tenants with Society.* Thesis for the Master of Architecture in Urban Design, Graduate School of Design, Harvard University, 1985.

DICKINSON, DAVID T. "The Cambridge Fire Department, 1846–1921," *Cambridge Chronicle,* October 8, 1921, 33–34.

DUNHAM, MARION JESSIE. "The Old Burying Ground in Cambridge," *Cambridge Historical Society Proceedings,* 35 (1953–1954) 23–5.

GREENE, HARDING U. "The History of the Utilities in Cambridge," *Cambridge Historical Society Proceedings,* 42 (1970–1972) 7–13.

International Association of Chiefs of Police, Field Operations Division. "A Survey of the Police Department Cambridge, Massachusetts." [1980] Available at the Cambridge Public Library, Reference Department.

KINGSLEY, CHESTER W. "Cambridge Water-Works," in Arthur Gilman, *The Cambridge of Eighteen Hundred and Ninety-six.* Cambridge, MA: Citizens' Trade Association, 1896, 113–118.

LANCASTER, SOUTHWORTH. "Fire in Cambridge," *Cambridge Historical Society Proceedings,* 36 (1955–1956) 75–92.

LEVINE, MAR D. *Working It Out: Crimewatch, Democracy, and Community Reconstruction in Cambridgeport.* Unpublished Ph.D. thesis, Union Graduate School, March 1986.

LINDEN-WARD, BLANCHE. *Silent City on a Hill: Landscapes of Memory and Boston's Mount Auburn Cemetary.* Columbus: Ohio State University, 1989.

MORRISSEY, LAWRENCE F. *History of the Cambridge Fire Department.* Unpublished, n. d.

SAUNDERS, GEORGE S. "Burial-Places in Cambridge," in Arthur Gilman, *The Cambridge of Eighteen Hundred and Ninety-six.* Cambridge, MA: Citizens' Trade Association, 1896, 133–141.

SAWYER, LISA. *Cambridge Housing Authority: Fiftieth Anniversary Report: 1935–1985.* Cambridge, MA: The Authority, 1986.

SCOTT, NANCY BELL. *A Legacy of Excellence: Mount Auburn Hospital, 1867–1986.* Cambridge, MA: Mount Auburn Hospital, 1984–86.

Thompson, Roger. *Sex in Middlesex: Popular Mores in a Massachusetts County, 1649–1699.* Amherst: University of Massachusetts, 1986.

Cambridge Workers Over the Centuries

CHAPTER FIVE

Cambridge Works

After its founding, and for the rest of the seventeenth century and for all of the eighteenth century, Cambridge's principal work and living was from farming and the College. It was not until the early decades of the next century that the community began to undergo some radical changes in the ways it made its living. If the College remained central, farming was slowly being phased out by light industry, and then during the last antebellum decades by factories. Yet the changes were such that for years Cambridge was at heart a hybrid community; in other words, it was both a rural and a developing urban settlement at one and the same time.

THE ERA OF FARMING

Cambridge farming, and farming as a way of life goes back thousands of years to the Neolithic Age, remained for decades the chief business of the town as it did in many of the other towns of Middlesex County.

William Wood noted in 1634 in his *New England's Prospect* that "the country wherein most of the English have their habitations: it is for certain the best ground and sweetest climate in all those parts" and that "the soil" was "a warm kind of earth, there being little cold-spewing land, no moorish fens, no quagmires." He observed further that its "marshes be rich ground and bring plenty of hay, of which the cattle feed and like" and that "the ground affords very good kitchen gardens for turnips, parsnips, carrots, radishes, and pumpions [pumpkins], muskmellon, isquouterquashes [Algonquin for squash], cucumbers, onions, and whatsoever grows well in England grows as well there, many things better and larger."

His survey also pointed out the excellent availability of such herbs as sweet marjoram, sorrel, yarrow and myrtle, as well as the seasonal abundance of strawberries, gooseberries, raspberries, and currants. Even bearing in mind that Wood's book was intended to lure further emigrants to New England, it remains a reliable source for understanding the first decades of farming in eastern Middlesex County.

Early colonial New England farms, because the land was so plentiful, often ranged from one hundred to two hundred acres. Usually, however, only fifty were under cultivation at any given time. In Cambridge the farms were much smaller than that average; small lots were about five acres, great lots were from six to sixty-three acres. They were cared for by their owners and their families although there was a bit of cooperation among neighbors during harvest, corn-husking season, and for barn raising. It was the male members of the family who worked the field except during harvesting when their womenfolk joined them; ordinarily female responsibility was the care of the dairy, the poultry, and the kitchen garden. Only occasionally was there a hired hand added to this labor force because those with poor land or who were landless could easily remedy their situation by moving to a new location.

While most of the inhabitants then were married to the agricultural way of making a life, the community also needed a few supporting occupations. Cambridge from its start had its share of carpenters, shoemakers, tailors, tanners, and blacksmiths. A century later there were even more non-farming workers such as barbers, brickmakers, coopers, glazers, hatters, sadlers, and distillers.

The tools used by southern New England farmers and their methods of cultivation hardly changed over the decades. Good farming habits, or what they believed were workable ways, were held to from generation to generation. Unfortunately, these ways—deforestation, over-grazing, plowing, ignorance of the concept of crop-rotation—eventually led to soil depletion; even the manure left in the fields by their herds as a fertilizer had only limited value. The result was that farmers had to begin to plant on less suitable acreage; in other words, on poor quality soil which proved to be embedded with rocks and outcrops of stone.

These southern New England farms were as a rule self-sufficient, and what they raised on their plot was basically consumed by themselves rather than sold. Milk, for example, came for generations directly from

A Cambridge kitchen.

household cows and small herds, and if it was sold at all it was done only locally. This was also the case with cheese, butter, meat, and vegetables. In Cambridge there was no common market until 1812.

Douglas McManis in his *Colonial New England* summarizes the accomplishment of the farming era rather nicely: "The first permanent settlers were aliens in a new habitat … decisions about resource use were based on trial and error—the colonists had only their European practices and techniques to fall back on, and the European methods did not always work. With the passage of time, however, they accumulated a greater knowledge of the region's resources, and eventually a distinctive, 'New England' way of doing things evolved … Independence gave New England a new and less restrictive political context. As a major region of the new and expanding country, it was able to broaden its resource base, the range of its markets, and the scope of its intellectual, political, and economic influences …"

There is, however, another layer of understanding to this early era of farming in Cambridge and in New England which is reflected also in the era that was in the process of getting developed. William Cronon in his study *Changes in the Land,* explains it this way: "By integrating New England ecosystems into an ultimately global capitalist economy, colonists and Indians together began a dynamic and unstable process of ecological change which in no way ended by 1800. We live with their legacy today. When the geographer Carl Sauer wrote in the twentieth century that Americans had 'not yet learned the difference between yield and loot,' he was describing one of the most longstanding tendencies of their way of life. Ecological abundance and economic prodigality went hand in hand: the people of plenty were a people of waste."

THE ERA OF URBANIZATION AND INDUSTRY

By 1860 with its population now over 20,000 Cambridge was one of the forty largest independent American communities. Boston at this time had more than 100,000 inhabitants crowded into a small very irregular land area, and so it began to annex its nearest neighbors in order to obtain space for its future growth as the "metropolis of New England." In 1868 it annexed Roxbury, in 1870 Dorchester, and in 1874 Brighton, West Roxbury, and Charlestown. (Hyde Park was not added until 1911.) Although it viewed Brookline and Cambridge as logical land areas for its needs, it failed to devour either which may not be the blessing that the inhabitants of those cities thought it was, for one of the keys to effective government remains deliverable services for all. Historic town and city boundaries, always artificial, created walls to the achievement of this goal.

One of the results of Boston's situation was that Greater Boston local government remained splintered (and often hostile to Boston.) Yet in order for all these cities and towns to function properly in the growing industrial age, intermunicipal cooperation and metropolitan planning became a vital necessity. This was to lead, fortunately, to innovative metropolitan approaches to such regional needs as water, sewage, parks, recreational uses, and transportation.

Meanwhile, as Cambridge rapidly filled up with new immigrants from abroad, especially from Ireland, new factories provided an economic basis equal to that generated by the College. For example, glass making soon gave East Cambridge a stimulus to growth just as brick making and the cattle market did for North Cambridge.

The sections of the town/city which had been isolated from the development and growth of the College

A Cambridge Smithy.

were invigorated and quickly took advantage of their new business opportunities. Possibilities and speculations abounded. Cambridgeport attempted to become "a port of delivery" and blossomed with new streets, building lots, waterways and canals. The immediate success that was expected did not result. But small business concerns—the making of soap, the building of cabinets, the making of carriages—took root here.

The business prosperity that blossomed out in East Cambridge was the result of its factories. It is important to keep in mind that two of the key factors which stimulated Cambridge business was its near location to Boston, whose own industrial base was expanding, and the development now taking place of railroads as a means of shipping and receiving goods and products quickly and economically.

The population of Cambridgeport and East Cambridge between 1848 and 1905 evolved into a mixture of Anglo-Saxons, Canadians (especially French Canadians), Irish, Scotch, Germans, Swedes, Spanish, Portuguese, Italians, Russians, Poles, Latvians, Armenians, and Lithuanians. African Americans, long time Cambridge residents, during this period were 4 percent of the community.

An examination of census figures helps in explaining Cambridge's growth from a post-revolutionary town of 2,115 people to an important industrial and commercial city whose population in 1930 was 113,643. That its dramatic population increases were due to immigrants is very clear. In 1830 there were a little more than 6,000 residents, by 1840 a little more than 8,000 but by 1850 it was over 15,000, by 1855 over 21,000, and by the end of the Civil War over 29,000. In the next twenty years it had doubled to 59,605.

The census figures also indicate the changing population base of the community. The breakdown of non-American residential nativity in 1855 shows that 4,483 were from Ireland; the next closest groups in the listing were British Americans 828 and English 547 with but a handful from any other country. Ten years later the census reveals that two-thirds of the population was American born and that 8,049 were born in another land. Of that total 5,588 were born in Ireland and 1,718 in England and Canada. About Canada, of course, it is important to understand that this category includes several significant nationalities: British, French, and the various populations that emigrated to the Maritime Provinces.

In 1915 with the population now 108,822, the state census shows the native and foreign born births of Cambridge citizens this way: native 72,757, foreign 36,065. The foreign births come principally from Ireland (9,846) and Canada (7,751). The next three largest groups are Italy (2,452), Russia (3,140), and Portugal (2,216). If we jump ahead to the close of the twentieth century when the city's population had fallen to under one hundred thousand (in 1990), the figures for the ancestry of most of its citizens break this way: Irish (16,619), English (11,781), German (10,208), Italian (8,220), and Portuguese (4,761). This federal census also reveals that Cambridge had 72,122 whites, 12,930 blacks, 228 native Americans, 8081 Asian/Pacific islands, and 6,506 Hispanics.

How did all these women and men earn their living? What toil and occupations defined their days and thus defined the broader life of their Cambridge community? Once again a few minutes studying census data is enlightening. In 1885 this is how many Cambridge folks earned their living: government workers (406), professionals (1,126), servants: from live-in to washerwomen to hairdressers (16,106), trade (4,163), transportation (1,828), agriculture (401), fisheries (8), manufactures (10,669), laborers (790), apprentices (334), and at home (7,357). One hundred and five years later this is how they did: managers and professionals (25,416), technicians, sales and administrative support (16,730), service jobs (6,148), government workers (5,700) and laborers, fabricators (3,260). So there it is: what a difference a century can make!

In the volume *The Cambridge of Eighteen Hundred and Ninety-Six,* issued to celebrate the first fifty years of Cambridge as a city, the extensive concluding section focused on the financial and manufacturing aspect of Cambridge's history. It included brief, and in some cases not so brief, accounts of the many business and industrial enterprises then a part of the community's life. It proved a fascinating survey and suggests that the creation of a similar photograph of Cambridge at work during its industrial and technological ages, if done with a less complete lens, would be the ideal way to pic-

ture the daily work of the folk of those times. But first it would be helpful to sketch the many businesses and firms that provided work for the women and men of Cambridge.

It was in 1850 that Edwin Dresser and Eben Denton started a company to produce diaries. Their business just grew and grew and employed members of both sexes in the printing and binding of these little books.

Then there were the people who made musical instruments. In 1854 Henry Mason and Emmons Hamlin joined together to make first melodeons, then parlor organs, and eventually pianos which were sold throughout the world. Church organs, more than eight hundred of them, were built in Cambridge by the S. S. Hamil Company. There was also the Ivers & Pond Piano Company which in the 1890's was turning out between 2,500 to 3,000 pianos a year. There were others, too, such as C. A. Cook & Company which made piano stools and the Standard Action Company which made pianoforte actions.

Meanwhile, other people were engaged in making machinery and boilers. Edward Kendall & Sons in their shops made boilers for many of the largest manufacturing plants in New England. Later Barbour, Stockwell Company, a union of three separate firms, also built boilers; in addition they made various kinds of engines and much of the track used by the Cambridge Railroad. The Rawson & Morrison Manufacturing Company was busy producing such varied items as hoisting-engines, fertilizer dryers, and hydraulic

Various Cambridge businesses.

pumps, while the Boston Bridge Works was busy making steel railway and highway bridges. Locally, they built the Harvard Bridge. The list of companies goes on and on as does what they made: brass items for plumbers, metal pipes, pulleys, hangers, pumps for ships, water tanks, and steam fire engine boilers for locomotives.

Cambridge workers made soap, too, a fact widely known by most of those who live in the city. And why not, since the slaughter houses were so handy! There was the firm of Curtis Davis which began in 1835, that of James C. Davis which was also founded in 1835, that of Lysander Kemp & Sons, John Reardon & Sons who also made candles, and C. L. Jones & Company, and in time Lever Brothers.

Yes, Cambridge was a soapy community; but it was also one that made carriages and cars. The Henderson Brothers of North Cambridge, whose building is still there on Massachusetts Avenue, were famous for their wagons, barges, caravans, hacks, sleighs, and pungs, just as Frances Ivers & Son was well known for its "Ivers" buggy. In addition to five other carriage makers, Henry Ford's company operated a plant down by today's Boston University Bridge from 1913 to 1926 which made and sold the cars and tractors it produced.

Furniture and cabinet work, slaughter houses and hog packing houses, paper collars, fish netting, twine, boxes, coffins, water proof hats, tin cans, feather dusters, step ladders, synthetic rubber, plastic shrink-wrap, and vinegar: all these things were made here and all the factories that produced them were active here at one time. Finding out how Cambridge folks made their living over the decades is just a bit like opening Fibber McGee's famous front hall closest.

Now for a closer description of some of the industrial and technological businesses that made Cambridge what it was and in part still is. In doing so one comes to appreciate the significance of the declaration made by Susan E. Maycock—in her recent study of East Cambridge—that this community had become by 1920 "an industrial city second only to Worcester in Massachusetts."

The Ice Cutting Business at Fresh Pond

The year is 1805, the season is summer, the farm is "Rockwood" in Saugus, and you are there for the wedding reception of Emma and Gardiner. As you sip your drink, cooled with winter ice from the farm pond, you overhear one of the bride's brothers say something dumb, like, "Wouldn't the folks in the hot and sunny West Indies love to have ice-cold drinks." You would probably have laughed with the others who heard this remark for you did not have to go to the College in Cambridge to know that ice would melt long before the ship carrying it from a northern port could reach the West Indies.

The above story, except for your presence, is true, and that was how the chance remark made by his brother William at their sister's wedding planted in the

The ice industry's buildings and the other key sites at Fresh Pond (ca. 1840): (A.) Fresh Pond Hotel, (B.) Ice Houses, (C.) Train Station, (D.) Tudor's Boat House, (E.) Charlestown Railroad, (F.) Fitchburg Railroad, (G.) Alewife Brook, and (H.) Brickyard Swamp.

mind of Frederic Tudor, soon to be New England's Ice King, the challenge that he wrote in his Ice Diary of "transporting Ice to Tropical Climates." Eventually this was to mean selling ice in Cuba, the West Indies, and India as well as in several American cities such as Charleston, Savannah, and New Orleans.

It made his fortune but it took him about eighteen years to do so. Those years were filled with hard, troublesome work, frantic pleas for cash, the accumulation of many debts (and time served in jail for the failure to pay them off when they were due), extensive travels to many ports, the curse to business of the War of 1812, the havoc of a commercial depression, petitions for the exclusive right to sell ice here, there, and everywhere, constant gifts to officials to get these requests granted, the building of ice houses, the harvesting of ice, and the shipping of it safely to its sunny destination. In short, it took patience and stubborn determination, and Frederic Tudor had those two qualities in abundance along with imagination. So in the end he was as he boasted he would be, "inevitable and unavoidable rich."

It began, however, with a failure, for his first shipment of ice in 1806 was a financial calamity although the trip did prove that ice could be transported quickly for it took his brig only twenty days to make the voyage from Boston to St. Pierre, and it also proved that most of the ice so sent would arrive whole. Getting it there Tudor now knew was possible. He also learned that was only half of the battle for the ice melted rap-idly after arrival unless there were suitable ice houses to store it while awaiting customers. At St. Pierre he had no such place, only the sun and the heat. It was the first of many lessons this Boston merchant was to be taught. But Frederic Tudor was a learner.

The Cambridge part of this story was Fresh Pond for it was one of the several sources of ice utilized by the 'Ice King.' It was also where he had hired Nathaniel Jarvis Wyeth in 1826 "to take charge of the active details of my ice business." It was a wise choice, for Wyeth was to create many of the tools and machin-

Interior of an ice house.

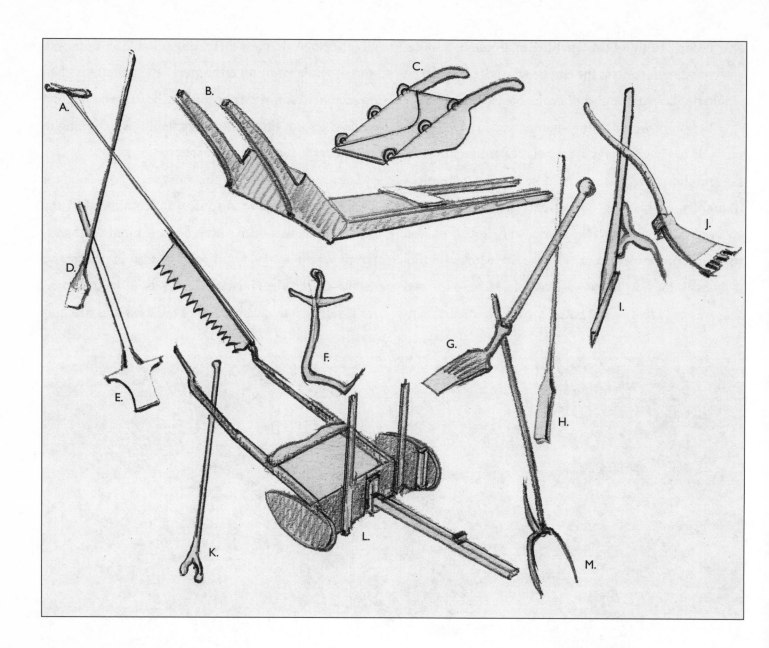

Ice tools:

A. Ice House Saw
B. Snow Scraper
C. Snow Scraper
D. Chisel
E. House Bar
F. Grapple
G. Floor Chisel

H. Canal Chisel
I. Cant Hook
J. Ice Adze
K. Line Marker
L. Snow Scraper
M. Elevator Fork

Nathaniel Jarvis Wyeth

ery that made running an ice business practical and profitable.

The Wyeth family's ties to Fresh Pond stretched back to the middle of the eighteenth century. Here his father had built on a bluff facing the pond (in the area of today's Kingsley Park) a hotel that was for many years a popular summer attraction for well-to-do Bostonians. It was there too that Nathaniel was born in 1802 and where he was working when Tudor made him his foreman. Later many of the employees of Tudor's ice business were to be housed at Wyeth's hotel.

Almost from day one Wyeth began inventing things to improve the harvesting of ice. Indeed most of the innovations in cutting and harvesting ice came out of his mind. For example, he arranged to have the ice blocks cut to a standard size and weight rather than the haphazard cuts of the past; he also started having ice cut by a horse-drawn cutter rather than sawing it by hand. The latter change not only saved time but saved Mr. Tudor money and had his boss call him "active & intelligent" and "just enough of a schemer & inventor to be valuable."

Improvements in the methods of operating the business continued over the years and clearly during the early years at least these two men worked as well together as anyone could have worked with "the Ice King." In time Wyeth was to make his own fortune thanks to his hotel business, his Oregon adventure, his western fur trade, and through shipping produce to the Caribbean which enabled him to leave Tudor's employment and to develop his own flourishing ice business and thus to become one of Tudor's "hated" competitors.

The ice business was a lively one and by 1834 thirteen ice houses had been erected at Fresh Pond; Tudor's were along its northern edge. Conflicts over ice-cutting rights led to a division of the pond in 1841 into areas where different concerns could cut it. That same year the newly built Charlestown Branch Railroad Company line between Fresh Pond and Charlestown began shipping Wyeth's ice directly to the port of Boston where it was loaded onto the ice-clippers. Previously it had been drawn by teams of oxen.

The ice trade peaked about the time of the Civil War and slowly declined throughout the rest of the nineteenth century although ice was still sold, especially for home ice box consumption, through the first decades of the next century.

The ice business at Fresh Pond meant jobs for the Cambridge community and an income for those working at the trade. Since it was a winter task it also proved to be a way for local farmers and others to supplement their regular income. It was not, however, an easy way to make a living for those actually harvesting the ice. Nor for the horse teams involved. But it was quite striking to watch. The poet Henry Wadsworth Longfellow did just that one afternoon in February 1847. He saw "the horses passing up and down among the pines; the green gloom above, the white snow beneath; the men on the lake; the square blocks of ice sliding along their canal, then borne up through the trees to descend the inclined plane on iron grooves into the great ice-houses."

Another vivid picture of the business is to be found in the journal entry of Benjamin Waterhouse for March 5, 1836: "The snow and thick solid ice still remains, and cubes of ice from 'Fresh Pond' incessantly, from before day-light to after sunset, pass in six-horse teams without an interval of half an hour…The quantity shipped is incredible, as there is as yet no tax upon it, the profit immense, compared with our laborious brickmakers. Besides this, which passes in front of my house, there are three other avenues to Boston through which this luxury is passing in quantities absolutely incredible."

The Glass Business in Cambridge

The New England Glass Company was started in 1818 as a result of the financial failure of the Boston Porcelain and Glass Company which had been established at Lechmere Point four years earlier. The new concern took over Porcelain's factory with its single six-pot furnace for the expressed purpose of making and selling the best "flint and crown glass of all kinds" available in America.

The manufacturing of glass was still fairly new in the States; indeed, the first significant glass company in Boston had not begun operating until 1787. New England Glass owed its establishment to Amos Binney, Edmund Monroe, Daniel Hastings, and Deming Jones; the latter while he was only 27 years old was selected due to his knowledge of glass making on Cape Cod to become the company's first business agent (he served until 1815) and proved to be an excellent choice.

The new company immediately constructed a second furnace and eventually several others. (The first three were nicknamed by the workers Etna, Vesuvius, and Trio.) Their plant had twenty-four steam powered glass-cutting mills and a red lead furnace that produced each week two tons of the stuff. These were clearly the days before the danger of lead poisoning was understood to be the peril that it is. The staff soon grew

Making glass objects

Glass factory salesroom.

to 140 workmen and by the middle of the century to 450 men and women. The women worked in the sales department and also assisted with cleaning the molds. New England Glass's capital was about half a million by now.

Glass making was a specialty craft that depended for good quality vases and jars on skillful employees and during the company's first decades many of these had to be lured from England and Scotland to Cambridge. The making of fine glass objects required manual ability for cutting and engraving as well as carefully controlled breathing for shaping objects. New England Glass soon became well known far and wide for the excellence of its products including both commercial items such as domestic house ware and highly prized unique items such as clear crystal glass, church chandeliers, beautiful vases, and decanters. At one period the company had agencies in New York City, Philadelphia, and Baltimore.

Business was excellent up to and really even during the Civil War; then the company's prospects began to dim. It suffered several financial setbacks as well as growing competition from other firms which led to its demise in 1888. Some years earlier one of its rivals had discovered a formula for making lime glass which proved to be cheaper to use than flint glass and which soon replaced it for everyday glass ware. New England Glass refused to adopt the new technique as its quality was not as high as the glass manufactured the old way. In time this decision severely limited its sales and profits.

In addition, during the 1870's a series of serious charges of poor management were leveled against the company along with questions of the honesty of some members of the staff. Talk of bankruptcy was in the air. To make a difficult situation more complicated, the iron roof on the largest furnace collapsed (fortunately killing no one.) The work force, which had become unionized now initiated several strikes. As bad as these developments were for the company, its death as a viable business was really due to the high cost of burning coal which had to be transported from Ohio and Pennsylvania to Cambridge and its obsolete plant. The only logical decision was the one taken to close its Cambridge doors and move to Ohio where it soon became the Libbey Glass Company. The old Cambridge plant was used for a while by the West End Street Railroad but was finally razed.

New England Glass was not the only glass concern in the city—others included New-England Crown Glass, the New England Glass Bottle Company, and the Bay State Glass Company—but it was the city's number one employer during its heyday. Perhaps its real legacy, however, is that surviving pieces of its artistic creations are still prized collectibles.

The Kennedy Biscuit Business at Cambridgeport

For Cambridgeport, it all started in the 1850's when Artemas Kennedy improved the cracker originally made in Arlington by his grandfather, also named Artemas Kennedy. The grandson's dough utilized in a special way the fermentation that occurred when yeast, dough, and water interacted. The result were crackers called the Kennedy Commons. These crackers were transported by wagons form his Cambridgeport factory to many Massachusetts towns and cities and eventually they even turned up as a part of the diet of the California gold miners.

Kennedy biscuits proved very popular with Americans and before long it became the largest bakery in the

Mr. Kennedy's Biscuits. *(Courtesy of the Rev. Dr. Janet H. Bowering)*

country. The company made numerous other eatables beside their Kennedy Commons: zwiebacks, pretzels, jumbles, gingersnaps, and, after 1892, Fig Newtons, which were named for the nearby Boston suburb. When Artemas died in 1861 he was succeeded by his son Frank.

Soon sales branches were opened in Philadelphia and New York city and a major bakery was constructed in Chicago in 1881. When that burned down three years later it was replaced by a six story building. A new Cambridgeport factory had been erected on Green Street in 1875; the company also had its own electric light plant. In 1890 Kennedy Biscuits had a staff of 650.

One should not forget that working conditions at the end of the nineteenth century were far different than they are just one hundred years later. As William Cahn pointed out in his study of the National Biscuit Company, "The employee in the biscuit manufacturing industry was typical of the new industrial worker of the era. He was without security; he worked long hours for meager wages under hazardous conditions...And when the demand for products slowed down, working people found themselves unemployed, without hope of finding other jobs or anything to eat."

It was at this time that Kennedy Biscuits was acquired by the New York Biscuit Company of Chicago, a corporation which had been formed from a number of baking firms and which soon became the leading baking company in the eastern half of the country. The bakery in Cambridgeport was its second largest and two members of the Kennedy staff were among those who soon led the newly created company: Henry J. Evans from its Chicago plant and James W. Hazen from the Cambridgeport plant.

This was a period of mergers and ever larger business organizations, and so it was quite natural that the various American baking establishments shared in this trend. Thus, eight years after the New York Biscuit Company was born, it was consolidated with companies from across the nation into the National Biscuit Company (and many decades later it ended up a part of RJR Nabisco, Inc.) The new concern represented about half of the bakeries in the states producing cookies, crackers, and biscuits and went on to become one of the dominant business companies of the next century. One of its many plants was continued in Cambridge until 1938.

The Brick Making Business at North Cambridge

Among the first workers in the brickyards were men from Ireland such as Tip O'Neill's grandfather and his uncles. As the grandson declared, they "settled in North Cambridge and worked in the brickyards, where they made bricks with nothing more than picks, shovels, and wheelbarrows. They would mix the clay, soften it, throw it in the kiln, and then bake the bricks." Later his father also worked in the yards "digging with a pick and an ax and loading the clay on a tram, with a horse to

The Cambridge brick yards.

pull it up the slope from the pit." In time the Irish parents encouraged their kids to get out of those pits; when this happened their places were filled first by French Canadians and then by Italian immigrants.

The making of bricks is thousands of years old. The ancient peoples of Egypt, Mesopotamia, and the Roman Empire made them and built with them. Among the early artisans of the Bay Colony were skilled brick workers. In nearby Medford bricks were manufactured and used in construction in the seventeenth century. Indeed, one of the earliest extant structures from that period is the two and a half story brick Tufts House (also known as the Cradock House) in Medford which was built between 1677 and 1680. From 1650 through 1750 the making of bricks was that town's largest business enterprise.

While Cambridge did not begin to utilize its glacial clay until the nineteenth century, there were in the 18th century small pits on the north side of the hill off Garden Street. The Sands family operated clay

Making bricks.

pits and brickyards in East Cambridge in the Brick-bottom neighborhood, off Harding Street, in the 1820s, and then along Putnam Avenue around Flagg Street in the 1830s, before moving out to Garden Street in the 1840s. Sands family brick houses still exist at 145 Elm Street and 22 Putnam Avenue.

Just where were Cambridge's major clay pits? First they were in Northwest Cambridge, and next more specifically in the Great Swamp near Alewife Brook, and finally, to be very specific, between Vassal Lane and Walden Street to Rindge Avenue and Alewife Brook. For a quick indication of where the pits were think of St. Peter's Field, Jefferson Park, Jerry's Pond, the Tobin School which are all former clay sites.

In the opening years of the nineteenth century much of this land area was owned by farmers and consisted of swamp willows, bramble thickets, and meadow grass. When the demand arose for commercially manufactured bricks, the land was sold or leased to a number of individuals and firms, and the result was the brickyards with their pits, drying kilns, and tramways of Northwest Cambridge. It is at this point of the story that men like Tip O'Neill's grandfather were hired to do the hard daily work of turning clay into bricks.

The bricks were made out of clay or shale and took their final color of yellow, red, and shades thereof, from the nature of the clay/shale deposits. Bricks were of two types: water-struck or sand-struck. In making bricks, a horse and a plough which literally "plowed" the clay as a farmer might a field were used. Once plowed, a harrow was rolled over the bed. Next, the clay along with more water and sand went into a "soaking pit" for about ten days. It was occasionally stirred and then put into a special machine, powered by a horse, which beat it until it was put into molds and set out to be dried by the sun. Burlap was used to help the bricks dry evenly or to keep out the rain. Eventually they were put out on flats for further drying and then put into "stone kilns" for firing. Later machines were used for much of the manual labor.

Although some bricks had been made in Cambridge during the colonial era, the real development of the business began when Nathaniel J. Wyeth of ice harvesting fame leased some clay land in 1844 to Peter Hubbell and Almon Abbott for the production of bricks. When this first enterprise proved successful, Wyeth leased out more land and finally got into the act himself with his own brickyard. That was all that was needed to create a clay rush. Among those who flocked to the business during the rest of the century were John Sands, Asa Murdock, Samuel Cofran, Charles Dana, Ben Parker, Jonas Wyeth, Royal Stimson, Solomon Sargent, and the four Parry brothers (John, George, Richard, and William.)

As with every business venture, brick making had its financial ups and downs, buyouts and mergers. It was adversely affected during the Panic of 1848; it experienced a boom period during the Civil War and another during the good economic years of the 1880s, and then once again a bad time during the Panic of 1893. In 1900 the Bay State Brick Company, which had earlier acquired a large chunk of the brick-making business, sold its holdings to the New England Brick Company (N.E.B.Co), a Boston firm. The brickyards continued to operate during both world wars and then declined and disappeared. The city in 1951 purchased some of the pits and filled them with trash until 1971. The last bricks were actually made as late as 1970 by Hews Pottery on Sherman Street.

Growing up in the city during the 1940's, Jack Tennis recalled the final years of making bricks here. "When we got older," he wrote, "we used to jump the train to the brickyards in North Cambridge. Those were raggedy buildings, a ramshack place, you or I wouldn't work in a thing like that today, you'd condemn it. We'd walk through there watching the guys firing up their ovens, making their bricks, until they found us and kicked us out. Then suddenly they quit. I don't know what happened, they must have run out of clay."

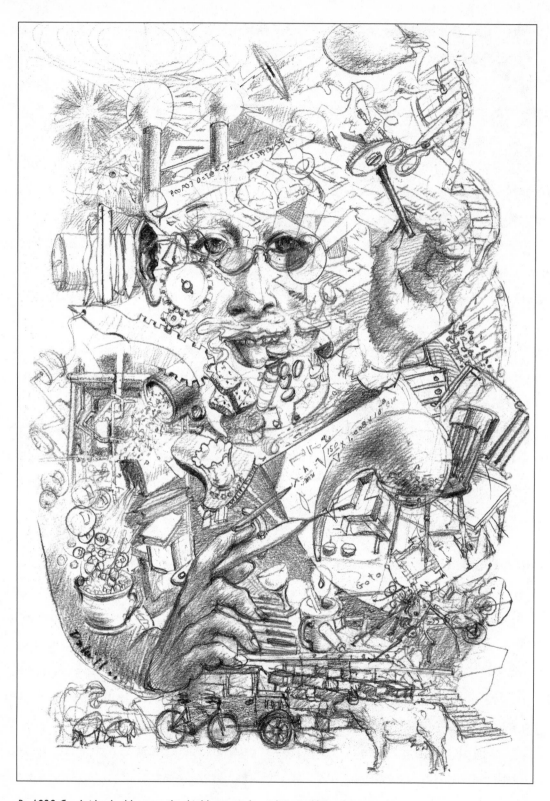

By 1920 Cambridge had become the third largest industrial city in Massachusetts.

The Hose Business at East Cambridge

The Boston Woven Hose and Rubber Company was launched in 1880 by Theodore A. Dodge in two rooms in the Curtis Davis Soap Factory on Portland street. It started with a staff of seven and a newly designed loom for the fabrication of fire and garden hose. Seven years later it had increased its staff to sixty and had erected a three-story brick building on the former Kinsley Iron property on Portland and Hampshire streets. By the end of the century its annual output of hose was more than a million feet.

Its early prosperity was based on its development of its Vim hose-pipe (single tube) bicycle tire. As its turn-of-the-century ad claimed, "one of the greatest if not the greatest features of the Vim tire is the pebble tread, the first non skid tread … The pebble tread makes the tire a wonderful hill climber. In fact it now holds the world's record in climbing the famous Corey Hill, the greatest number of times in an hour."

The Broad Canal which connected to the Charles River ran through the company's property; it was used by them to bring their coal barges to its power plant and also for cooling its turbines, rubber mills, and calendus. Several more buildings had been added by now including a foundry, a brass shop, and a mill room, and in 1952 a million dollar reclaim plant was constructed. Adjacent to its property were two railroad sidings making transportation of goods convenient.

Just prior to the First World War, Boston Woven ran into financial difficulties which resulted in its being acquired by new owners and managers. For most of the twentieth century it offered employment to 1,600 workers, two-thirds of whom lived in either Cambridge or Somerville. This work staff consisted of a good number of talented engineers and chemists whose discoveries produced patents which enabled the company to stay commercially viable. An example would be the Rotocure machine "for the continuous vulcanization of sheeted and plied rubber products."

Over the decades Boston Woven produced cuspidor mats (for brass spittoons), rubberized fabrics for cars, carriage tops and curtains, heels and soles (six thousand a day in 1915), flat belting for moving items, conveyer belting, V-Belts for direct drives, rubber and plastic garden hose, rubber rings for fruit jars (at one time ten tons a day), garden hose nozzles, fire hose couplings, and friction tape.

Modern technological progress made Boston Woven's plants and equipment obsolete and inefficient by the 1950's. As a result it began to lose large amounts of money and, therefore, when the American Biltrite Rubber Company in nearby Chelsea acquired in 1956 enough of its stock to control the business, it was merged in 1957 into that company.

The Candy Business at Central Square

It all started in 1927, this making of candy in Cambridge by the New England Confectionery Company or

The Mark 1 and the Imac Ruby

NECCO as it is more commonly known to the friends of eating candy. But of course it really did not start in 1927. That was simply the year that this Boston firm moved into its just built six-story brick, stone, and concrete two and a half acre plant on Massachusetts Avenue. Its making of candy really goes back some eighty years before to 1847.

So it really all started that year when the Chase brothers—Oliver, Silas, and Daniel—got into the business. Oliver invented the candy wafer and the machine to produce it in bulk and some years later Daniel did the same for what was to become one of NECCO's most popular products, the small heart-shaped pieces of candy with printing on them such as expressing such sweet romantic Valentine messages as "I LOVE YOU" and "BE MINE" and "KISS ME."

The present company was created in 1901 when Chase merged with two other candy makers to create The New England Confectionery Company. Eventually, just as MIT had done, it crossed the Charles to relocate in Cambridge beside, at that time, such companies as Ford and Lever Brothers. In 1963 it became a vital part of the United Industrial Syndicate, the New York-based holding company. While the candy business is seasonal, and therefore its need for workers is also, NECCO remains at the start of the twenty first century an active part of the Cambridge business landscape. When you walk by it pause and remember the city's good nineteenth century industrial past.

THE AGE OF TECHNOLOGY

The story of Cambridge business after the Second World War is as varied and remarkable as it was during the nineteenth century and the first four decades of the twentieth century. So it is somewhat unfair to highlight just a few of the many companies that were, and in many cases still are, active and vigorous components of the business scene here especially since the end of the Second World War.

Of course the end of that war was no magic curtain coming down on one kind of industrial scene and then opening to a very different business focus. The roots, for example, of both Raytheon and Polaroid reach much further back than that. Yet it is right to say that it was after that terrible conflict that technology emerged in a major way to change both the business culture and the character of the society of Cambridge and indeed of the world.

Cambridge and the entire Greater Boston area proved to be a popular place for research in many new fields of endeavor as the twentieth century began its historical march. One of these fields was that of electronics. Examples of Cambridge firms working in this area would be the Clapp-Eastham Company and its offspring, the General Radio Company. The former sold early radio receiving sets called Radak; the latter also produced radios. Other concerns working in the wireless field here were the National Company, the

Cutting and Washington Company, Harvey Radio, Hermon Hosmer Scott, and the Krohn-Hite Instrument Company. Dwarfing them all eventually was Raytheon. In time, work in the field of electronics grew from radios to include computers, geophysics, guided missiles, and much more. Truly, as Harold B. Richmond put it in his 1952 talk to the Cambridge Historical Society, the city was "a pioneer home of electronics."

Yet it also proved to be a pioneer home for engineering as well as a center for other kinds of research and development firms. These included organizations like Biogen, which produces among other products drugs to make people healthy through genetic engineering, the Lotus Development Corporation, whose software products are used internationally, and the technological research company of Arthur D. Little, which has its offices and laboratories in Cambridge.

The Raytheon Company

The American Appliance Company was born on July 7, 1922; three years later its name was changed to the Raytheon Manufacturing Company. Raytheon at the end of the twentieth century was the largest private employer in Massachusetts. It took its name from the rectifier tubes or S tubes for radios developed by C. G. Smith that it was producing. While Raytheon did not invent the radio, its early innovations made it possible to operate them from wall sockets. More important to the consumer, it made radios affordable for everyone. None of this would have happened, however, without the involvement of two men whose vision, drive, and abilities made the company's growth possible: Dr. Vannevar Bush and Laurence K. Marshall.

Strangely enough, the company's first product was refrigerators and its roots traveled back to a defunct company called the American Research and Development Corporation (AMRAD) which was active during the First World War. Its first lab was located in the Suffolk Engraving Company building in Kendall Square. By 1926 it was leasing a two-story building on Carlton Street.

A basic re-organization of the company took place in 1928 and a brand new name—the now familiar Raytheon—was created for it. From this point the Raytheon story becomes complicated with, as one of its historian put it, "big dreams; large sums; big business." In short the Raytheon Company became the Raytheon Companies.

It had prospered almost immediately and had soon become a million dollar a year corporation. While this may sound impressive, the fact remains that at this point in its history it was nothing more than a small Cambridge business with a staff just over three hundred.

It came out of the Great Depression in pretty good shape and in 1934 it opened a factory in the nearby town of Waltham, and by the 1950's it had grown from one to twenty-five buildings with plants and labs in many Massachusetts locations such as Newton, Quincy, Wayland, Burlington, Bedford, Lowell, as well as with numerous operations outside of the state in such places as Chicago and Rhode Island, England, France, and Switzerland. During the 1960's it moved its main headquarters to Lexington, Massachusetts.

It was the Second World War with its technological needs that helped to make Raytheon the company it is today. By the end of that war its production was forty times that of 1940 and the number of its employees exceeded 16,000. But the war was not the only component of its success. This was due as much to the ability of its management teams, their financial boldness, some luck, and the company's willingness to collaborate and bond with other firms in expanding the electronic possibilities now driving one section of the Technological Age. An example is its association with another Cambridge outfit, the small Acme Delta Manufacturing Company whose transmitters and magnetic components were ahead of its competitors. Working as Acme Delta, they joined together their creative skills to produce equipment for radios. Eventually Raytheon bought Delta outright.

The working philosophy of management was simple during these years. First, they always kept in mind that the raw material for their business success lay in their close access to the technological brains produced by colleges and universities, especially those of the Bay State. Second, they always made sure that they had workers "who wanted to do things." If Raytheon is no longer located in Cambridge, it was Cambridge and its rather unique mixture of intelligence and daring that made its conception and birth possible. For Cambridge the significance of the Raytheon story is the fact that businesses which operate in Kendall Square near MIT and Harvard operate in a brilliant location.

The Polaroid Corporation

"The era of immediately visible, living images is now at hand." These are the words of Edwin Herbert Land one of the founders of the Polaroid Corporation who was born at Bridgeport, Connecticut in 1909, who attended Harvard University but did not graduate from it or from any college, who invented the revolutionary Polaroid Model 95 Land camera in 1947, the SX-70 instant color camera in 1970, and who uttering the above words introduced his latest invention Polavision instant motion pictures in 1977. Of course the Polaroid Corporation is also well known for many other now common day items such as its sunglasses and glare-free desk lamps.

Land opened his first lab at age seventeen in the Big Apple, his next at Harvard when he was a student and just twenty, and when he was only twenty-three invented his first usable product which artificially polarized light and was later called Polaroid. Then with George Wheelwright III, his Harvard physics section leader, he started in a Wellesley, Massachusetts barn, the Land-Wheelwright Laboratories, the fore-runner of the

Polaroid Corporation which was formed later in Cambridge in 1937.

The story of Polaroid, its inventions and business growth, involves many locations and individuals outside of Cambridge. Its importance to this city, however, is three-fold: first, it retains its corporate headquarters in Technology Square in East Cambridge; second, it is the community's third largest employer; and lastly, it continues to maintain here its research facilities.

In Mark Olshaker's recent study of Polaroid he points out that if its Cambridge complex of buildings are not "readily identifiable" and that if the corporation does not dominate the community as does its two main universities or as does the Eastman Kodak Company in Rochester, New York, it has nevertheless made a significant and positive set of contributions to the community's history. He goes on to say that while "it is difficult to determine exactly what portion of Polaroid's corporate development has been influenced by the intellectual character of Cambridge, and what portion has been the result of Dr. Land's personality," it is clear that Dr. Land "is a product of this intellectual tradition" and that "even the naming of Technology Square, a modern development built by MIT, indicates a certain orientation and acknowledges the value and faith placed in science."

The important key here is the welcoming intellectual atmosphere which has played such a vital role in fostering the city's twentieth century business base. Therefore, when Harvard awarded Land an honorary Doctor of Science degree in 1957, the citation quite properly said: "Through his ingenuity we can portray ourselves in 60 seconds; through his industry the life of our city becomes more abundant."

Draper Laboratory

It reads just like a mission statement, this self-generated and succinct description of its purpose and service and so is worth quoting in part. "Draper Laboratory is a non-profit organization dedicated to engineering of prototype systems, research and development and education. Functioning as a Design Agent and skilled in the efficient and orderly transfer of advanced technological application and methods to industry." In 1998 the Lab celebrated its 25th anniversary as an independent corporation. However, its historical roots are much older than 25 years.

It all started with the amazing Charles Stark Draper, a 1926 graduate of MIT who never really left the Institute, and his equally amazing Aeronautical Engine Lab which he started in the 1930's. Here Draper and his staff developed inertial navigation, which enables an airplane pilot to operate his plane without reference to visual or radio signals. The plane you fly today is guided by the incredible accuracy of this innovation. The basis of inertial navigation is Draper's invention of the "single- degree-of-freedom gyroscope" as applied to his accelerometer.

During the Second World War the Draper Lab, now

The lead pencil of the 20th century.

a series of laboratories, applied this basic navigation and guidance concept to all human made things which use the sea, the land, the sky, and space. In other words, the reality behind the images conjured up by the terms Polaris, Poseidon, Trident, Titan, the MX/Peacekeeper, Apollo, Skylab, Space Shuttle, Navy Hydrofoils, Deep Submergence Rescue Vehicle, and Aerial Profiling of Terrain System, function because of the pioneer work of Charles Draper and his colleagues. The Lab went on, as one of its publications states, to delve into "fault tolerant computing, energy systems, software systems, oceanographic sciences, precision instruments, and precision pointing and tracking systems."

MIT in 1973 gave the Instrumentation Lab its freedom and separated it from the control of the Institute. So it moved its several labs with its staff out of the MIT complex, incorporated, and set up its teaching and working laboratory next to—one might say—Mom at 555 Technology Square. At one time Draper employed over 2,000 staff members but the number of its employees fluctuates according to the "fatness" of the budget of the United States Department of Defense.

At its 25th celebration the Chairman of its Board declared: "I believe that Draper can look forward with confidence to the future…It has a very, very good reputation, it has a solid base of current customers, it has really good people, it has good leadership." Its president, Vince Vitto, put its future this way: "You can't just walk up to someone and tell them what the capabilities are—you have to be able to conceptualize the problems and demonstrate to people how the technology and the fundamental capabilities of Draper Laboratory play into a major government or commercial research and development project."

THE AGE OF CYBERSPACE

This intellectual reliance on science and its method and approach to knowledge and development will continue to be an important and basic ingredient of the new age of cyberspace. Dr. Edwin Land put it this way:

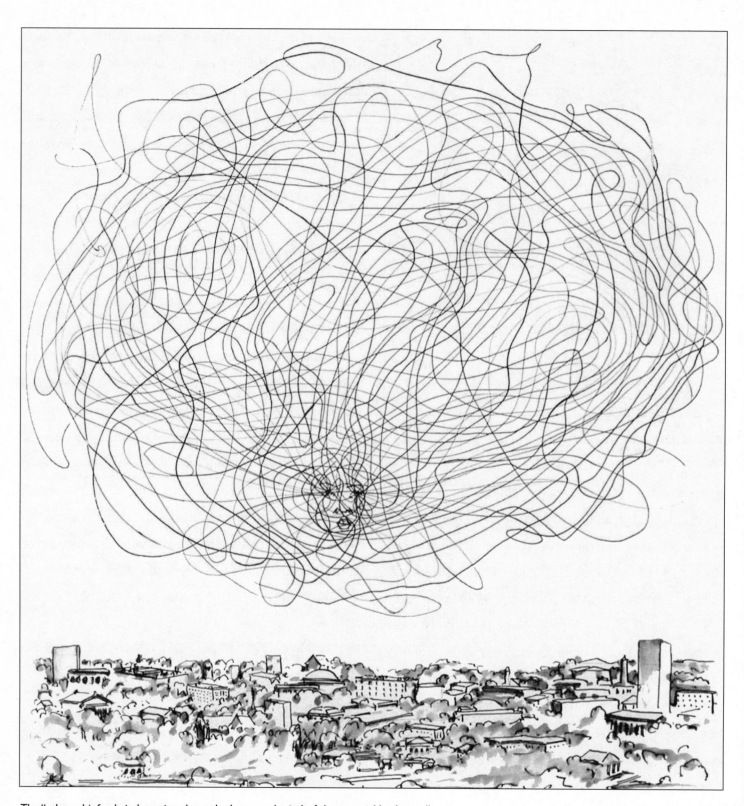

The "ethereal info-skein hovering above the bump and grind of the material landscape."

"An essential aspect of creativity is not being afraid to fail. Scientists made a great invention by calling their activities hypotheses and experiments. They made it permissible to fail repeatedly until in the end they got the results they wanted. In politics or government, if you made a hypothesis and it didn't work out, you had your head cut off. The first time you fail outside the scientific world you are through."

Certain older concepts will continue to symbolize the nature and drive of Cambridge business and industry during this new age. Some of these are creativity, innovative inventions, luck or chance, risk, persistence, and determination. As in all business ventures, daring to take a risk and the brilliance of the invention and the business undertaking do not mean success. As in the past there will be many failures in the age of cyberspace. However, granted that fact, it seems more than appropriate to close this survey of Cambridge business with two examples from this new era of companies which have succeeded.

Cognectics, Inc.

Today's Cognetics, once located in the industrial complex at Cambridge Park Drive just back of the Alewife T station, is an example of a business that was seeded by MIT. It came into existence in 1983 when a group of economic and business researchers from the Institute under the leadership of Dr. David Birch and William L. Parsons wedded their knowledge about employment, business growth, and the changing world of economics to their knowledge of data analysis, economic modeling, and computer mapping techniques.

As its 1999 "Overview" states, "The foundation of Cognetics' knowledge is a collection of public and private databases, the largest of which currently contains recent historical information on approximately 14 million United States business establishments." Utilizing this database, the company "is able to examine business formation and growth patterns" for long periods of time and in great depth which enables them to study both what is happening to corporations and also "to convert analyses and forecasts directly into sales leads, tenants for buildings, and job openings for people." Its three main business products are Targeted Marketing, Real Estate Information, and Cognetics Job Search. The operations of the company are carried out by a small staff working in a pleasant, friendly, efficient, and environmentally clean and healthy space. As has been rightly observed about the cyberspace age, less is more. In 2000 Cognetics became a subsidiary of the MacManus Group and moved its operations—due in part to a large rental increase—to Waltham

Plantall, Inc.

In 1995 Warren Adams graduated from the Harvard Business School; in 1996 with Brian Robertson, a graduate of MIT, he co-founded Plantall, Inc., a web site that invites and encourages individuals to develop their own on-line "community in cyberspace." When called up, its home page allows members to access among other categories their own address books, calendars, change of address, as well as to contact people and groups that share their views, experiences, and professional interests.

Two years after its establishment in rented space in Central Square the company had 1.5 million subscribers; also two years after it was started it was acquired for almost ninety million dollars by Amazon.com, the leading bookseller on the Internet, whose chief executive called Plantall "one of the most innovative things I've seen on line, period."

Cognectics and Plantall, working out of small spaces—for business in the cyberspace age does not require lots of space— serve as a working example for many new Cambridge businesses. The individuals behind them have solid connections with the city's two giant educational institutions, which not only stimulated them to be both creative and knowledgeable about things and services that could effectively serve people all over the world, but encouraged them to locate their activities close to one of the basic sources of ongoing scientific investigations. So as Cambridge once provided bricks, glass vases, and biscuits to the larger community, it now develops and "exports" services once undreamed of by the human mind but services that render life easier and more enjoyable.

FURTHER READING

BIDWELL, PERCY WELLS AND FALCONER, JOHN I. *History of Agriculture in the Northern United States 1620-1860.* NY: Peter Smith, 1941.

BRAY, HIAWATHA. "Amazon.Com Grace: Deal Made at St. Peter's Gate," *Boston Globe* (August 5, 1998) F1, F12.

CAHN, WILLIAM. *Out of the Cracker Barrel. The Nabisco Story from Animal Crackers to Zuzus.* New York: Simon and Schuster, 1969.

CRONON, WILLIAM. *Changes in the Land: Indians, Colonists, and the Ecology of New England.* New York: Hill and Wang, 1983.

CUMMINGS, RICHARD O. *The American Ice Harvests: A Historical Study in Technology, 1800-1918.* Berkeley: University of California Press, 1949.

ELIOT, SAMUEL A. "All Aboard the 'Natwyethum'!," *Cambridge Historical Society Proceedings,* 28 (1942) 35–54.

FEENEY, MARK. "Cambridge and the Candy Factory," *Boston Globe Magazine,* (December 5, 1993) 10, 24–29.

FOSS, ALDEN S. "Boston Woven Hose and Rubber Company: Eighty-four Years in Cambridge," *Cambridge Historical Society Proceedings,* 40 (1964–1966) 23–42.

GILMAN, ARTHUR., ED. *The Cambridge of Eighteen Hundred and Ninety-six.* Cambridge, MA: Citizens' Trade Association, 1896.

GILMAN, ROGER. "The Wyeth Background," *Cambridge Historical Society Proceedings,* 28 (1942) 29-34.

JONES, JOSEPH C. *America's Icemen: Am Illustrative History of the United States Natural Ice Industry 1665-1925.* Humble, Texas: Jobeco Books, 1984.

LONG, G. BURTON. "The Romance of Brick," *Cambridge Historical Society Proceedings,* 42 (1970–1972), 67–76.

McELHENY, VICTOR K. *Insisting on the Impossible: The Life of Edwin Land.* Reading, MA: Perseus Books, 1998.

McMANIS, DOUGLAS R. *Colonial New England: A Historical Geography.* NY: Oxford, 1975.

MAYCOCK, SUSAN E. *East Cambridge.* Cambridge, MA: MIT Press, 1988.

OLSHAKER, MARK. *The Instant Image: Edwin Land and the Polaroid Experience.* NY: Stein and Day, 1978.

RAND, CHRISTOPHER. *Cambridge, U.S.A.: Hub of a New World.* NY: Oxford, 1964.

RICHMOND, HAROLD B. "Cambridge, a Pioneer Home of Electronics," *Cambridge Historical Society Proceedings,* 34 (1951–52) 111–124.

RIZZO, PHILIP. *Cambridge Brick Details.* Cambridge, MA: Rotunda, 1984.

SCOTT, OTTO J. *The Creative Ordeal: The Story of Raytheon.* New York: Atheneum, 1974.

SEABURG, CARL AND STANLEY C. PATERSON. *The Ice King: Frederic Tudor and His Circle.* Edited by Alan Seaburg. Boston: Massachusetts Historical Society, 2002.

SHARPLES, STEPHEN P. "Nathaniel Jarvis Wyeth," *Cambridge Historical Society Proceedings,* 2 (1906–1907) 33–38.

WATKINS, LURA WOODSIDE. *Cambridge Glass 1818 to 1888: The Story of the New England Glass Company.* Boston: Marshall Jones, 1930.

WILDES, KARL L. AND NILO A. LINDGREN. *A Century of Electrical Engineering and Computer Science at MIT, 1882-1982.* Cambridge, MA: MIT Press, 1985.

WILSON, KENNETH M. *Glass in New England.* Sturbridge, MA: Old Sturbridge Village, 1969.

WYLIE, FRANCIS E. *MIT in Perspective.* Boston: Little, Brown, 1975.

The Faces of Cambridge's school students.

CHAPTER SIX

THE PUBLIC SCHOOLS

"And by the side of the Colledge a faire Grammar Schoole, for the training up of young Schollars, and fitting of them for Academicall Learning." (*New England's First Fruits,* 1643) The year this faire schoole was begun is unknown but it was certainly in the early 1640's. The name of the first Cambridge public school teacher, however, is known: Master Elijah Corlet or Corlett "is the Mr. who has very well approved himselfe for his abilities, dexterity and painfulnesse in teaching and education of the youth under him." (*First Fruits*) Corlett held his position until his death in 1686–7.

The first public school had only a handful of students and its pupils were both English and Native Americans. Its financial support came from tuition fees and town appropriations. After Corlett's death the school was conducted by a series of graduates from the College. The first permanent school house was erected on Holyoke Street in 1648 through private gifts from concerned citizens, and a school was maintained on this site until 1769. The town took possession of it in 1660, replaced the original structure in 1670, in 1700, and in 1769 when the fourth building was put up, the location was moved to Garden Street, just west of Appian Way.

The early public schools, which were required in all towns with one hundred families by the Commonwealth of Massachusetts after 1647, emphasized the

Cambridge Educates Its Community

teaching of Latin grammar rather than English grammar, and their mission was the preparation of boys (girls were not allowed public schooling until late in the seventeenth-century) for entrance to college. Eventually, reading and writing schools were also created.

The American orator Edward Everett, remembering his own school instruction in neighboring Boston in the early 1800's, declared that its curriculum contained but "a very little grammar" and that was "very indifferently taught." A generation later Sarah Jacobs, who in 1880 was one of the first two women to be elected to serve on the Cambridge School Committee, wrote about her Cambridge school days in the 1820's with about 60 other children in a single classroom heated only by a wood. They sat on long benches, worked at "clumsy desks or tables," their teacher wore a white flannel dressing gown full of ink spots "caused by the frequent wiping of his pen," and discipline was kept with a cowhide (a leather whip) and a slap or sudden smack. A bad boy might have "to stand on a bench with a bag of unbleached cotton tied over his head" and a bad girl "to wear a split stick shaped like a clothes-pin on her nose."

By 1845 Cambridge had 13 active public schools: the Boardman (built 1802), the Franklin (1809), the Third Street (1818), the Putnam (1825), the Thorndike (1832, enlarged 1840), the Washington (1832), the Mason (1835), the Bridge (1836), the Auburn (1838), the Broadway (1838), the North (1841), the Otis (1843), and the Harvard (1843).

School days in the 1840's varied throughout the year. From May to October the scholars went mornings from 8 to 11, and from October to May, 9 to 12; the afternoon hours were 2–5 March to November and 1:30 to 4:30 November to March. There were four stated holidays, several weeks of vacation carefully spread throughout the year, and five kinds of schools: alphabet (where the very young pupils learned the simple rudiments for two years), primary (2 years), middle (2 years), grammar (3 1/2 years), and high school (4–5 years). This totaled 11 1/2 years of public school instruction. Until the Commonwealth passed in 1844 a law providing students with free textbooks, their parents had been required to purchase them along with their writing slates unless they did not have the means to do so. Gradually, especially beginning in the 1830's, the schools had become co-educational.

The typical school day in Cambridge in the 1840's opened with the reading of the Bible, the singing of a hymn, and the repetition of the Lord's Prayer. But there was opposition by some parents to this practice from the very beginning. The curriculum emphasized reading, spelling, and arithmetic. Primary school children were expected to commit to memory the multiplication table; later they had to Master Warren Colburn's *First Lessons in Arithmetic.* In 1845 the teaching of music became a part of the curriculum.

When the town began its public school system, it was the Selectmen who regulated and monitored its activities; but on May 21, 1744, the town appointed a committee of five to be in change of inspecting "the Grammar School in this town" and to determine "what proficiency the youth and children make in their learning." Later the committee was enlarged to nine, although the Selectmen still kept a close watch on their schools until 1795 when a new committee of seven was "chosen for the purpose of superintending the schools." So they have been doing for more than two hundred years with, since 1869, the help of a Superintendent to oversee the day to day operations.

Most of the early school teachers were men; only gradually were women allowed to instruct the community's youth. Although as early as 1680 Corlett was assisted by "schooldame" goodwife Healy who was responsible for teaching English. Eventually it came to be that women were in predominance except at the highest ranks. For example, even as late as 1895 when the city maintained nine grammar schools their principals were all males except at one.

Master Corlett, the first teacher, did not become rich at his chosen profession, nor have his successors of either sex. For the next century teachers' pay continued meager—first 12 pounds a year, later 20, and when the Grammar Schools were made free schools, 40 pounds. After the Revolutionary War which so upset the currency, the stipend was established at 30 pounds. In 1845 the yearly salary of grammar school teachers was $250 and of principals $700; by 1895 it was $620 and $2,000 respectfully.

Cambridge opened its first high school for English instruction for both sexes in 1838; within a few years two additional high schools for classical education had been established in other areas of the town. In 1847 this arrangement was re-organized and the three schools were united as just one under the direction of Elbridge Smith assisted by Ms N. W. Manning. In June 1848 a new schoolhouse was dedicated on Amory and Summer streets to accommodate the growing needs of the high school. During the next decade the student body doubled from 100 to 200, the teaching staff tripled, a school library was opened, and the study of English literature was instituted. The income from the Hopkins Fund (an endowment established in 1657 by the will of Edward Hopkins for classical education, one fourth of the income of which was to be used by the public schools of Cambridge and which for some years had not been available to the city) was returned by the State Legislature to create a Hopkins Classical Master.

As the high school continued to grow with additional pupils, there soon became a clear need for a more commodious structure, and so money was appropriated and a building was erected in 1864 at the corner of Broadway and Fayette streets. As with the earlier building it soon became crowded with an ever expanding student body, and by 1878 it housed 500 scholars. Eventually Cambridge turned its high school into two institutions: Cambridge Latin School, which specialized in the classics, and Cambridge English High School, which focused on the other subjects of study. The Latin School occupied a yellow brick structure for

The classroom, 19th century.

many years on Ellery and Trowbridge streets. This new arrangement lasted for almost a generation before the two schools were again united in 1910 as the Cambridge High and Latin School. Leslie L. Cleveland was its headmaster to 1941.

One of the students at the Latin School at the beginning of the twentieth century was the poet and playwright e. e. cummings. He was just 12 when he entered and the courses of study he followed consisted of English, Algebra, Geometry, Latin, French, and Greek, but not a single science course. Cecil T. Derry, his Greek teacher, deeply influenced the young poet, and encouraged him to attempt his own poetical translation of Greek poetry. Eventually, as a result of his study of Greek culture and language at the Latin School, he chose to major in Greek at Harvard. One of his biographers, Richard S. Kennedy, has noted that this study of language and linguistics "stretched his vocabulary and embedded a sense of syntax in his very bones."

To train students who did not wish a more formal college preparatory education, the city had founded in 1888 through the generous gift and support of Frederick Hastins Rindge the Cambridge Manual Training School for Boys. It soon was called the Rindge Manual Training School, and after 1912 just the Rindge Technical School. Almost 90 years later it was merged with the High and Latin School, and today the city has again but a single high school: the Cambridge Rindge and Latin School.

A comparison of the school system in 1845 just before the town became the city with the system in 1872, in 1895, and finally, with the schools of today (1996/7) provides a quick and reliable "photograph" of public education in Cambridge.

	1845	1872	1895	1996/7
Students	2,151	7,554	12,174	8,077
Teachers	30	176	322	809

Clearly there was a long period when the student body increased its numbers (Master Corlett had only 9 students in 1644) followed by a shorter period of decline in the 20th century.

Maria Baldwin, Headmaster from 1889–1922 of the Agassiz Grammar School and the first African American in the north of our country to serve as an elementary school principal.

Throughout both periods the people of Cambridge have insisted on having the best possible teaching staff to serve the growing and changing educational needs of the next generations of Americans and Cantabrigians. One further statistic reveals an important change in the make up of the student enrollment. Once the schools taught children who were primarily of one "color"; today's schools reflect the wonderful diversity of urban American cities, and so 34% are Black, 43% White, 8% Asian and 14% Hispanic Americans.

The citizens and parents of Cambridge have always been concerned for their schools and the quality of education provided to the students. If at times this has meant lively moments of debates and strong differences of opinion (sometimes perhaps difficult and heated), in the long run it has been beneficial to the process of educating the young.

The last fifty years have been particularly prone to such sharp conflicts and opposing viewpoints. Several factors influenced the discussions, such as the need in the 1950's to rebuild and consolidate a number of schools, and the political, racial, and student unrest of the 1960's and 1970's. When you throw into this mixture the word "labels" liberal and conservative, town and gown, the Cambridge Civic Association and the Independents, the result was that for many a day and many a night, as the old song goes, there was a hot time in the old town.

The issues were complicated and important ones. They included the instability created by a succession of superintendents, racial tensions that led to a riot, the best way to maintain discipline, and the denial of full accreditation to the high school by the New England Association of Secondary Schools. If these were not enough problems, there were additional ones: labor conflicts, differing educational and curriculum points of view, the impact of an economic recession, falling enrollments, the issue of fiscal austerity, and finally, the need to either build a new high school complex or to renovate the existing one.

Solutions to many of these issues were eventually determined through dialogue and concession. If not all the problems were solved successfully or the exact way some felt they should have been, the school system survived its serious challenges. The old Latin building was replaced with a modern structure and Rindge Technical was renovated and expanded. The school administration was reorganized, and future superintendents and administrators were appointed only after a national search had been conducted. Parents were now made welcome by the system as active and positive partners in the educational process. The Agassiz and Haggerty elementary schools were replaced with new ones.

In addition, school libraries were drastically improved and made "media centers," computers were purchased for each classroom as well as the libraries, improved programs were initiated for Spanish and Portuguese speaking children, and a controlled-choice program where parents can opt for one of three types of elementary school educational approaches for their children—fundamental, innovative, or computer-assisted instruction—was put in place.

In 1997 Nancy Walser, as a concerned parent, prepared an excellent and helpful *Parent's Guide to Cambridge Schools* which lets everyone know what is happening in the individual schools along with their particular teaching emphases, their special programs, their problems (if any), and the educational options available to parents.

The standard reference work—Peterson's Guide *Public Schools USA*—in its latest edition rated Cam-bridge in 1991 as "good" in its school leadership, instruction, and environment; as old Master Corlett might say, that is not bad for a large urban diverse school system that strives to provide educational excellence for children and young adults with differing cultural, socio-economic, and ethnic backgrounds and traditions.

Perhaps, however, the best way to understand today's public schools is through the words of its students. In 1986 Olive Pierce, whose three children all graduated from the Cambridge Rindge & Latin School and who was a teacher of photography there, published a

Two school scenes, ca. 1930s.

delightful book of photographs and interviews with some of the students of the high school. Here in some of their thoughts and feelings one finds the essence of today's public education in Cambridge:

~

"One thing I like about this school
is its diversity.
I'm Russian, Puerto Rican, Jewish,
and politically different, it seems…
The way I see it is that,
in order to learn,
you have to have contrast."

~

"I come from the ghetto…
A lot of people are afraid to say
they live in the projects.
It doesn't really get to me
because it's not a lifelong thing…
There's no school better than ours.
It's mixed balance,
and you don't have
that many racial fights anymore.
Society's changing."

~

"The first day I came to this school,
I was nervous.
The size was over-whelming.
It took me twenty minutes
to find the swimming pool
and by the time I got there
I was in tears.

The gym teacher
put his arm around me
and calmed me down.
When I went into my first class,
I could tell
it was going to be different.
Not just because
I was only one of two girls,
but because
the boys were what in my other school
would have been classified as 'thugs.'
They were so friendly to me
that there was no way
I could keep that description in mind.
It's been rewarding
because the people I've gotten to know
have completely
shattered my prejudices."

~

"If I hadn't gotten in Bill's class
[a program for boys with legal
and disciplinary problems],
I would have quit school,
definitely.
I woulda just quit.
I can't deal with the regular school…
Bill's good.
He say,
'Hey, you don't wanna do shit,
just don't come.'
It's like, if I do it it's for me.
I've been in here three years,
and I've done fine.
I got all my credits."

Buckingham Browne & Nichols School

A young graduate of Harvard (Class of 1878), George H. Browne, switched in 1882 from public to private school teaching. He began with five students, three of them sons of his former Harvard professors. The next year along with his friend Edgar H. Nichols he opened the Browne & Nichols School with seventeen scholars; its aim was to teach students to think rather than merely memorize, and this approach immediately proved popular in Cambridge. As one of the first students expressed it at the school's fiftieth anniversary: "The successful teacher, as they saw it, was not the man who could spoon-feed knowledge but who could arouse in his boys an appetite for knowledge. Once the mind is stimulated, education will follow."

By 1897 the school had replaced its initial three buildings with a new brick structure at 20 Garden Street which was to be its home-base for the next fifty years. In 1948 the entire operation moved to ten acres at Gerry's Landing near the Charles. The maximum number of boys enrolled while at Garden Street was about 160 (there had been, however, periods of ups and downs over the years since 1883); by 1955 the enrollment had climbed to 250, and in 1969, just a few years before its merger with Buckingham, it was at 359.

The Buckingham School—it was not called that until 1902— started in 1886 when twenty-two year old Jeanette Markham from Kansas newly enrolled in The Annex (Radcliffe College) started to teach the daughter of her host and friend at the latter's house on Buckingham Street. Her host was the wife of Col. Thomas Wentworth Higginson. Three years later she moved her co-educational "school" to a neighbor's living room and in 1892 to a brand new wooden school house financed by Mrs. Richard H. Dana. Her sister joined her on the staff and gradually others were added; at the end of the century the enrollment stood at 30. The school was called simply "Miss Markham's School."

When "Miss Markham" left to be married, the school was incorporated as The Buckingham School and Katharine M. Thompson was made its Principal. Slowly the school developed and the need for additional buildings had to be met. A brick building was constructed next to the original school house, and later a house on Craigie Street purchased for the kindergarten. Later yet in 1949 another larger house on Sparks Street was bought for the Upper School. Enrollment rose steadily from 27 in 1902, to 250 in 1952, to 449 in 1966. Just prior to the merger the two schools started to combine several of the courses they offered.

In 1974 the extensive programs of these two schools merged to form the co-educational Buckingham Browne & Nichols School (BB & N). Twenty-five years later the enrollment in its Upper, Middle and Lower schools neared a thousand students drawn both from Cambridge and from other Greater Boston communities. While each of the three education divisions has its own campus, the entire plant consists of fifteen buildings, a library of 12,000 volumes, several language labs, as well as two gyms, a boathouse, ice rink, and other athletic facilities. The endowment is more then eleven million dollars.

Shady Hill

When the Agassiz School was torn down in 1915 to be replaced by a more modern structure, Agnes and Ernest Hocking wondered where to send their eight-year old son during the interim. They tried one of the other city schools but were not satisfied and so they decided that they would create their own school until the new Agassiz opened. So was born the Shady Hill School.

The Hockings—he was a philosopher teaching at Harvard and she had previously been a school teacher—ran their school from their commodious house on Quincy Street with just a handful of teachers and about twenty pupils. It was an immediate success and they soon moved to Charles Eliot Norton's Shady Hill estate—hence its present name. In 1925 it purchased 8 acres (now 11) on Coolidge Hill and started construction on a series of small wooden buildings around a central assembly building. It currently has 16 buildings.

Shady Hill was from the start a co-educational school with a very different approach to education; its curriculum has always attempted to bond and blend traditional knowledge and constructive imagination with children's own life experiences. It has served as an important educational model for other progressive educational schools in the United States. Today it has over 60 faculty members, about 500 elementary students, and an endowment of 11 million dollars.

Fayerweather Street School

The Fayerweather School was started in 1967 by a group of local parents and educators as a co-educational elementary school whose classes were open and ungraded so that the children would learn about knowledge and problem solving in a mixed age setting. Its enrollment was purposely therefore kept small. Two years after it opened its doors it had 114 students and 6 faculty members, in 1982 120 students and 16 teachers, and currently it has 180 youngsters and 31 teachers. It operates in four buildings and its plant includes a gym and playing field.

An excellent example of the school's approach to learning today is in a booklet put together over five months in 1996 by its 5th and 6th graders entitled *Voices of Central Square*. The students went out, met, and talked with some of the residents of the Square who shared with them their stories, memories, and hopes. In the booklet you find their "interviews, demographics, graphs, creative writing and poetry, drawings, oral histories and much more."

THE RELIGIOUS SCHOOLS

Catholic Schools

At first the Catholic churches in North America encouraged their parishioners to send their children to public schools; later concern for the proper religious education of the young led the Third Plenary Council of Baltimore in 1884 to vote in favor of establishing an American parochial school system.

In Cambridge Catholic parents and their religious leaders had also been uneasy over the public schools drift to what they felt was a secular education at the expense of necessary moral beliefs. A further complaint was that when the schools did read from the Bible and allow prayers they were always Protestant in nature. Thus the creation of a parochial school system in Cambridge for these faithful parents was a logical attempt to redress this situation. In this effort Cambridge was a leader in the local area for the Boston Archdiocese only slowly implemented the 1884 decision.

In 1869 the city's first parochial school was opened at St. Mary's of the Annunciation Church in Cambridgeport; it was for girls, cost but one dollar a month, and was staffed by the Sisters of the Congregation of Notre Dame, Montreal. In 1875 they closed their school and returned to Canada.

Meanwhile, the church's pastor, Thomas Scully, had been thinking how important it was for a Catholic

A teaching nun.

child to have a Catholic education. He wanted that education to be free to all especially since many of the families in his congregation were poor. To help raise money for his projected school he started *Our Young Folks Magazine*. Finally his school was built and opened in the fall of 1875; its mission was to teach "all the branches from A.B.C. to the classics, and from arithmetic to algebra and geometry." During its first year it had over six hundred students including the girls from the now closed school of the Sisters.

Soon other parishes opened their own schools: for example, in the Harvard Square area St. Paul's in 1889 acquired through the Archdiocese the estate of Gordon McKay between Arrow and Mt. Auburn streets. His mansion served both as a school and a residence for its teaching staff, the Sisters of St. Joseph. St. John the Evangelist in North Cambridge opened its school in 1913 with just the first grade and then each year added another grade and eventually a high school in 1921. Its school was staffed by the Dominican Sisters.

Today there are in the city two Catholic elementary schools and two high schools: St. John the Evangelist Elementary School, St. Peter's School, Matignon High School (named for the French Father Francis Matignon) and North Cambridge Catholic High School. These are not all the parochial schools that have served the needs of Catholic families. Several that were once active have for various reasons been closed at St. Hedwig's, St. Patrick's, St. Paul's, the Sacred Heart High School, St. John the Evangelist High School and others. Indeed, as late as 1966 there were sixteen parochial schools in the city: one kindergarten, eleven elementary, and four high schools.

St. Peter and St. John's are today coeducational, open to both Catholic and non-Catholic children, and to students outside the confines of Cambridge. Their grade level is kindergarten through the eighth grade; their total enrollment currently is about 400 pupils. Parochial schools in Cambridge have seen the same decline in their enrollment as have the public schools For example, St. John's Grammar School in 1930 had 1000 students and its High School 320.

Matignon, established in 1947 as the first Central Catholic High School in the Boston Archdiocese, has currently about 600 students, almost 40 teachers, and three buildings on a 5-acre campus. North Cambridge Catholic High School which opened in 1958 as a diocesan High School is also the successor to the High School once maintained by St. John The Evangelist Church. Its enrollment today is about 160.

Tip O'Neill, Cambridge's "Man of the House," was a product of the parochial school system, and remembered that the discipline at St. John's Grammar School was "pretty strict." If "you were late or you didn't know your catechism, the nuns would hit you on the hand with a piece of rattan." But he also remembered with fondness "a wonderful teacher named Sister Agatha" who, when she learned that after high school he had become a truck driver instead of going to college, cornered him on the street and told him to make something of himself by going to college. So he enrolled in Boston College and did.

Louise Forrest who graduated from St. Paul's in 1904 remembered her education this way: "We were given a diploma after eight or nine years' instruction by the Sisters. I ought not to say instruction, for what we received was far more reaching and deeply effective than mere instruction. It was part of themselves, their enthusiasm, their ambitions for us, their love, their very life, it was what those good Sisters gave us. And they gave it so that we might go out fully equipped, both morally and mentally to do good work in life."

Special recognition needs to be made of the Boston Archdiocesan Choir School, also known as the Boston Boy Choir, which was founded at St. Paul's in 1963 and is still based there. Its membership, drawn from all the parishes in the Boston Archdiocese, is currently at 54; it sings not only on church occasions but also with various musical organizations such as the Boston Symphony Orchestra and at Harvard University concerts at Sanders Theater and Memorial Church. The school motto is the first line of an antiphon suggested by Pope Pius XII for church choirs: *Repleatur os meum laude tua*, "let my mouth be filled with your praise."

It is clear that parochial schools have been and will continue to be a significant partner in the education of the young people of Cambridge. The decline in the number of parish schools does nothing to diminish this role. As the church itself is evolving from its initial role of serving Catholic immigrants to one striving to meet the challenges created by Vatican II and modern demands, so are its parochial schools.

How the North Catholic High School sees itself today describes the other Cambridge parochial schools, too. They aim to provide their "students with an opportunity for developing personal responsibility, global awareness, spiritual growth and an environment for learning…within the context of a multicultural community which seeks to affirm all students…(with) a strong commitment to Catholic values as well as a respect for the individual learning styles of students."

Cambridge Friends School

A very different kind of religious school is the Cambridge Friends School, which was founded in 1961 by the Cambridge Meeting of the Society of Friends. Its birth grew out of discussions held between 1958 and 1960 by several of the Meeting's parents concerning the need for Quaker values as an essential component of their children's general education. In the fall of 1960 the Meeting agreed to be responsible for a Friends School; a committee was appointed to secure funding, a staff hired, and classroom facilities located.

The School opened in North Cambridge with sixty girls and boys the following September in the educational wing of St. James Episcopal Church. A year later about five acres, also in North Cambridge in the area known as the Clay Pits, was purchased from the City, architectural plans drawn up, the money to construct the building raised, and in September 1964 the School opened in its new quarters at 5 Cadbury Road. Some years later a gym was added.

Today the School has an enrollment of about 200 pupils and a teaching staff of over twenty. The student body consists both of Quaker children and those from other communities of faith; it also reflects the economic and population mix of the city of Cambridge. The grade level goes from kindergarten through the eighth grade, the endowment is over four millon, and it continues to emphasize Quaker principles and practices.

SOME OTHER SCHOOLS

These schools by no means exhaust the list of educational institutions associated with Cambridge. Private schools have come and gone: examples would be the various "dame schools" run by older women in the community which taught girls of kindergarten age; the three free kindergartens run for 11 years by Mrs Quincy A. Shaw which were taken over in 1889 by the Cambridge Public School; the Fitting School for Boys and Girls started in 1879 by Ms K. V. Smith which was the first private co-educational school that prepared its students for college; the Agassiz School (1855–63) for young women run by Professor Agassiz of Harvard and his family in their home on Quincy Street, now the site of the Fogg Art Museum; the New Preparatory School, a non-profit school for boys, which was started in 1924 in a bank building in Harvard Square but which after 1940 occupied a mansion built by Longfellow for his daughter Edith on Brattle Street and which ceased in 1987; and the Charles River Academy, an urban day school for adolescent boys with learning problems, which was started in 1965. Its property was between Harvard and Central Squares.

If some Cambridge private schools then no longer exist, there are others, if smaller and more focused than those discussed, that very much do exist. Examples would be the Cambridge Community Hebrew School, the Cambridge Montessori School, and the James F. Farr Academy which opened in 1972 to serve students with significant educational and emotional needs.

THE CAMBRIDGE PUBLIC LIBRARY

The Cambridge Public Library is yet another way that the city educates its citizens. It is the felicitous legacy of the Cambridge Athenaeum. When the city purchased in March 1858 that organization's building at Main and Pleasant Streets for use as a City Hall, it also acquired its library which it agreed to maintain "for the benefit of the inhabitants of Cambridge, under reasonable regulations" forever. Initially the library was called The Dana Library in recognition of the 1850 gift from Edmund T. Dana of the land upon which the building stood; it was not until 1879 that it was officially named the Cambridge Public Library. The Athenaeum librarian, Caroline F. Orne, was made the city's first librarian and trustees were appointed to oversee its activities.

Ms Orne, who wrote and published short stories and poetry, served for 16 years. She was succeeded by Almira L. Hayward, a former teacher in the Cambridge school system who served until her accidental death in 1894. It was the work and devotion of these two directors and their small staff over 36 years that laid the foundation which has enabled the public library to

Caroline Frances Orne..

play a vital role in shaping the educational and cultural life of the Cambridge community.

In the beginning the library occupied but a single room in the new City Hall, had a collection of only about 1400 volumes, and was open only on Saturdays between 4 and 8 pm. Gradually the days and hours were expanded until by 1880 the library was opened six days a week. As more books were added, it became clear that more space was needed, and so in 1866 the library moved into rented rooms in the nearby Masonic building where it remained for the next 23 years. In 1874 the city allowed the library to drop the rule establishing an annual fee to use it, and since then the Cambridge Public Library and its resources have been freely available to all.

As the city grew so did the collection of its library and its use by its many patrons. Although its has always been one of the city's most popular services, there has never been enough funds to underwrite fully its programs and activities. For years one of its most pressing needs was related to space, and this problem was not resolved until Frederick H. Rindge came to the rescue.

In 1887 he wrote to the Mayor, William E. Russell, offering land and a public library building. His only requirements were that part of the land should always serve as "a play-ground for children and the young" and that five tablets bearing his own words of testimony to the Christian religion must be displayed within the building. The city agreed to his conditions and the library was built at a cost of 80,000 dollars and dedicated on June 29, 1889.

The new library building was designed by the architectural firm of Van Brunt & Howe. It is a "modified Romanesque" structure in the style of H. H. Richardson and was constructed using Dedham granite and Longmeadow brown sandstone; it sits on two and a half acres with the main entrance on Broadway; and its features included a multi-arched portico and a round tower. The stacks have iron floors, stairs, and bookcases and when originally built had space for at least 60,000 volumes. In 1894 a children's wing, catalog

Almira Leach Hayward.

volumes and the circulation that year was 5,460; in 1889 the library had 22,398 books and the circulation that year was 79,961; in 1907 73,555 books with a circulation of 283,688. By the time of the 1967 addition the book collection was edging toward 270,000 and circulation to 580,000. At the end of the century the library's holdings are at the half million mark and it circulates more than a million loans each year. If the library began by collecting books and soon thereafter serials, that collection today is far more diverse containing reproductions of paintings, prints and sculptures, music, tapes, CD-Roms, films, and audio-visual materials.

The library, however, was not content with merely reaching the public at one location and so gradually it pushed its "walls" further outward. The staff established in 1889 six outside delivery stations in various areas of the community where material could be received and returned several times a week; soon a similar delivery service was instituted for the school system. Eventually a series of branch libraries came into being: the first in East Cambridge (1897) and the second in North Cambridge (1906). In time branches were also opened in Cambridgeport (1914), at Cambridge Field and Mount Auburn (1915) and in Central Square (1976). Today these are known simply as the Boudreau, Central Square, Collins, O'Connell, O'Neill, and Valente branches.

Some of the other programs the library developed to meet its mission included the creation of a special area

room, and office for the librarian were added; in 1902 the stack area was further enlarged; and in 1967 a second wing was added to meet the growing need for additional reference and reading/study space as well as a modern facility for the children's programs and collections.

Central to the library's mission has been the best service possible for its patrons. One measure of this service is evidenced in its book collection and in its circulation statistics. In 1859 the library owned 1,722 and collection for children; the establishment of story hours for the youngsters; the publication of printed catalogs updated as necessary; the production of reading lists, bibliographies, and monthly surveys of books; the delivery of materials to nursing homes, senior centers, and other community locations; visits and talks to local groups to let them know about the library and what it had to offer them such as large-print books for the visually impaired; and for a while a bookmobile. The library also made sure that it did not ignore the needs of the increasingly diverse population of the city as regards services, programs, and resources.

After World War II, the mission and services of all libraries were enhanced and sharpened by the rapid developments and improvements provided by modern technology. While librarians Orne and Hayward might be surprised by CD-Rom products and on-line catalogs, they would also probably have been excited by the possibilities offered by the new tools of technology. The Cambridge Public Library kept in step with all these transforming changes. Its patrons have access to the advantages of photocopiers, microfilms, readers and printers, and through computers and modems to regional and national networks including the Minuteman Library Network and the World Wide Web.

In 1998 the Public Library Trustees and the Cambridge Community Foundation, a private philanthropy group organized in 1916, established an endowment fund to be administered by the Foundation for the benefit of the Library's programs and services. And in

Librarian with books. This figure is on one of the Library's porch pillars.

1999, as a result of a generous gift by the Rotary Club of Cambridge, the library opened a Technology Learning Center at the Central Square Branch Library. Here patrons and various community organizations and agencies are trained to use new computer resources and software. At the close of the 20th century the library had almost 48,000 active library cardholders.

Along with the other opportunities of the Information Age, these changes have once again affected the setting in which the library conducts its business. During the 1990's, therefore, the city administration, the library trustees, the staff, a special Library 21 Committee, and the public engaged in a careful and thoughtful process, including a survey by mail of 5,000 citizens chosen randomly, to determine the appropriate goals and needs of its library at the opening of the 21st century.

In the fall of 1997 the Library 21 Committee, which

was responsible for conducting an independent and wide ranging study, published its recommendations calling for a new, dramatically larger main library (not necessarily on its present site), charged with providing the community in collaboration with other city agencies, especially with the School Department, and with other appropriate cultural organizations, a variety of information and human services to make the library "the civic heart of the city." To meet this goal the library would require both a highly trained staff and an expansion of its print and electronic resources.

Finally, after several years of public discussion concerning the new library's location, the decision was made by the City Council in 2000 in favor of its present site.

THE PROSPECT UNION

This educational association for "workingmen" was started in 1891 at Cambridgeport by a Congregational minister, Robert Erskine Ely; its name came from the former hotel (the Prospect House) where Ely hired rooms for its first classes which were taught by students from the College. It began with 44 members. Soon faculty members from Harvard were added to its faculty and eventually classes were offered in many fields including languages, science and math, the various disciplines of the liberal arts but also the practical arts.

Through a gift in 1894 it was able to acquire its own building.

Though initially successful, by the time of the First World War it met several serious problems. The first was the war, which took away many of its students and teachers. Of more lasting significance was the subway system which enabled its students to take advantages of the growing educational courses and lectures now available for people throughout Greater Boston. As a result, after studying the situation, the Union sold its building in 1923 and changed its mission from one primarily of teaching to one which assisted people seeking ways to further their adult education. It did this by issuing annually a catalog and guide to "Educational Opportunities of Greater Boston." It continues to do so as the Educational Exchange of Greater Boston.

THE CAMBRIDGE CENTER FOR ADULT EDUCATION

Cambridge's Center for Adult Education traces its roots to 1871 when a group of concerned citizens meeting in Lyceum Hall founded an organization whose aim was to stimulate and improve the educational and cultural life of the city's young people. In April 1876 their effort was incorporated as the Cambridge Social Union. The present name was adopted in 1938.

Cambridge Center for Adult Education, the former William Brattle House (1727).

The Union initially operated its program in several rented locations until 1889 when it purchased the William Brattle House (built 1727) at 42 Brattle Street for $17,000 as its permanent headquarters. The Blacksmith House where Longfellow's blacksmith once worked was bought in 1972. Still later when further classroom space .was needed, the Center secured ten additional rooms, one of which is an art studio and two of which are computer labs, at One Story Street.

At its start, the Center's programs consisted of "social singing" on Wednesday nights, "musical entertainments, lectures, talks and exhibitions" on Thursday nights, and "spelling-matches" just for men on Saturday nights. They also had a library reading room stocked with Boston newspapers and some of the leading magazines of the day and an "amusement" room where the young people played chess, checkers, backgammon and dominoes. Eventually the activities expanded to include some educational classes (at 50 cents a class) taught by Harvard students.

The Center of today with its stress on active and interactive learning in a cooperative atmosphere began to take shape after World War II. Between the two world wars the Center had experienced a decline in membership and activities, and as a result during the 1940's was forced to share its space with the Red Cross, the League of Women Voters, and two local businesses. This decline in membership and programs, however, was only of short duration. Now the Center, operating on a budget of three million dollars, with a faculty of more than 500, and with an annual student enrollment of more than eighteen thousand, offers 2,500 educational courses and programs a year for adults on a wide spectrum of subjects which include the humanities, the arts, language instruction, business skills, computers, cooking and social issues. It offers $115,000 in financial aid to students who need assistance. The Center's goal is "lifelong learning" and during the last half century its activities and courses have involved the minds and lives of more than half a million folks.

ELECTRONIC EDUCATION

The last half of the twentieth century witnessed the rapid development of electronic means of communication. As a result such devices as Email, fax machines, modems, computers, word processors, home pages, networks, the World Wide Web, and cable television opportunities offer additional methods of continuing the community's education. Cambridge Community Television (CCTV) and Cambridge Municipal Television (CMT) provide citizens the chance to view city council and school committee meetings as well as a varied collection of programs about the community.

In addition, programs are shown that have been produced by local residents covering a wide assortment of topics and issues. As a part of its agreement with the city, Continental Cablevision, the city's cable operator, also does some programming especially for the Cambridge audience. Without question electronic education with its open access to all in Cambridge has since the 1980's become a lively communications schoolyard.

NEWSPAPERS

The city's first real newspaper—there had been several short-lived occasional papers since 1839—was the *Cambridge Palladium* which came out in 1843, but unfortunately for its publishers did not live out the year. That was not to be the fate of the community's second newspaper which is still a vital institution today. It is the *Cambridge Chronicle,* which first hit the newsstands at four cents the copy on Thursday, May 7, 1846. Its arrival coincided with the launching of the town as a city and so, quite appropriately, the first issue focused on that exciting event. Since then the *Chronicle* has been consistently on the job under a series of capable editors who with their staffs have faithfully "recorded the growth of the city and the life of its people."

If Cambridge had to wait a couple of centuries to have its first two significant local newspapers, it did not have to wait very long before others appeared on the scene. In April 1866, a second major newspaper, the *Cambridge Press,* was started, followed within twelve years by *The Cambridge Tribune,* and then in 1879 by yet a fourth newspaper, *The Cambridge News.* There were still others published in the city. The undergraduates at Harvard, for example, began their colorful *Crimson* as early as 1873 and in 1930 the free *Cambridge Sun* was established; its separate existence was short-lived however and it merged in 1935 with the older *Chronicle.*

The *Chronicle* is the only paper to survive from the nineteenth century, and it is the only one that covers Cambridge events in any real detail. The community is served by a number of other newspapers; two of these are the freely distributed *Cambridge Tab,* which is but one unit in a larger chain of community newspapers under the collective *Tab* banner, and since 1972 the Spanish-language weekly *El Mundo.*

The latter was started by Alberto Vasallo, Jr., a refugee from Cuba, in a single room on Magazine Street. It is still published in Central Square, but its staff now includes all his family as well as several photographers and reporters and two news services. During its first years, the focus was on international news important for Hispanics, but more and more local Hispanic news and culture activities have come to fill its pages. Also while for years it was printed just in Spanish, today some of its stories are also printed in English. Eventually the editors hope that it will be entirely bilingual. *El Mundo* also operates a Spanish radio station, Radiolandia. While both are Cambridge-based, the scope of news coverage is directed to the entire Hispanic community of Greater Boston.

THE CAMBRIDGE HISTORICAL SOCIETY

On April 19, 1905 fifty Cantabrigians associated themselves with the intention of forming a corporation to be known as the Cambridge Historical Society. Eighteen of these subscribers later met on the night of June 17th at the Cambridge Social Union at 42 Brattle Street and, with Richard Henry Dana in the chair, adopted By-Laws, elected the necessary officers and directors, and the Cambridge Historical Society became a reality. It has a membership presently of more than four hundred.

The Historical Society's headquarters—the Hooper-Lee-Nichols House—at 159 Brattle Street, originally built as one of the mansions which line the old "Road to Watertown," was left to it in 1957 through the will of Mrs. Frances White Emerson. She further gave the Society twenty thousand dollars, the interest of which was to keep the old house in good condition. Today it contains the Society's collection of eighteenth and nineteenth century books, manuscripts, maps, photographs and slides, and provides work space for its paid staff and its volunteers. The house with its furnishings is also open to the public.

The purpose of the Society is to collect and preserve all material which relates to the history of Cambridge and to foster interest in the life and activities of the city. This is accomplished through various public lectures, walking tours, and numerous special programs and activities, and through individual publications. An example is the historical booklet *A Tale of Three Cities* by George H. Hanford which was put out for the sesquicentennial of the incorporation of the city. Other publications include "*For the Entertainment of Strangers": the Inns & Pubs of Cambridge* also authored by Hanford, the monograph *Cambridge on the Cutting Edge: Innovators and Inventions,* John Langone's *The Cambridge Rindge and Latin School,* and the periodic volumes of its own *Proceedings.*

Complementing the mission of the Cambridge Historical Society is the work of the relatively newly organized Cambridge Black Cultural and Historical Association. The Association was initially an informal group of community leaders who worked with staff from the Public Library to celebrate their "experience in Cambridge, the United States, the Caribbean, and Africa." As their programs and efforts increased, they became a non-profit educational organization known first as The Cambridge Black Cultural Association. While the group has several aims, one of its main purposes is "to see that Afro-Americans in Cambridge are a visible part of the cultural mosaic that defines Cambridge."

The Hooper-Lee-Nichols House, 159 Brattle Street, headquarters of the Cambridge Historical Society.

Charles Sullivan, Executive Director, Cambridge Historical Commission, 1974–.

Another resource for the community's history is the Cambridge Historical Commission which was established in 1963 by the City Council as an agency within the municipal government. Its mission is the "co-operative and intelligent planning for the growing needs of the families, the industries, and the institutions which make up our city, and at the same time of procuring for the enjoyment and understanding of present and future generations as much as possible and practical of our rich heritage in Cambridge of historic landmarks, both buildings and sites, and of examples of architecture surviving from earlier periods."

It enforces all the ordinances that apply to the preservation and restoration of historically significant buildings, places appropriate markers where applicable, and offers technical assistance when needed and preservation grants as allowed by law. The Commission has a small staff, a fine library of photographs and other visuals, and was responsible for bringing into publication between 1965 and 1977 the excellent five volume *Survey of Architectural History in Cambridge*.

FURTHER READING

BRADBURY, WILLIAM F. *The Cambridge High School: History and Catalogue.* With its Early History by Elbridge Smith. Cambridge, MA: King, 1882.

Cambridge, Ma. Library 21 Committee. *In Brief Program Report.* Cambridge, MA: Cambridge Public Library, October 1, 1997.

Cambridge, MA *The Rindge Gifts to the City of Cambridge, Massachusetts.* Cambridge, MA: City Council, 1891.

DERRY, CECIL THAYER. "Pages from the History of the Cambridge High and Latin School," *Cambridge Historical Society Proceedings,* 35 (1953–1954) 91–109.

DOYLE, EDWARD G. *A Commemorate History of the Cambridge Public Library.* Cambridge, Ma.: Cambridge Public Library, 1989.

ELIOT, THOMAS H. *Two Schools in Cambridge: The Story of Browne & Nichols and Buckingham.* Cambridge, MA: Windflower Press, 1982.

GILMAN, ARTHUR., ED. *The Cambridge of Eighteen Hundred and Ninety-six.* Cambridge, MA: Citizens' Trade Association, 1896.

HILL, FRANK A. "The Public Schools of Cambridge," in Arthur Gilman, *The Cambridge of Eighteen Hundred and Ninety-six.* Cambridge, MA: Citizens' Trade Association, 1896, 187–217.

HOWE, ROSAMOND COOLIDGE. "The First Cambridge Historical Commission," *Cambridge Historical Society Proceedings,* 39

LANGONE, JOHN. *The Cambridge Rindge and Latin School: Yesterday and Today.* Cambridge, MA: Cambridge Historical Society, 1998.

LIONS, ZELDA AND GORDON W. ALLPORT. "Seventy-five Years of Continuing Education: the Prospect Union Association," *Cambridge Historical Society Proceedings,* 40 (1964–1966), 139–158.

LITTLEFIELD, GEORGE E. "Elijah Corlet and the `Faire Grammar School' at Cambridge," *Publications of the Colonial Society of Massachusetts* 17 (1913–1914), 131–142.

McCOY, W. KEITH. *A History of the Public Schools of Cambridge.* Cambridge School Department, 1974.

PAIGE, LUCIUS R. *History of Cambridge, Massachusetts. 1630–1877.* Boston: Houghton, 1877. *Supplement and Index.* Mary Isabella Gozzaldi. 1930.

PIERCE, OLIVE. *No Easy Roses: a Look at the Lives of City Teenagers.* Cambridge, MA: No publisher listed, 1986.

RETTIG, ROBERT BELL. "Cambridge Historical Commission: Progress and Prospects," *Cambridge Historical Society Proceedings,* 42 (1970–72) 31–47.

ST. JOHN THE EVANGELIST CENTENNIAL COMMITTEE. *St. John the Evangelist Church Centennial: 1893–1993.* Dallas, TX: Taylor Publishing Company, 1992.

SPALDING, ELIOT B. "The Founder and Three Editors of the Cambridge Chronicle," *Cambridge Historical Society Proceedings,* 36 (1955–56) 107–21.

SULLIVAN, MARY XAVERIA. *The History of Catholic Secondary Education in the Archdiocese of Boston.* Washington, D.C.: The Catholic University of America Press, 1946.

WILLS, JEFFREY, ED. *The Catholics of Harvard Square.* Petersham, Ma.: Saint Bede's Publications, 1993.

WRIGHT, GEORGE GRIER. "Early Cambridge Newspapers," *Cambridge Historical Society Proceedings,* 20 (1927–1929) 84–90.

———. "The Schools of Cambridge, 1800–1870," *Cambridge Historical Society Proceedings,* 13 (1918) 89–112.

Some Harvard and MIT graduates: Helen Keller, Gertrude Stein, Henry Thoreau, Franklin Delano Roosevelt, Yo Yo Ma, Gen. Jimmy Doolittle, Florence Luscomb, William Barton Rogers, "Buzz" Aldrin, Robert Taylor, Gordon Brown, Robert Burns Woodward, and Norbert Wiener.

CHAPTER SEVEN

HARVARD UNIVERSITY

Cambridge Educates the World

The Puritans arrived in Massachusetts Bay in 1630; the Great and General Court of Massachusetts voted 400 pounds "towards a schoale or colledge" in 1636; a Board of Overseers (magistrates and ministers) was appointed, land and a house acquired in Cambridge in 1637; and with teachers and a few students studies began in 1638. That year one John Harvard of Charlestown, "a godly Gentleman, and a lover of learning," died and willed the new "colledge" half his estate, less than 800 pounds, and about 400 books for a college library. At the next session of the General Court it was "ordered, that the new colledge agreed upon formerly to bee built at Cambridge shalbee called Harvard Colledge."

The college was incorporated in 1650, and its charter stated its purpose as "the advancement and education of youths in all manner of good literature Artes and Sciences," and "all other necessary provisions that may conduce to the education of the English and Indian youths of this country in knowledge and godliness." In 1702 the Reverend Cotton Mather declared that Harvard College was "the best Thing that ever *New-England* thought upon." While it was not the first college established in the New World—Mexico and Peru had started universities in the previous century—it was the forerunner of all centers of higher education in the United States.

The Seventeenth Century

The college struggled for existence throughout its first century. During the first four decades it barely had a teaching staff and but two or three youthful and badly paid tutors, and those were constantly leaving to take up the calling of the ministry which had always been their goal. Not until 1680 did gifts to the college generate enough money to maintain a regular teaching staff. Further, its first "head" of the college, Nathaniel Eaton, was a disaster; he was soon dismissed and eventually fled the colony in 1639 probably with some of John Harvard's legacy. For the next year the "colledge" on the "spacious plain" adjacent to the Charles was just about extinct. Then the Overseers appointed Henry Dunster, just three weeks in the colony, as the first president of Harvard. He served the college well.

Eaton did accomplish one thing. He initiated the plan which has resulted in today's College Yard which for so many students and graduates is still the sentimental, and perhaps even the mystical center, of the university. The Yard began as one of several plots of land called Cowyard Row for here the cattle owners lived and kept at night their herds. To the northeast was the town's old Ox Pasture, to the east the planting fields, to the south the town, and to its west Watch House Hill and the Burying Field. Samuel Eliot Morison observed in his history of Harvard that "anyone who has seen stockyards can imagine what the Harvard yard looked (and smelt) like before the College was

founded." What Eaton did was to fence it in, plant thirty apple trees on some of it, and begin the construction thereon of the first Harvard building, which came to be called the "Old College." The Yard slowly grew over the years and reached its present size in 1835. While other American colleges have their campuses, thanks to Eaton Harvard has the Yard.

A Cambridge University graduate, Henry Dunster reopened the college, assembled its scattered scholars, and as the sole teacher, educated them so that the first class graduated in 1642. The A. B. was then only a three year program; it was another decade before Dunster made it four. Old College, the building Eaton had begun was completed by that first graduation. It was a clapboard structure of three stories with a main hall and wings at either end, making an open quadrangle. It had turrets, a bell, and served as dormitory, commons, lecture hall, kitchen, butteries, and library. There was also the necessary "House of office" (outhouse.) Viewed from the old Ox pasture, framed by farm houses and the village, it was a "very faire and comely" scene. Old College was about where Grays Hall is today.

When the students were not in the Yard having their "bevers" (breakfast), afternoon lunch, beer or ale—and beer was then as now as vital as books in the quest of an education—they would be hard at their learning. The average age of the freshmen was 17, and at its best in the seventeenth century the total enrollment at any time was fifty. The curriculum was not easy. To get in, a student had to sight-read Cicero and be at ease with

Latin and Greek. His studies were similar to those taught at Oxford and Cambridge and consisted of lectures, debates, private reading, and work with his own tutor. At the end of three years when he received his bachelor's degree, he had been exposed to the Latin classics, logic, Aristotle, Greek literature and composition, and just a bit of history, botany, physics, math, and astronomy. Harvard under Dunster's leadership insisted on such a high educational standard that from the start its degrees were honored by Oxford and Cambridge, an honor not accorded so quickly to later American colleges.

Perhaps the most significant event of Dunster's tenure was that the Great and General Court of Massachusetts in 1650 granted the college and its Overseers complete corporate autonomy. The legislature also voted the basic Charter by which the College is still governed. Dunster was also instrumental in establishing the first set of "Lawes Liberties and orders of Harvard Colledge." Among these rules are ones compelling the students to speak Latin and not their "Mother-tongue" while at college and one banning "oathes, Lies, and uncertaine Rumours" and "all Idle, foolish, bitter scoffing, frothy wanton words offensive gestures." It is worth noting also that Harvard has never required from its community a religious test. Clearly Henry Dunster, was, as Josiah Quincy wrote in 1840 in his history of Harvard, "as true a friend, and as faithful a servant, as this college ever possessed." One hundred years later Samuel Eliot Morison could but re-affirm

John Harvard in his study. (Dahill conceptualization)

this opinion. It was indeed fortunate that Dunster had laid the foundations of the college solidly, for during the rest of this century it was never able to solve its leadership problem satisfactorily until the election of John Leverett as president in 1708.

For the college during these years there was the disturbing matter of money and how to get enough of it to properly run a college that had been founded without land to rent, annuities, invested funds, or scholarships. In the early years tuition and other student bills were often paid with bushels of barley malt, parsnips, barrels of salt beef, casks of butter, even by hogs and cows. For a time the state allotted the income from the Charlestown ferry to the college, and farmers in the various colonies contributed some of their corn to support the scholars at Cambridge. The first endowed scholarship—to assist a "poore scholler"—came from Lady Mowlson in England. Her maiden name was Anne Radcliffe. At the end of the nineteenth century when a woman's college was organized, it was appropriately named Radcliffe.

Along with the financial problems was the matter of improving and keeping in shape the physical plant, a headache no Harvard president escapes. The college now consisted of the Old College building and the president's house, which was about where Massachusetts Hall is and which had been paid for largely by the president. In 1652 the home of Edward Goffe was bought and then a small brick building was constructed as an "Indian College" but it did not last long as only a few Native Americans ever enrolled. The Old College was always a maintenance problem and finally, as Cotton Mather noted in 1695, it just "mouldered away." Its function had been replaced in 1677 by Old Harvard Hall.

From its founding in 1636 the Puritans had one clear purpose for their college and its graduates: "to know God and Jesus Christ." In the twentieth century Bernard Bailyn put it this way: "Harvard was founded as an institution from which the leadership of the church, state, and trade was expected to emerge and that leadership, like the community as a whole, was expected to remain deeply and correctly Christian." As one century ended and the next began that was still the clear purpose of the college.

The Eighteenth Century

If Henry Dunster was the president who firmly established the roots of Harvard, John Leverett was the president who established the college's commitment to the spirit of free inquiry in every area of education. Leverett was installed as president and given the college seal, keys, records, and the Charter of 1650 on the 14th of January 1708. Previously he had been a tutor and Fellow of the College, a lawyer, the Cambridge representative to the General Court, Speaker of the House, and a judge of the Superior Court. In religion he was liberal, in politics a conservative. He was also the first lay person to be president of Harvard.

His administration, which saw an increase in the student body, made few changes in the curriculum although courses in Hebrew were offered now for the first time and also for the first time, serious attention began to be paid to scientific research. Eventually a separate room was set aside in Massachusetts Hall for the college's growing collection of scientific apparatus.

Leverett was proud of the fact that Harvard was training men not only for the ministry but to be scholars, judges, physicians, soldiers, and even farmers. This fact along with Leverett's religious views were of deep

"The Great Leverett"—John Leverett, president, 1708–1724. (Dahill conceptualization)

scholarships. Leverett hinted a need for a professorship too, and the result was Harvard's first endowed chair, and the first endowed professorial chair in the United States, the Hollis Professor of Divinity. In 1721 Edward Wigglesworth, a young minister who could not find a church because of his deafness, was appointed to the new professorship. It proved an important appointment.

The students who studied at the college under Leverett always spoke of him as "The Great Leverett." He deserved their praise, for he freed the college in Cambridge of its "provincial orthodoxy" yet kept it "a house of learning under the spirit of religion."

In the new eighteenth-century there was obviously a need for additional college buildings. In 1698 Stoughton Hall had been built as a student dormitory, which made the college a quadrangle with old Harvard Hall to the left of Stoughton and the president's house to the right. The focus of the college was shifted as a result to the western edge of the Yard where the main entrance still is. In 1720 the president's house was replaced by Massachusetts Hall, now the oldest surviving college building although its interior has been altered several times. In 1726 a new residence was built for the president and was so used during the next century. This is the familiar wooden yellow house facing Massachusetts Avenue called Wadsworth House after its first occupant. Harvard's first building used just as a chapel was not built until the construction of Holden Chapel in 1724; and when another dormitory, Hollis

concern to the orthodox divines, and when some of the students proved troublesome—they swore, played cards, took in horse racing and similar "riotous Actions"—they raised alarms, and led by that troublesome divine Cotton Mather, created their own set of riotous actions. Fortunately, the college was to survive both vexations.

During Leverett's tenure and due directly to his liberalism, Thomas Hollis, London merchant and Baptist, started sending funds for library books and

Hall, was added in 1762 just beyond Holden, the Yard had its second quadrangle. Slowly, then, the Harvard Yard familiar now was emerging.

Then a first-class disaster struck! During the evening of January 24, 1764, in the midst of a northeast snow storm, old Harvard Hall burnt to the ground. The greatest loss in this fire was the college library whose 5,000 volumes made it the largest library in the colonies. Fortunately, there was an immediate and generous response from the public towards rebuilding the library and the hall. Within two years, the Harvard Hall of today had been constructed with space for the library, the commons, a chapel, and even a museum.

Then the college had to deal with the problems caused by the war between the colonies and Britain. During the siege of Boston, it packed up and moved to the safety of Concord where it remained for the next eight months. The students were boarded in taverns and private homes; classes and chapel were held in the court house, the school house, and the First Parish. The college eagerly returned to Cambridge as soon as the British troops had sailed out of Boston in March, 1776, for New York. Back in Cambridge one of the first things it did was to thank the future president, George Washington, for ridding the area of the redcoats, the hated Lobster-backs, by granting him an honorary doctor's degree.

Harvard might be home; but there was still a revolution, and that meant that the college had fewer students and that supplies, textbooks, and related items were hard to procure. Further, the soldiers who had been quartered in the college had done a fair amount of mischief to the buildings. Currency inflation played havoc with the budget. On the brighter side, however, was the fact that the new General Court reaffirmed all the rights and privileges Harvard had been given during colonial rule. A new president now assumed the leadership of Harvard; and if the Reverend Joseph Willard was not a brilliant president, his administration did successfully begin to turn the college into a university by creating in 1782 the Harvard Medical School. It was not a bad gift to give the new Republic or future generations of Americans.

The Nineteenth Century

In 1805 the liberal Christian Henry Ware became the Hollis Professor of Divinity. This appointment was really a momentous act, for it enabled the intellectual life of the college to move away from its restrictive Puritan foundations and to develop in the freer atmosphere of secular knowledge and scientific inquiry that has characterized humanity's search for understanding since the eighteenth century. Fortunately for Harvard, Ware's choice was followed in 1810 by that of the Reverend John Thornton Kirkland as the college's fourteenth president.

The Kirkland years, and to some extant those of his successor Josiah Quincy, saw the firm establishment of liberalism at Harvard and the increasing emergence of

Harvard University. Eliza Susan Quincy's drawing of the September 1836 procession of Harvard alumni leaving the First Parish Meeting House and walking to the Pavilion. *(Courtesy of Dr. Conrad Wright)*

its graduates—Emerson, Thoreau, Theodore Parker, Jared Sparks, George Bancroft, Francis Parkman, Wendell Phillips—upon the national and international stage. These years saw too the foundation of the Divinity School, the Law School, and the creation of numerous endowed professorships. Major improvements were also made to the physical plant including in 1841 Gore Hall, the first separate building for the expanding college library of 41,000 volumes. When Harvard celebrated its bicentennial in 1836 and when Quincy penned his detailed two-volume history of Harvard in 1840, it was possible to declare "that the noble purposes of the clergy and laity, the founders of New England and of its institutions, have not failed."

As with all institutions Harvard developed fitfully and the next significant leap forward took place during the presidencies, 1869-1933, of two of Harvard's most gifted educators, Charles William Eliot and Abbott Lawrence Lowell. The university of today took shape and developed as a result of their remarkable vision and effective leadership. In six decades the university at Cambridge went from a provincial institution into one of the leading institutions of higher learning in the world.

Charles William Eliot, President, 1869–1909

ious fields. Further, students were encouraged to ask questions and teachers to show them methods of research and to share with them their own discoveries. These changes required more teachers not fewer, better salaries, increased library resources, and the enlargement of the college plant. During his years some thirty-five buildings were constructed or improved for use as dormitories, classrooms, laboratories, museums, and athletic facilities.

During his administration the Graduate School of Arts and Sciences was established, the Law School reformed, its *Review* begun, the Medical School and the Dental School drastically improved, and the biological and natural sciences finally came of age. Indeed, the much-admired glass flowers came during this period. Almost more important, however, than these acts was that from this period onward the earned Ph.D. became the degree at Harvard and elsewhere that represented the attainment of knowledge.

After forty years of service, Eliot retired in 1909. In his first commencement address in 1870 he had declared, "We mean to build here, securely and slowly, a university in the largest sense." This had happened. He had transformed Harvard from a local New England college to a world-class research institution (largely because of the development of the Graduate School of Arts and Sciences.) Now it was time, as he told the undergraduates who came to the president's house upon hearing of his plan to retire, for "a man who will take up this extremely laborious and extreme-

Eliot believed that "universities are teachers, storehouses, and searches for truth." He believed learning was vibrant and opened-ended and that students should be exposed to all known human knowledge and experience. As president, and against some faculty opposition, he relaxed the curriculum requirements and permitted the young scholars to elect their own subjects to investigate and study. Recitation was largely abolished, replaced by lectures given by experts in varly influential position with untiring energy and carry this university to a higher plane than it now occupies."

That individual was Abbott Lawrence Lowell.

The Twentieth Century

Lowell is perhaps best remembered for the attractive, pleasing Harvard Houses built along the Charles River in an area that at the end of the nineteenth century was a fairly unattractive collection of commercial buildings, small homes, coal yards, a power plant, irregular streets, wharves, and, at low tide, mud flats. The reason that Lowell had them built is not as well remembered. It was an effort by the institution and the president to provide for the growing college, growing in numbers of students and from a wider social and financial base than in earlier centuries, a more integrated and intimate sense of belonging and sharing. "The task before us," Lowell stated at the beginning of his presidency, "is to frame a system which without sacrificing individual variation too much or neglecting the pursuit of different scholarly interests, shall produce an intellectual and social cohesion, at least among large groups of students, and points of contact among them all."

Slowly the college purchased the necessary land, and after much planning and the building of a series of related dormitories, construction on the first House began in 1929. The initial funding came from a Yale graduate, Edward S. Harkness, who eventually gave over $13 million to the project. He had suggested earlier to his own alma mater the House concept, and when for various reasons the college had not yet responded, he proposed a similar concept to his friend Lowell, and Harvard Houses was the result.

The concept was simple: while each would have its own architectural style, partly determined by its site and the space available, each would provide students with rooms, a dining hall, lounges, courtyards with trees, and their own sense of privacy. Not foreseen originally was the fact that over the decades each of the Houses was to develop its own character and individuality.

Meanwhile, across the Charles, the Harvard Business School, which had been established in 1908, began to construct in the twenties its own rather extensive and eventually most luxurious complex. The Education School had come into being in 1920. It was also during Lowell's period that the Fogg Museum was erected as was the Memorial Church which faces Widener Library which had been opened in 1915. The area between these two impressive structures is where Commencement is held each June.

The most recent sustained building program came during the presidency of Nathan Pusey (1953–1971.) He initiated a plan to improve undergraduate education at Harvard, a plan sorely needed because of the rapid growth of the student body and all that that implied. He successfully completed the single largest financial drive ever undertaken by Harvard up to that time: almost 100 million dollars. The money went for new professorships, library resources, building repair and upkeep, housing for married students, more laboratories and classrooms, a new infirmary, and a theater. The new buildings included the Carpenter Center for the Visual Arts, Gund Hall (the home of the Graduate School of Design), Holyoke Center in the Square, William James Hall, the undergraduate Science Center, and the Loeb Drama Center.

Sometimes it is difficult for Cantabrigians to recall

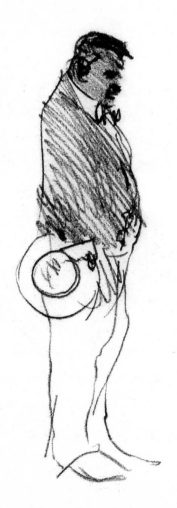

Archie C. Epps, Senior Associate Dean of Harvard College.

Harvard's slender and tentative beginning in 1636 or the belief in learning and knowledge that called it forth, that caused it to take root, struggle, preserve, and finally become the major international educational center it is today. Harvard, after all, is just Harvard, and one cannot imagine Cambridge without its first college—if for no other reasons than that it owns over 400 acres of land, over 460 buildings, is the city's largest employer, and its band seems always to be marching through Harvard Square playing football songs or "Fair Harvard."

Today well over 30,000 students from over 100 countries taught by more than 2,200 faculty members attend the university not only in Cambridge but also at the Medical and Dental Schools as well as the Business School and School of Public Health all in Boston, at the Arnold Arboretum in Jamaica Plain, at the Harvard Forest in Petersham, at the Center for Hellenic Studies and at Dumbarton Oaks both in Washington, and finally at the Center for Italian Renaissance Studies in Florence, Italy.

The university's endowment is valued at more than thirteen billion; it employs a staff including those who work in its teaching hospitals of more than 20,000, and has a quarter of a million living graduates. This immense and complex institution is governed by the "President and Fellows of Harvard College"—a self-perpetuating corporation—and its charter of 1650. The Harvard Corporation is charged with making all appointments within the university and with conduct-

Two of the architectural styles at Harvard: Memorial Hall (1864–1878) (*left photo*) originally designed by the firm of Ware and Van Brunt is shown here with its restored tower (2000) and the Carpenter Center for the Visual Arts (1963) (*right photo*), the only American building designed by the French architect, Le Corbusier.

ing its business. Its major decisions are subject, however, to the consent of the Board of Overseers whose 30 members are now elected at large by the graduates of Radcliffe and Harvard.

Yet a university is so much more than such facts and figures as these words of President Lowell indicate: "As wave after wave rolls landward from the ocean, breaks and fades away...so the generations of men [and now women] follow one another, sometimes quietly, some-times, after a storm, with noisy turbulence. But whether we think upon the monotony or upon the violence in human history, two things are always new—youth and the quest for knowledge, and with these a university is concerned. So long as its interest in them is keen, it can never grow old, though it counts its age by centuries. The means it uses may vary with the times, but forever the end remains the same."

Along with students and their quest for knowledge

another essential ingredient is always necessary. At the Overseers meeting of December 27, 1643 it was voted "that there shall be a College seale in the forme following." Someone then drew in the record book a shield with three books, the first two open, the lower one face down. On those symbols of learning appears the Latin word Veritas, meaning truth. With this simple image, with this one concept, the Puritans established a standard for their college in the wilderness, and indeed for all institutions of higher learning.

MIT

The year was 1861. On March 4th Abraham Lincoln took the oath of office as the 16th president of the United States; on April 12th the rebels bombarded Fort Sumter in Charleston Harbor; and on April 16th Lincoln called for 75,000 volunteers to defend the Union. The War Between the States had begun but so too, and without as much media attention and fuss, had MIT, Cambridge's other major educational enterprise. On April 10th of that year The Great and General Court of Massachusetts had voted to Incorporate the Massachusetts Institute of Technology. For its first fifty-years the Institute was located in Boston and was popularly known as "Boston Tech". Since 1916 it has been in Cambridge and is now called by most everybody simply MIT.

William Barton Rogers, MIT's first President.

Boston Tech

The founding of MIT in Boston's Back Bay was due largely to the vision of William Barton Rogers and his brother Henry. The "Brothers Rogers," there were four of them, were esteemed scientists and teachers in early nineteenth century America. Eventually William and Henry located in Boston, one of the important developing centers for industry, engineering, and applied science. Quite quickly it became apparent that there was a need for scientific and technical education as well as for liberal arts education, and so William in 1846 wrote a proposal for a polytechnic institution in Boston that would offer courses in such fields as mining, chemical analysis, engineering, and machinery. It took fifteen years, several attempts, two redrafts of his proposal, before his vision of an Institute of Technology became a reality. When the General Court granted MIT its charter in 1861, William Barton Rogers was elected its first president.

If it had been a struggle to found the Institute, it was just as much of a struggle to get it launched, especially in an America involved in a civil war. From the start there was a desperate need for financial support, and this only materialized when Dr. William J. Walker, MIT's first significant benefactor, gave the school sixty thousand dollars. He was to give additional funds, and the Walker Professorship of Mathematics honors his generosity.

Walker's gift made possible the erection on Boylston Street, still but a muddy roadway, of MIT's first building, an impressive four story structure, eventually named for the first president. Soon the new officers and faculty decided upon a proper curriculum, and on February 20, 1865 the Institute opened its doors. Rogers noted in his diary: "Organized the School! Fifteen students entered. May not this prove a memorable day!" Since the new building was not yet ready, the first classes were held downtown in one of the rooms of the Mercantile Library Association.

Once established, Boston Tech, as the Institute was soon called, took a firm hold on life and its reputation for excellence quickly developed. By 1868 the student body was 175, and in 1871 the first woman was admitted, Ellen H. Swallow. She also became the first woman instructor, joining the teaching staff in 1878. Although there were always some women at the Institute, not until 1960 was their presence in laboratories and classrooms firmly secured.

Ellen H. Swallow, MIT's first coed, who received her degree in 1873. She was also its first female instructor.

As the school grew, the teaching staff was increased. One of the first appointments was Charles W. Eliot who had begun his teaching career at Harvard as professor of analytical chemistry and metallurgy. Eliot taught at MIT until he was elected president of Harvard in 1869. He was to attempt more than once to have Harvard annex MIT but always failed to realize this hope. Other attempts were to be made; but all met the same fate and MIT has always retained its independence as an educational institution.

The early history of Boston Tech was not smooth. The basic problem was money, the lack thereof. During the decade of the 1870s tuition had to be increased with the result that there was an immediate decline in the student body, which meant that fewer faculty were necessary and that they were paid smaller salaries. However, during the next decade Boston Tech weathered the financial crisis and was again on the move. Several new buildings were constructed including the Walker Building on Clarendon Street. To help pay for it, MIT had sold to Boston the small triangular plot of land in Copley Square facing the Boston Public Library. It should be noted that the Walker Building was close to the Buckminster Hotel and its bar, a place friendly to Boston Tech students and nicknamed by them The Chapel.

During this period the most popular courses were those related to civil engineering, and more than a third of the graduates chose this field as their major. Among the other courses taught were electrical and mechanical engineering, metallurgy, philosophy, literature, and modern languages. As practical experience was stressed both in the field and in the classroom, MIT established in 1869 the first physical laboratory in the United States.

At the beginning of the twentieth century Boston Tech could boast of a student body over 1,200, a competent and widely recognized teaching staff, a distinctive curriculum and philosophy of education, and a sound financial base. Its future appeared solidly rooted in Boston. Yet at this time MIT made a dramatic decision to move its campus across the Charles River to Cambridge.

As early as 1902, it had become apparent that if the Institute was to be able to grow and play the role it should in higher education it needed more space than was available in the Back Bay. Several possible options were discussed in the opening decade of the century. Not only was more space essential but also the funds to move and erect a new campus. When the decision finally was made in 1911 it was to move to Cambridge, and this was done in 1916.

MIT Cambridge

In June of 1916 MIT Cambridge became a reality. The Institute celebrated that month both its past fifty-five years as Boston Tech and its future as an educational institution poised for rapid growth and service to its own country, and as it has turned out, to

MIT Boston crossing the Charles to Cambridge.

the world community, too. For several days a great gathering of graduates, professors, officers, staff, and friends marked the occasion by programs and events that included a march from the Back Bay to the new campus by the Charles River.

The vision of William Barton Rogers had been responsible for the founding of the Institute; now it was that vision enlarged by president Richard Cockburn Maclaurin, supported by the generous donation of T. Coleman du Pont for the purchase of land in Cambridge and the equally generous gifts of George Eastman, the inventor of the Kodak camera, for the erection of the initial buildings, that made the move to larger quarters and more effective service possible.

The new MIT campus with its Great Court (after 1974 called Killian Court for the first MIT graduate to be its president), side wings, and Great Dome over the original library were built on land that had been made from mud pumped up from the Charles and on earth dug up from the construction of the new Boston subway system. Before building could commence, 22,000 piles needed to be driven. The architect was one of MIT's own, Welles W. Bosworth, as were the engineers, Charles A. Stone and Edwin S. Webster. Bosworth took his concept from Thomas Jefferson's use of the Pantheon motif at the University of Virginia and used Indiana limestone for the facade.

As new ones were added to the main buildings, each with a name but often referred to by a number, they were tied together by corridors and tunnels. In time an east and a west campus were developed. The additions include the Spectroscopy Laboratory in 1931; the Eastman Laboratories (Building 6) in 1932; the elegant Rogers Building (Building 7) in 1938 where architecture and urban planning courses are taught; the Kresge Auditorium and Chapel designed by Eero Saarinen in 1955; a sixteen-story married students residential center in 1962; the Sherman Fairchild building in 1973, the largest building erected since those of 1916; and the I. M. Pei building for the department of chemical engineering in 1975. When the whole is viewed from the Boston shore of the Charles, it has a graceful and attractive appearance.

During the First World War, the Institute offered its facilities and specialized skills to the nation. Among the war-related work it undertook was the training of pilots, radio engineers, and even the building of a prototype 45-ton tank. The campus again became almost a military camp during the second world conflagration. Karl Compton, the president, along with many of the Institute's faculty and graduates, worked just about full-time for the National Defense Research Committee and for the Office of Scientific Research and Development on one of the largest cooperative scientific and technological projects ever attempted by a national community.

For this effort the Institute created its Radiation Laboratory, occupying fifteen acres and employing over four thousand persons, to pioneer research into all aspects of radiation including Long Range Navigation for ships and airplanes, and its Servomechanisms Laboratory which worked with Charles Stark Draper, its professor of aeronautics, to research fire-control problems connected with the various weapon systems. Finally, its cyclotron contributed to research in the areas of metallurgy, medicine and chemical warfare, and its High Voltage Lab constructed five large x-ray machines for the Navy. Such efforts and programs on behalf of the nation's war effort had a lasting impact on the Institute and profoundly influenced its future development as an educational center.

During the decade after the First World War, MIT meandered along without any special distinction, and then in 1930 Karl Compton, well-known and respected scientist and physicist, assumed its presidency. One of his first acts was to revive the department of Physics by appointing John C. Slater from Harvard as its chair and George R. Harrison from Stanford as Director of the Research Laboratory of Experimental Physics. Later Harrison was to head MIT's School of Science from 1942 to 1963. Vannevar Bush was made a vice-president and dean of the engineering school, and the Division of Humanities was established. These acts indicated the importance being given to the need for excellence in all of the Institute's scholarly undertakings.

The course charted by MIT was not always an easy one during these years due first to the Great Depression and then to the World War when so much of the talent and energy at MIT was helping the democratic nations deal with the challenge of Fascism. After its defeat, the Nuclear Age moved onto center stage.

In 1958 a nuclear reactor was built on the campus and a department for Nuclear Science created, which resulted in MIT becoming the leading center in the United States for nuclear research and education. The old Radiation Lab became now the Research Laboratory of Electronics. One of the most basic changes that took place was that more and more scientific efforts became interdisciplinary endeavors. While a Magnet Lab was started in 1960 and an Energy Lab in 1972, the real future for science lay in the area of cooperation between researchers, schools, and the government, and so MIT faculty and students worked and learned not only in Cambridge but in a number of localities such as at the Brookhaven National Laboratory on Long Island and the Lincoln Lab in Lexington, Massachusetts.

When James R. Killian, Jr. became the Institute's tenth president in 1949, one of his first tasks was to implement the recommendations in the report of the Committee on Educational Survey, popularly known by the name of its chair, as the Lewis Report. This report was the result of a far-ranging study of the Institute, its past policies and its possible future directions. It concluded that "technological and social problems are so inextricably interwoven that the humanities and social sciences are also components of man's professional life." This was in keeping with the views first promulgated by William Barton Rogers. Killian moved, therefore, to make the Humanities Division the School of Humanities and Social Science.

To carry out the educational goals expressed in the Lewis Report, Killian and the staff went to work to secure funding. The Alfred P. Sloan Foundation gave over five million dollars to establish the School of Industrial Management and the Mid-Century Development Fund Drive raised over twenty-five million. In 1960 the Second Century Fund Campaign of MIT raised an additional sixty-six million, and in 1980 the MIT Leadership Campaign raised two hundred fifty million. The Institute, its programs and teaching faculty, had come a long way from those first classes in 1865 at the Mercantile Library Association.

The Institute continued its remarkable educational role as it entered its second century. The emphasis was

The Ambulatory Network of MIT.

clearly now on interdisciplinary efforts and on cooperation. Several centers were established, including one for cancer research, one dealing with earth sciences, and one for materials research in archeology and ethnology. The work done at the Lincoln Lab was expanded and computers, satellites, and the concept of cybernetics came into their own and flourished. The faculty also won several Nobel Prizes. For MIT students, faculty, and graduates, their curriculum had literally become anything and everything in the expanding universe.

Today MIT occupies 146 acres of Cambridge land and the campus runs for more than a mile beside the Charles River. It has a teaching staff of about 2,000 and a support staff of over 8,000; its student body exceeds 10,000 and comes from around the world; its graduates number more than 88,000. Its annual budget is $1,230.8 million, and its endowment is valued in the billions.

At the beginning of the twenty-first century how does one define the history and educational philosophy of the Institute? President Henry S. Pritchett stated it this way at the celebration of MIT's first fifty years: "Today more than ever men ask truth, but truth related to human needs and human aspirations. If the Institute of Technology stands for anything distinctively, it stands for these two things." In 1971 Jerome B. Wiesner at his inauguration as president added another human task to these two when he declared: "We are all gathered here, teachers and students, to expand man's knowledge of the universe. No doctrine, no orthodoxy, no conventional discipline or gust of political passion can be allowed to divert us from this purpose."

View of MIT's east campus, 2001.

Radcliffe students studying, 1879.

RADCLIFFE COLLEGE

Efforts for opening Harvard education to women first started in 1855, when Elizabeth Cary Agassiz, wife of the Harvard naturalist, opened her home for a school for girls between the ages of 15 and 18, with lectures being provided by her husband and other Harvard professors. She ran her school until 1863. That same year the college's president, Thomas Hill, established courses of University lectures given by various respected scholars. These were open to the general public, so women were able to attend. Then came the Bussey Institution in Jamaica Plain where three sum-

mer courses were offered without credit for women in natural history.

Finally, efforts for giving women Harvard-quality education led, in 1882, to the incorporation of the Society for the Collegiate Instruction of Women, nicknamed the "Harvard Annex," a permanent program created by Arthur and Stella Scott Gilman. With Elizabeth Cary Agassiz as its president, and with Harvard professors providing the instruction, it was empowered to give a certificate but no credit or degrees. In 1894, the Society was chartered as Radcliffe College, and empowered to award undergraduate and graduate degrees. The College was named after a woman who made her mark in 1643, Anne Radcliffe, and who had established Harvard's first scholarship fund, presumably without any thought of women's education in mind.

While the first seventeen students of the society were housed in four rented rooms on Appian Way, the first Radcliffe President was very forward looking as she acquired the Fay House on Garden Street and most of the land that is known today as the Radcliffe Yard. Next came another large estate on Garden Street where the Hemenway Gymnasium and the first dormitory (1901) were built. This building program continued aggressively through to the construction of the college's Hilles Library in 1966.

It was the Second World War that made it necessary for a basic change in the College's relationship to Harvard. The result was that Harvard and Radcliffe agreed to coeducation, and Radcliffe made plans to phase out it its credit courses and degree-granting programs. This took time and it was not until 1963 that all Radcliffe seniors received Harvard degrees. In 1971 all Harvard dorms became coed, and by 1995 women comprised nearly one-half of the Harvard College student body. In 1999 the two colleges agreed to full merger.

In the agreement signed that year by the Harvard Corporation and Radcliffe's Trustees, the former College was replaced by the Radcliffe Institute for Advanced Study. The Institute is led by a Dean who has the same relationship to Harvard as do the Deans of its other faculties and was established with an endowment of 300 million. It continues Radcliffe's present programs: the Schlesinger Library on the History of Women in America, the Public Policy Institute, the Bunting Institute, and the Murray Research Center, and establishes another that will "focus on the study of women, gender, and society."

LESLEY UNIVERSITY

In 1909, in the early days of the kindergarten movement in America, Lesley University was founded to prepare women for careers in kindergarten and primary education. It was started by Edith Lesley, a former Cambridge school teacher, in the living room of her family home at 29 Everett Street, which is now the school's main administration building. It was called appropriately enough Miss Lesley's School, and its student body at the beginning was about a dozen young women. She directed the school into the 1930's, assisted in the beginning by her sister and invalid mother, and then by Gertrude Malloch.

Although the enrollment remained small for many years, it acquired throughout the country a reputation for excellent teacher training. In 1942 it was incorporated as a nonprofit institution, and in 1943 its named was changed from the Lesley Normal School to Lesley College. Its growth from this time has been steady, and in 2000 it became a university.

Its home campus, situated on five-acres off Massachusetts Avenue just west of Harvard Square, serves over 6,000 women and men a year in a great variety of programs. In addition, classes are also offered in about forty other locations in Massachusetts, fourteen other states, and in several other countries. Lesley offers certificate and degree programs in its School of Undergraduate Studies, Graduate School of Arts and Social Sciences, School of Education, and School of Management. The aim of all the programs is to blend the theoretical with the practical; in 1995 Lesley granted 451 bachelors and almost 2,000 masters degrees.

CAMBRIDGE COLLEGE

Cambridge College plays a unique role in the higher education community of the city in that its primary goal is to help working adults, of an average age of 40 years, obtain graduate education in the fields of education, counseling, management, and integrated studies. Special preparation programs make it possible for persons, even those without undergraduate degrees, to enter the program. Further, Cambridge College emphasizes multicultural diversity in its admissions and curriculum and as a result 45% of its students and faculty are now from minority groups.

Started by a small group of educators in 1971 without endowment but with a clear idea of its mission, it was connected first with the Newton College of the Sacred Heart and then with the Antioch University Network. In 1981 it became an independent institution and now has nearly 1000 students in its undergraduate program and 1700 in the graduate.

Located between Central Square and Harvard Square at 1000 Massachusetts Avenue, the College boasts a modern building purchased in 1994, furnished with conference tables, comfortable chairs, study areas, lounge areas, a computer lab, and a writing lab. A second campus is located in Springfield for the convenience of students in western Massachusetts and Connecticut. Courses are offered also in a number of satellite centers around the state: Worcester, Brockton, Beverly, Revere, Plymouth and Sandwich. The college does not have its own library but its students have full use of the Gutman Library at Harvard, the Sawyer Library at Suffolk University, and the Wheelock College Library.

THE EPISCOPAL DIVINITY SCHOOL IN CAMBRIDGE

The Episcopal Divinity School was created in 1974 when Pennsylvania's Philadelphia Divinity School moved to Cambridge and merged with the Episcopal Theological School. The local component of this combination had been established more than a hundred years earlier when Benjamin Tyler Reed of Boston gave 100,000 dollars to found at Cambridge a theological school for the training of men for ministry in the Protestant Episcopal Church.

The new school opened its doors on January 1, 1868, in temporary quarters on Mount Auburn Street with two professors and one student. Within a few months it started to acquire its present eight acre campus on Brattle Street and construction was begun on its first building, St. John's Chapel. By the end of the century several additional buildings had been added including today's dormitories, Lawrence and Winthrop Halls.

The student body averaged forty during this period, and it was not until the conclusion of the Second World War that the enrollment climbed to one hundred. Today the merged school has 15 full-time faculty members and about 130 women and men studying in its various programs. While many of them are headed for service in the Episcopal church, at least a quarter of them will seek ministry in other denominations.

THE WESTON JESUIT
SCHOOL OF THEOLOGY

Weston College, the forerunner of the present institution, was founded in Weston, Massachusetts, in 1922 for pretheology students in the Roman Catholic order of the Society of Jesus. At first its instruction was limited to philosophical studies, but four years later its core courses were increased when the faculty of theology was created, and then in 1959 Weston became a constituent college of Boston College from which its students received their degree for the next several years. In 1972 this arrangement ceased, and Weston was empowered by the Commonwealth of Massachusetts to grant its own professional degrees.

A few years earlier in 1967 the College had helped to launch the Boston Theological Institute, a cooperative movement between several of the Boston-based theological schools, and so its move a year later from Weston to the campus of the Episcopal Theological School in Cambridge was both appropriate and logical. So too were the decisions to share library resources, classroom space, the EDS chapel, and to enlarge its student body by admitting others than those headed into the Jesuit order. Since 1972 it has housed its administrative and faculty offices in the White Building on Phillips Place immediately adjacent to the EDS campus and maintained a dormitory on nearby Hawthorn Street. The present name of the school was adopted in 1994, and today as both a graduate divinity school and as a Pontifical faculty of theology it is engaged in training over 200 women and men to be Roman Catholic priests (about half of the male student body enters the priesthood), lay ministers, and vowed religious.

Longy School of Music.

school's Board of Trustees and for the gift from the Pickman Fund which had made the wing possible.

Longy has by choice remained a small conservatory of less than 100 professional students with a strong emphasis on solo and ensemble performances. However, the school in its many other divisions provides training for more than 1200 children, young adults, adult learners, and amateur musicians. In 1998, as a result of its overall increasing student enrollment, it purchased a second building [on the corner of Garden and Chauncy Streets] less than a minute's walk from the Abbot mansion. This building doubled the school's classroom and office space. Each year in its concert hall Longy hosts over 250 musical events for its pupils and the general public.

THE LONGY SCHOOL OF MUSIC

This music institution was started in 1915 in Boston by the Boston Symphony Orchestra's principal oboist Georges Longy. In 1930 it moved to Cambridge, first to a small house on Church Street (where the Atrium Building is now), and then in 1937 to the Follen Street Victorian mansion (1889) of the railroad tycoon Edwin Hale Abbot. A concert hall was added to the mansion in 1970, and named for Edward M. Pickman in acknowledgement of his service as president of the

THE AMERICAN ACADEMY OF ARTS AND SCIENCES

In the fall of 1980 the American Academy of Arts and Sciences moved its headquarters from Brookline where it had been since 1957 to its brand new red brick building with its copper roof in Cambridge. It was designed in the style of an oriental pagoda for the lovely woody site where the first mayor of Boston, John Phillips, had built in 1807 his summer mansion eventually called Shady Hill. The area is now known as Norton's Woods because Andrews Norton when he lived there had been the one to have the trees planted. Its construction had been made possible thanks to the generosity of the Rowland Foundation and one of the Academy's former presidents and his wife, Mr. and Ms. Edwin H. Land.

The Academy had been formed in 1779 to promote and nurture all the arts and sciences in the new United States; it was incorporated a year later in Boston. It consists today of over 2,400 fellows and 400 foreign fellows who are elected to the Academy from the disciplines of math, the physical and biological sciences, the social arts and humanities. It sponsors various publications, one of which is its widely circulated journal *Daedalus,* awards prizes, and holds seminars and conferences.

THROUGH PUBLISHING AND PRINTING

It was in Cambridge that the first press in America was established. That press, a font of type, a stock of print paper, and a Stephen Day to do the printing, arrived from England aboard the *John* in 1638 as part of the entourage and possessions of the Rev. Jose Glover and his family. Unfortunately for the minister he died on the way over, and so it was his good wife Elizabeth who bought a large house where today's Holyoke Center is in Harvard Square, set up the "print-

ery," and produced the next year an almanac and a broadside of the freeman's oath. In 1640 the press put out its first book, the justly famous Bay Psalm Book. Cambridge printing and publishing had been born and christened.

The widow Glover married Harvard's first president (Dunster) and the young press was soon moved to a lean-to attached to the presidential house and became the college's first printing office. Eventually, Samuel Green became the printer and served in that position for the next forty-three years. His first book was "The Platform of Church Discipline" which had been drawn up for the churches of the Standing Order by a synod meeting in Cambridge. Later, with the assistance of Marmaduke Johnson, Green published the first Bible printed in America, John Eliot's Indian Bible of 1663. During excavations in the Yard in 1979, some type from this press were discovered; they can be seen at Houghton Library. In 1675 the first Boston press was started, and as others were begun Green's business declined and by 1692 ceased to exist. Harvard did not get back into the printing business for more than one hundred years.

In 1802, the Harvard Corporation created the University Press and hired a young Boston printer, William Hilliard, to run it. He was told to print with quality paper and the best available fonts. Of course he also was able to publish books on his own. His earliest imprints included textbooks and various documents needed by the college. The relationship between Harvard and Hilliard worked unevenly for two decades and then Harvard decided in 1827 to get out of the printing game and sold the business to Eliab Metcalf who had become Hilliard's partner. It retained, however, the printing building it had erected on Holyoke Street although it did rent it to Metcalf.

The University Press

The new firm continued to do business with Harvard, and on the university catalog it was listed as "Printers to the University." It moved its operations in 1865 to an old hotel in Brattle Square, and in 1895 it

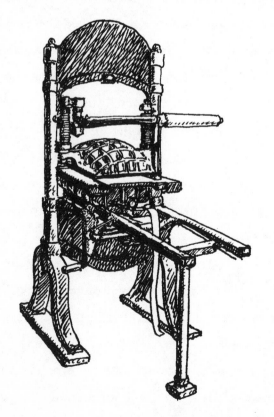

A Washington handpress press used at the Athenaeum Press.

built its own commodious plant on University Road near the Charles. By then it had been sold several times, and its imprint was now The University Press: John Wilson & Son, Inc."

Wilson, a Scot and self-taught scholar, made the press a force to be reckoned with, and under his leadership it developed a progressive reputation, and its print list included almost every important writer of the day. Eventually its plant had fifty-eight presses and a staff of more than three hundred, and for a while the press was the major rival of another Cambridge printing firm, The Riverside Press. That rivalry ceased in 1928 when the University Press was acquired by Tolman Print of nearby Brockton. Although Tolman added "University Press" to its name and continued in business during the 1930's, it ceased to exist itself in 1942; and the printing plant on University Road was eventually demolished in 1970.

The Riverside Press

The Riverside Press was founded in 1852 by Henry Oscar Houghton, a young man from Vermont who had come to Cambridge and learned the printing trade at the small firm of Freeman & Bolles. When Freeman retired, Houghton became Bolles' partner and soon took over the firm on his own. One of its chief customers was the publishing house of Little, Brown, and shortly after Houghton had taken over the operation of the business, they suggested buying the old Cambridge

Alms House Estate on the banks of the Charles and leasing it to him. He accepted, and after renovations and the addition of steam power to the six Adams presses, the Riverside Press, drawing its name from its location, came into existence.

The new firm had fifty employees and did printing for Little, Brown, Ticknor & Fields, and the *Atlantic Monthly,* and in 1863 it signed a contract to print and bind the new dictionary of G. & C. Merriam Company. However, Houghton soon had several problems on his hand. For unexplained reasons, Little, Brown moved their business to another Cambridge printer, the University Press, and when Ticknor died his partner also moved their business to the same printing house.

Houghton was not easily deterred and in 1864 acquired a new partner, Melancthon Montgomery Hurd, who brought with him $50,000. With this, Houghton rented a building close to his plant to serve as a bindery (previously the Riverside Press had none) and hired English workers with bindery knowledge to come to Cambridge. Within three years the staff of the firm had grown to 300, and in 1867 it purchased outright its property from Little, Brown and replaced the original structure with a large four-story brick building.

By the 1870s the staff grew to 400, in the next decade to 600, and expanded, acquiring in 1875 the lithographic firm of Armstrong & Company, which enabled them to become involved in commercial work such as advertising circulars and book illustrations.

Houghton died in 1895, but the firm continued under the leadership of the partner he had accepted in 1872, George Harrison Mifflin. The firm now had 9 proving presses, 6 steam lithographic presses, and a skilled team of designers including for several years Daniel Berkeley Updike and Bruce Rogers. The latter worked for Riverside for 15 years and designed 200 books, many of them still regarded as works of "imagination, taste, and brilliance."

Riverside Press continued to grow and prosper even during The Great War. Additional buildings were added to the original ones, and there were now 60 steam presses and 700 workers. In 1921, however, there was a bitter industrial strike in the Boston printing business when the employees went out to bring the working week down from 48 to 44 hours. Riverside expected its workers to be loyal; and when the printing firms broke the strike, many of the Riverside workers who had dared to go out were never allowed to return to their jobs, creating bitter feelings that unfortunately never healed.

Henry W. Laughlin now took over running the operations at the Press. He was an energetic and charismatic individual and business was good during the twenties, so good that a new bindery was built on Blackstone Street in 1924. Four years later an addition was started, and then arrived the Great Depression. Riverside survived it, but the bindery addition had to be delayed, and for a while employees worked only a few days every other week. But then the second great war arrived, and slowly business improved, partly due to government work, so that once again employees worked a 40 hour week.

During the next few decades, new printing technologies, often costly, brought dramatic changes to Riverside including offset publishing. When the plant was modernized it was necessary also to move to an offsite warehouse for storing paper as there was no more space available in Cambridge for all of the press' activities. Even with the accommodation to change, it became increasingly clear to the owners of the Riverside Press, the Houghton Mifflin Company, that its real profits were not in the printing side of the business but in the publishing side. Thus, in 1970 Riverside Press was sold to Rand McNally and the business relocated at Taunton. Three years later the Cambridge buildings were demolished, and in 1977 much of the land was acquired by the city for a park and playground site, today's Riverside Press Park.

The Athenaeum Press

In 1896 Ginn & Company, the Boston-based educational publishers, decided to have their material printed in Cambridge and so built on the banks of the Charles their own printing establishment which they called the Athenaeum Press. It was named for the Boston Athenaeum Library which was near the original office of Ginn and for the goddess of wisdom, and a statue of the latter made in Italy adorned its roof.

The building, which had four floors and a basement, covered three acres and was made of brick and steel; it had automatic sprinklers and sliding metal doors to make it fireproof and so was considered very modern. It also had telephone connections between the various departments—composition, engraving, electrotyping, printing, binding—and with the editorial offices in Boston. Initially the presses could generate ten thousand books a day, a figure that rose eventually to forty thousand a day. At the start of the twentieth century the Press employed 450 men and women.

Lewis Parkhurst directed the Cambridge operations for the first ten years (all told he worked for Ginn for 46 years.) One of the characteristics of Ginn was that they were among the earliest companies to produce text books that were attractively designed and printed.

After using the plant to produce all of its books for more than five decades, Ginn, which was to merge in 1968 with the Xerox Corporation, realized that to continue to do so was uneconomical and so sold the building in 1950 to the John F. Cuneo Press of Chicago. The Cuneo company, which had started in Chicago in 1907 as book binders but which quickly and successfully went into the printing business too, utilized the plant for thirty years and then sold it in 1979 to the Athenaeum Group who renovated it (1979–1983) from a printing plant to the modern office building it is today.

Appropriately, the statue of Athena on the pediment which had come down before the First World War was replaced with a replica and the building was named Athenaeum House. The new owners also put on display on the ground floor several of the original printing presses used by the Athenaeum Press and mounted on the walls two original tablets erected after the Second World War by the plant's work force in memory of their fellow workers who gave their lives in that conflict for freedom.

Harvard Printing and Publication Services

This printery, Harvard's third, traces its beginning to 1872 when President Charles William Eliot was directed by the Corporation to "cause a printing office to be fitted up." Eliot did what he was told to do and an office was fitted up in Wadsworth House. Later, as its staff and work grew it expanded to two rooms in the basement of University Hall, and still later it moved into Randall Hall, now the site of William James Hall. Finally, it moved in 1962 to its present modern plant in Allston.

The office came into being because Harvard was unhappy with the work of the various local printers it had been doing business with and decided it could produce a higher quality product less expensively itself. The printery did the Harvard catalogs, of course, but also its circulars, envelopes, tickets, library forms, examinations, etc. But this inhouse business again had its financial ups and downs, as had been true since the days of Glover and Day. When the university hired a "publication agent" in 1892 to be in charge of all of its publishing efforts, he also quite quickly became the boss of the printing shop. Even after the Harvard University Press was formally established in 1913, the dual role of publishing and printing was maintained for three more decades even though it was clearly an unhappy duality.

The Harvard University Printing Office, as it was called after 1912, gradually adopted the various new printing methods, monotype machines instead of setting type by hand and then linotype machines, which 20th century technology had made possible. Nevertheless, many at the university complained that the press charged too much for its products. The result was that in 1942 Harvard publishing and printing separated and each went its own way.

Yet even after its divorce from the press, the printery continued to be mauled with problems, criticism, and financial woes. As a result the university again pondered getting out of inhouse printing operations but finally decided to make one further effort and in the early 1980's changed the name of the printery to the Office of the University Publisher (OUP) under the able leadership of Robert A. Rotner. Daniel J. McCarron, who was serving as the Art Director and Production Manager of Harvard Magazine as well as Associate University Publisher in OUP, was named University Printer. McCarron's design and sales skills brought a new dimension to the business of printing at

Harvard. The organization flourished during the 1980's as new technologies gathered momentum in the printing world. No department or individual within the university needed to use its services; its work, products, and charges had to be, therefore, as good or better than the best outside service and price. This its production staff and union printers came to provide, and the plant in Allston eventually worked three shifts a day.

In 1996 the OUP and Harvard University Copy merged their related activities under the name Harvard Printing & Publications Services to provide for Harvard "quality digital print, network, and copy services at below market prices." The new organization continues to operate in Allston. As a result, printing at Harvard as the new century begins will be a far technological cry from the initial work produced in the lean-to attached to President Dunster's house in the Yard.

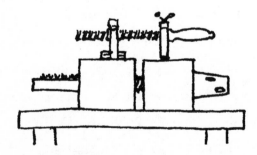

The Harvard University Press

Although the roots of the Harvard University Press extended from the 19th century, it was not until 1913 that it was officially set up by the Harvard Corporation to publish volumes "of a high scholarly character" that would "aid in the advancement of knowledge." It proved easier to state the goal of the press than to solve the problems of running it and keeping it financially afloat. As Professor Ralph Barton Perry was to note some decades later, a university press was not in business to make profits, although it should pay its way, but existed to share with "honesty and accuracy" the creativity of its faculty and the treasures of its libraries. Later one of the press' directors put it more sharply: a university press "exists to publish as many good scholarly books as possible short of bankruptcy." This the press has done, but at times the wolf was knocking at its door.

The press has been quartered in several college buildings including a house on Quincy Street, a faculty residence on Francis Avenue, and now in Kittredge Hall on Garden Street. In its first year it published just 7 titles; now it regularly issues about 140 titles and has a backlist of more than 2800 titles. In 1913 its annual sales were $61,000 and in 1995 they were a little over 13 million. The staff at the beginning consisted of just a few individuals; today it numbers almost one hundred. A few of the press' many notable books are D. B. Updike's *Printing Types*, George Foot Moore's *Judaism*, Arthur O. Lovejoy's *The Great Chain of Being, The Harvard Dictionary of Music*, the *Adams Papers*, and the Loeb Classical Library.

Printing and publishing has always had at Harvard a checkered history; yet it survives as a partner in Cambridge's long involvement in the dissemination of knowledge to the rest of the world.

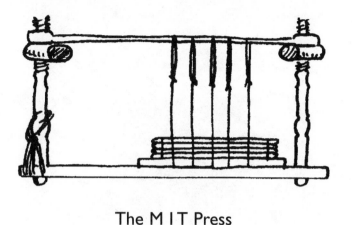

The M I T Press

It was in 1932 that MIT, which up to this point in its history had not had its own press, established The Technology Press. Previous to that time it had worked with commercial and scholarly publishers as the vehicles to serve its needs. The new venture was launched by James R. Killian, Jr., who was then the editor of *The Technology Review,* and was a very modest undertaking. In its first five years it issued but 8 titles.

In 1937 an agreement was reached with John Wiley & Sons to handle all the publishing matters except for the selection of the manuscripts to be produced. Under this arrangement 175 titles were printed. The arrangement with Wiley was in force until 1962 when, after careful thought and discussion, the Institute decided it should cease being an occasional publisher and have its own press. The break with Wiley was completely amicable, and on January 1, 1963, The M.I.T. Press was born.

In its early years the Press focused on books aimed at the scientific and technical market. While its mission was to meet the educational needs of specialists, it was aware also of the need of the general public for nontechnical volumes by competent scholars and encouraged such publications. In general, this was the operational approach until 1975 when the Institute decided that the Press needed to reshape its program and publications. The task of accomplishing this was given to Frank Urbanowski, the new director.

The major thrust of the new program was the development of "core publication lists." These lists, in the words of Larry Cohen, the Editor-in-Chief of the Press in the 1990's, combined "professional, text, trade, and reference components." They came to include such subjects as computer science, artificial intelligence, networking, nanotechnology, virtual reality, economics, architecture, aesthetic theory, design, genetic algorithms, cognitive and brain science, and the environment. Besides the major core lists, there were other more limited series such as those dealing with social theory and technological studies.

A few of the significant titles that the Institute through its Press has brought to the public are Hans Wingler's *Bauhaus,* Noam Chomsky's *Aspects of the Theory of Syntax,* Norbert Wiener's *Cybernetics,* the *Encyclopedic Dictionary of Mathematics,* and Carole Gallagher's *American Ground Zero.*

At the close of the 20th century the MIT Press publishes about 200 books a year and over its lifetime has published about 4900 titles, has a backlist of 2000 titles, and annual sales of 14 million dollars. It also publishes 40 journals, some of which are completely electronic, has a web site, and in 1995 put out its first web-accessible volume. In 1986 it consolidated its operations from two locations into one, 55 Hayward Street. In the words of one of its directors, the MIT Press continues today as it has done in the past its willingness to be "on the leading edge of scholarship and research".

Private Presses

Cambridge has clearly been a significant commercial printing and publishing center since its foundation. The Riverside Press, the University Press, and the Athenaeum Press support this claim and in their heyday employed hundreds in their large plants beside the Charles which at the time was a kind of mini-Route 128 industrial area. In addition to these major players, there were much smaller, much more individualized efforts, the work of the private presses whose motives were not money or reputation but fine design, craftsmanship, and the publication of titles that the public should have access to but for several reasons were not commercially viable volumes.

These include those described below, some of which are still active while others have done their thing and then quietly vanished. Still other presses which started their life in Cambridge have moved away to other locations. An example would be Apple-wood Books which

Hand colored drawing by the English artist, Ted Williams, for the cover of a book of poems about Virginia Woolf issued by the Anne Miniver Press. Its inspiration was from the illustration done by Virginia's sister Vanessa for an early catalog of the Woolf's Hogarth Press.

Phil Zuckerman began in 1976 in the basement of his brother's Cambridge house but now runs out of Bedford, Mass. It issues about eleven titles a year mainly dealing with such varied subjects as cooking, parenting, travel, sports, and children's literature. Its first title, however, was most unusual: a hand-bound volume of medieval poetry.

AT THE SIGN OF THE GEORGE, the press of the scholarly librarian George Parker Winship, was active in the 1920's. Winship was always interested in special printing and limited editions, but he did not have his own press until 1920 when a friend presented his young son with a hand press and type for it. For the rest of the decade Winship published several whimsical pieces setting the type with the aid of his offspring at home but having the work actually done at a commercial house which is why the colophons said, "Put into type at the Sign of the George." There was actually such a sign, a dragon fierce, which was painted by a friend, but the sign was so heavy it never got hung.

The character of the Sign of the George is reflected in this 1920 piece, "How the monkey got its tail" and in the 1929 piece, "John Donne's letter to Sir Nicholas Carey, written from his house in London in the early Summer of the plague year 1625, and printed from the original manuscript which is preserved in the Charles Eliot Norton collection of Donne's writings which is now a part of the Harvard College Library." It was produced with original terra cotta wrappers, a paper label on the front cover and had a cloth case. Style!

THE BOW AND ARROW is a more recent and still active press in Harvard Square which also shares a devotion to excellent typographical work. It was started in 1978 when two Harvard students living in Adams House discovered by chance an old 1912-ish galley-proof press in the House's basement. They fixed it up, got some type, raised some money, and began printing as the Bow & Arrow Press.

Their first effort was a poster with the words: "It Works!" Since then they have published numerous posters and over the years have built a collection of more than 150 different fonts. But they have printed more than the posters; their work has always been in very limited editions, usually consisting of just a few pages but printed in rare typefaces on fine paper. These include *Aphorisms* by William Cole with woodcuts by Damon Lehrer, *Herna* a story by Melinda Marble with illustrations by Michael Mazur and *Prelude* by George Eliot which the artist A. Beresford put out on Bodleian paper using the typeface known as Perpetua. Although others have joined the staff from time to time, and a second press added to the original, the aim and purpose of the press remains the same: good letterpress printing in the age of computer-based printing and technology.

ALICEJAMESBOOKS was founded in 1973 as a cooperative for publishing women's poetry although it has on occasion published poetry by men. Its members are called "Alices". In the spring of 1993 it celebrated its first 20 years with a series of 24 readings in New England and New York City as well as a gala benefit at Boston College. At any given time there are eight authors under contract who serve for a period of two years; it is their responsibility to select, design, and publish the titles issued during their contract period. Usually four new volumes come out each year, and so far Alicejamesbooks has published more than 80 poetry titles. One of their more notable authors has been Ruth Whitman.

THE ANNE MINIVER PRESS, started in the neighboring community of Medford in 1990 by the then Curator of Manuscripts at the Harvard Divinity School Alan Seaburg and now in Cambridge, is a writer's cooperative with members in Massachusetts, Ohio, Indiana, and Connecticut. It publishes The Aster House Broadside Series, leaflets, keepsakes, bookmarks, pamphlets, calendars, postcards, cookbooks, music, mysteries, autobiographies, and poetry volumes. In 1997 it put out for the Medford Historical Society and the Middlesex Canal Association a bicentennial history of that canal which ran from Charlestown to Lowell entitled *The Incredible Ditch*. It exists to bring to print works by authors and artists that deserve public attention.

ZOLAND BOOKS is more than a decade old having been started in 1987 and presently has over thirty titles in print. Roland Pease, Jr., the publisher, usually adds an additional nine new fiction, nonfiction, poetry, and photography titles a year. Zoland promotes readings for its authors as well as a newsletter concerning its publications; their books are available to the book trade through Consortium Book Sales and Distribution.

VAN VACHTOR & GOODHEART, it sounds like a dance team or a vaudeville act, but it is a husband and wife publishing team who got their initial small press experience putting out their own little magazine *Canto*. One of the by-products of the magazine was getting to meet writers and others in the publishing field. There was also the possibility of making money in publishing, and so the partners expanded their activity in 1978 and incorporated themselves as a small press to be run out of their Cambridge row house.

Their first two books were paperback editions of previously published novels. Six years later that was all they had put out for they almost immediately got interested in film producing and writing scripts for film tie-ins. "My view," Van Vachtor told the *Christian Science Monitor* in 1984 "is that these days a book almost has to have a tie-in. Otherwise, a book is not newsworthy, and it is very difficult for a book to exist by itself in the market today … You need the backup of exposure to talk shows, mass-market sales, book club, etc." That philosophy still remains their approach to publishing.

YELLOW MOON PRESS, as with several of the other small presses listed here, comes out of the 1970's, having been founded in 1979. It is interested in poetry, story telling, music, and oral tradition and prints about five new titles a year and has in its backlist 34 titles.

FURTHER READING

BOWEN, CARROLL G. "Publishing at M.I.T.," *Technology Review,* (Dec. 1962) 11–3, 46.

BURTON, JOHN D. *Puritan Town and Gown: Harvard College and Cambridge, Massachusetts, 1636–1800.* Thesis (Ph.D.), College of William and Mary, 1996.

COHEN, LARRY. "The MIT Press: An Overview." Unpublished, 1993 with corrections in 1996.

GILMAN, ARTHUR., ED. *The Cambridge of Eighteen Hundred and Ninety-six.* Cambridge, MA: Citizens' Trade Association, 1896.

Glimpses of the Harvard Past. Bernard Bailyn, Donald Fleming, Oscar Handlin, Stephan Thernstrom. Cambridge, MA: Harvard University Press, 1986.

GRAFFAN, GRAY. "A Discovery of Seventeenth-Century Printing Types in Harvard Yard," *Harvard Library Bulletin,* 30 (April 1982) 229–31.

GRANNIS, CHANDLER B. "MIT Press: At the Leading Edge," *Publishers Weekly,* 230 (Dec. 1986) 23–4.

HALL, MAX. "Cambridge as Printer and Publisher: Fame, Oblivion, and Fame Again," *Cambridge Historical Society Proceedings,* 44 (1976–79) 63–83.

————. *Harvard University Press A History.* Cambridge, MA: Harvard University Press, 1986.

The Harvard Guide: The Faces, History, and Lore of America's Oldest University 1998–2000. Cambridge, MA: Harvard University Office of News and Public Affairs, 1998.

HIGHTOWER, MARVIN. "At Bow and Arrow Press, Printing Remains an Art," *Harvard Gazette* (March 18, 1988) 5.

HOWELLS, DOROTHY ELIA. *A Century to Celebrate Radcliffe College, 1879–1979.* Cambridge, MA: Radcliffe College, 1978.

KNOX, JEAN MCBEE. *Longy School of Music: the First 75 Years.* Watertown, MA: Windflower Press, 1991.

MORISON, SAMUEL ELIOT. *The Founding of Harvard College.* Cambridge, MA: Harvard University Press, 1935.

————. *Three Centuries of Harvard.* Cambridge, MA: Harvard University Press, 1936.

PRESCOTT, SAMUEL C. *When MIT was "Boston Tech" 1861–1916.* Cambridge, MA: Technology Press, 1954.

QUINCY, JOSIAH. *The History of Harvard University.* 2 vols. Cambridge, MA: Owen, 1840.

RHEAULT, CHARLES A. *In Retrospect: The Riverside Press, 1852–1971.* Boston: Society of Printers, 1979.

SOLLORS, WERNER, TITEMB, CALDWELL, UNDERWOOD, THOMAS A. EDS. *Blacks at Harvard: A Documentary History of African-American Experience at Harvard and Radcliffe.* New York: New York University Press, 1993.

WILDES, KARL L. AND NILO A. LINDGREN. *A Century of Electrical Engineering and Computer Science at MIT, 1882–1982.* Cambridge, MA: MIT Press, 1985.

WINSHIP, GEORGE P. "Recollection," *The Colophon,* 3 (1938) 210–222.

WRIGHT, CONRAD EDICK. "John Harvard," *Harvard Magazine,* 102 (January–February 2000) 40.

WYLIE, FRANCIS E. *MIT in Perspective.* Boston: Little, Brown, 1975.

Cambridge Worships.

CHAPTER EIGHT

THE PURITAN CHURCH

Cambridge Worships

The spiritual life of Cambridge remained fairly constant during its first two hundred years as a community. Throughout this period it was the undivided Puritan church that was its people's chosen way of worship. While there were a few exceptions to the elected way—the English Quaker Elizabeth Hooten, for example, was arrested, imprisoned, whipped, and then banished in 1663 for wandering the town urging the "Cambridge Scholars" to repent—there was no real challenger to Puritanism in Cambridge until 1760.

In that year a small group of wealthy Boston merchants who had recently moved to Cambridge formed Christ Church next to the Burying Ground and opposite the town common. It followed the practice of the Church of England and its first rector was East Apthorp. This new institution ran into trouble with the start of the American Revolution for most of its members remained loyal to the crown and as a result were forced to flee from Cambridge. Indeed, in 1777, the church was broken into and ransacked by a mob of Cambridge "patriots".

As a result, the building became a ruin, "the doors shattered, and all the windows broken out ... its sanctuary defiled, the wind howling through its deserted aisles and about its stained and decaying walls." It was not repaired until 1790, for after the war only two members remained of the original congregation. Even

The First Parish in 1896, watercolor by Mary Winlock, daughter of Joseph Winlock, Director of Harvard College Observatory, 1866–1875.

house of today, a Folk Gothic structure, was built; in it until 1873 Harvard held its annual commencement exercises.

The pastor before the division, Abiel Holmes, who had written the town's first history, now became pastor of the newly organized First Church in Cambridge also known as the Shepard Congregational Society. In 1830 this group built a small wooden meeting house on the northwest corner of Mt. Auburn and Holyoke Streets. After twice enlarging it they sold it in 1872 to St. Paul's Catholic Church and moved to their present structure on the corner of Garden and Mason Streets.

This split between the Orthodox and the Liberal Christians was not a gentle one. Probably no religious separation ever can be when each side believes its theology contains the truth of God's revelation. As a result, during the course of this controversy passions ran high on both sides. For example, the Orthodox asked, "Shall we have the Boston religion, or the Christian religion?" while the Liberal Christians responded, "Are you a Christian or a Calvinist?" While these slogans seem mild today, they were not two hundred years ago and caused hurt and anger to those at whom they were directed. Cambridge knew its share of such partisan attacks. Such feelings did not fade away easily just as later Protestant prejudice toward Cambridge's growing Roman Catholic population did not.

The Reverend Abiel Holmes, Cambridge's first historian.

THE RISE OF OTHER DENOMINATIONS

Religious life in Cambridge evolved during the nineteenth-century into the pattern we are still familiar with. In other words, individuals were able to chose and form religious organizations which best met their deepest needs and which reflected and expressed their ideals and values. It was a parallel development to the break-up of the undivided Puritan church and one which would have happened even if that way had survived in tact its internal division.

Initially the range of available choices locally were limited to Protestant Christianity. In Cambridge the Baptists opened their first church in 1817, the

Father Manasses Dougherty, "Apostle of the Catholic Church in Cambridge."

although several of its parishes are indeed handsome structures.

While all this was occurring, the Protestants had also been expanding from their original congregations. Congregationalists by the century's end had several additional houses of worship: the First Evangelical Congregational Church (often referred to as the Prospect Congregational Church), the Second Evangelical Congregational Church, the Pilgrim Congregational Church, and the North Avenue Congregational Church. The Universalists had established two more churches, the Unitarians three more, and the Episcopalians now had, beside the venerable Christ Church, St. Peter's in Cambridgeport, St. James' in North Cambridge, St. John's Chapel at the Episcopal Theological School on Brattle Street, and St. Bartholomew's Church on Harvard Street. That was composed of African Americans as well as Canadian and West Indies immigrants who had once belonged to St. Peter's but who no longer felt welcome there. Such local church growth was also reflected by the other Protestant denominations.

Federal and state census statistics confirm the rather dramatic religious change in the once Puritan and Protestant town/city. The eleventh census of the United States, that for 1890, indicates that Cambridge had 29,094 members belonging to its forty-one religious organizations. Of this total, 20,056 were Roman Catholics; in other words, two-thirds of the total. To help understand the significance of the Roman Catholic total, here are the figures of the largest Protestant groups for 1890: the Congregationalists 2,510, the Baptists 2,367, the various Methodist churches 1,593, and the Protestant Episcopal Church 1,067. Almost at the bottom of the scale were the two most liberal groups, the Unitarians with 450 and the Universalists with 308.

St. John the Evangelist Church

St. Anthony's Church

St. Peter's Church

Sacred Heart Church

Blessed Sacrament Church

St. Paul's Church

St. Francis of Assisi Church

Notre Dame de Pitié Church

Roman Catholic parishes..

"You are and I am many things and we are defined in many ways....
But fundamentally, you and I are made in the image of God.
Nothing and no one can take that away. Therefore, don't give up, keep the faith."

Rev. Dr. Peter Gomes addressing a demonstration against discrimination of gay and lesbian people from the steps of Memorial Church, Harvard University, in 1991.

1884 called the liberal minister George A. Gordon to its pulpit some members of the council called to approve his installation severely questioned his orthodoxy. On that ecclesiastical council were members and ministers from the neighboring churches of Greater Boston, including representatives from the First Church and the North Avenue Church in Cambridge. So once again Cambridge Congregationalism was involved in another internal conflict between liberal and orthodox thought. Eventually, the council voted overwhelmingly in favor of installing Gordon. As no record of how its membership voted exists, it is impossible to know clearly how the Cambridge delegates voted. Yet the pastor of First Church, the Rev. A. McKenzie, took part in the act of installation so we can assume that he voted with the liberals as probably did the other member from First Church.

Another example of the conflict caused as a result of changing and evolving ideas occurred during the rectorship of James Field Spalding at Christ Church. While Spalding's crisis of faith was a personal one and not a crisis with his congregation, it serves well to explain the conflict in thought and belief that continuously is present in any organized religious tradition. In his farewell sermon Spalding said, "What first set me thinking in the direction that has resulted thus far ... was the rational, the free-thinking, and the unbelieving in the Episcopal Church and the entire Anglican Communion.... The point with me was that it was unchecked.... I refer to scouting of the doctrine of the apostolic succession, to the so-called higher criticism of Holy Scripture, to the weakening of the doctrine of the Incarnation, to the out and out denial of the Virgin Birth and the bodily resurrection of our Lord, or the making of these truths only a matter of interpretation." In these few words Spalding touched upon issues that affected all mainline Protestant church in the last century. To these can be added Darwin's theory of evolution and all of what scientific method is revealing now about our species and the universe. Indeed, Darwinism—especially in the twentieth century—continues to be the most powerful idea affecting the currents of religion's evolving understanding of *Homo sapiens* and their world.

Upon reflection, one sees that it is not only Protestantism that can be defined by differences of opinion but religion itself. More than that, it is also a vital part of any philosophical definition of America's working experiments in democracy.

THE TWENTIETH CENTURY

As the twentieth century opened it too saw a continued growth of mainline Protestant churches and also of Roman Catholic churches. But the century did not forever sustain this momentum. Several factors account for this. One is that the population eventually ceased to increase throughout the new century; indeed it

mainline Protestant institutions did not establish new churches here for some did. The Lutherans started University Lutheran (or, as it is popularly called, UniLu) in 1928 when the University Lutheran Association of Greater Boston was created. After worshipping in temporary quarters for some years, it began construction of its present building in 1950, the first church to be erected in Cambridge after the Second World War.

Orthodox Christianity also opened another church in the city in 1954 when Holy Trinity Armenian Apostolic Church of Greater Boston acquired for its congregation the former home and estate on Brattle Street of the ornithologist William Brewster. In 1958 the congregation authorized the building of the present handsome grey brick structure with its memorial bronze doors which were designed in the tradition of 12th century Armenian architecture. The building was consecrated in 1961. Next to it is the church's rectory and offices and William Brewster's private museum; their Cultural Hall stands in Brewster's old garden where he grew trees and shrubs for their beauty and for their ability to attract birds.

The Quakers serve as yet another example. After several failed attempts at starting a viable meeting here, the Cambridge Quakers met for ten years with their counterpart in Roxbury. Then in 1936 they acquired the brick Georgian-style house owned by Longfellow's granddaughter in Longfellow Park as a Friends Center. On the vacant plot next to it a simple Meeting House

for worship was constructed the next year. Eventually the Society became a seedbed for the founding of societies in several nearby communities as well as a second one in Cambridge.

As significant as these developments proved for the Christian experience in Cambridge, a very different input to the religious complexion of the community also occurred in this century. That was the slow but gradual shifting away from the traditional Christian context of Cambridge worship which had been so dominated since its founding by the Puritans. The city began in this century to welcome all the major world religions to its neighborhood. It started with Judaism.

OTHER WORLD RELIGIONS COME TO CAMBRIDGE

Boston was not to have a synagogue or a permanent Jewish community until the 1840's, and even by the 1890's it consisted of no more than five thousand individuals. It is not surprising, therefore, that Cambridge did not have its own synagogue, Congregation Beth Israel, until 1901. Before this there had been a minyan held in a private home in 1842, and in 1898 some Jewish immigrants from Russia had formed a synagogue called Anshai Sfard, but when they built their temple in 1906 it was to be in Somerville and not in Cambridge. Eventually the city was to have three synagogues, but

"You are and I am many things and we are defined in many ways....

But fundamentally, you and I are made in the image of God.

Nothing and no one can take that away. Therefore, don't give up, keep the faith."

Rev. Dr. Peter Gomes addressing a demonstration against discrimination of gay and lesbian people from the steps of Memorial Church, Harvard University, in 1991.

Plate 9

The ice industry's buildings and the other key sites at Fresh Pond, ca. 1840: (A.) Fresh Pond Hotel, (B.) Ice Houses, (C.) Train Station, (D.) Tudor's Boat House, (E.) Charlestown Railroad, (F.) Fitchburg Railroad, (G.) Alewife Brook, and (H.) Brickyard Swamp.

Interior of an ice house.

Plate 10

Making bricks.

The Cambridge brick yards.

Plate 11

The cattle market.

Plate 12   The Rand Estate.

Glass factory salesroom.

Mr. Kennedy's Biscuits. *(Courtesy of the Rev. Janet H. Bowering)*

Plate 13

"Art Triumphs Over History," The stage curtain of the University Theatre: Washington takes Command of the Continental Army, Cambridge Common, 1775.

The American Repertory Theatre.

Plate 14

Mt. Auburn Hospital from the air, ca. 1940.

Beat the Belt, wall painting by Bernard LaCasse, 1980.

Plate 15

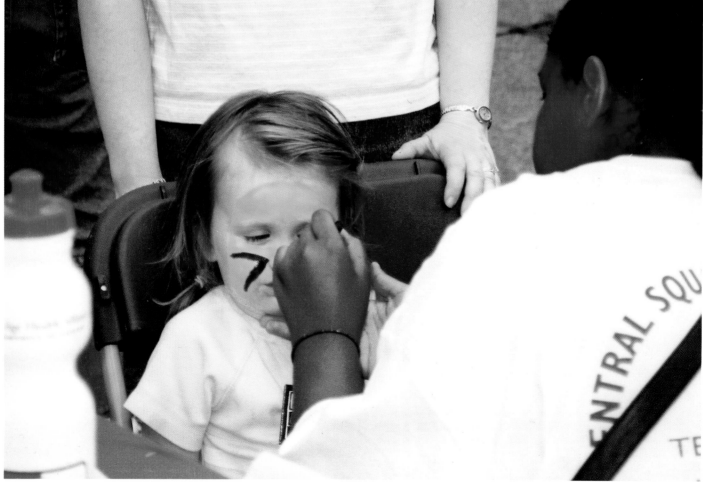

Plate 16

a decline in Jewish life here at mid-century resulted by 1976 in the joining together of all three as Temple Beth Shalom. Cambridge also has a gay, lesbian, and bisexual congregation Am Tikva (they meet however at Temple Sinai in Brookline) and a "post denominational congregation" Eitz Chayim Harvard Hillel. The city's first public menorah-lighting ceremony for Hanukkah was celebrated on the Common in 1997.

Buddhism in Cambridge owes its origin to a growing interest at Harvard in the 1950's in Zen Buddhism and to the 1957 visits to the city of the Buddhist scholars Daisetz Teitaro Suzuki and of Dr. Shinichi Hisamatsu from Kyoto University in Japan. One of the results of these visits was the formation of the Cambridge Buddhist Association by Elsie and John Mitchell and others who had persuaded both teachers to stay and help them organize a Western-style spiritual center. Suzuki also agreed to become the Association's first president, a position he held until his death in 1966. Also in this decade Larry Rosenberg brought into being the non-residential and non-profit Cambridge Insight Meditation Center for the practice of meditation which allows its practitioner to reach a state of "mindfulness," or awareness, and true understanding through sitting and walking meditation "which sees without judgment."

In 1973 the Cambridge Zen Center, the oldest Korean Kwan Um School of Zen Buddhism in Greater Boston, was formed by Seung Sahn, a Korean Zen Master, and in 1980 the Sakya Institute for Buddhist Studies and meditation was established in Central Square by the Tibetan abbot His Eminence Deshang Rinpoche. These organizations have paved the way for further Buddhist groups to settle in the community.

It was not until 1993 that the city was to have its first mosque. That year the Islamic Society of Boston opened on Prospect Street an Islamic Center and Mosque to serve the needs of the community's growing Muslim population as well as those of the Islamic students attending Harvard, MIT, and other local colleges.

It was not the first Islamic organization here, however, for as early as 1958 three Harvard students had started the Harvard Islamic Society. Later, as more Muslim students went to Boston area institutions of higher education and started their own student groups, there became a clear need for an umbrella organization to offer them support and guidance, and so in 1982 the Islamic Society of Boston was born. Cambridge also has had since 1971 a practicing Sufi group, the Boston Center of the Bawa Muhaiyadeen Fellowship.

The first appearance of a Hindu organization was in 1976 when the Dhyanyoga Center for the practice of meditation and chanting according to Kundalini Maha Yoga was opened by Dhyanyogi Madhusudandasji. Fifteen years later the Hindu Sri Premananda Center of the U. S. A. was established by Christopher Germer and Clare Moore who had met in India its religious teacher Swami Premananda. Its members gather for meditation, singing, and fellowship according to the Bhakti Yoga tradition.

Twentieth century religion in Cambridge also saw the emergence of two groups—probably for the first time here—which needed no supreme being: the Society for Ethical Culture and the American Humanist Association. Although some find this fact at odds with the very word religion, the concept has a long and honored tradition in the world's religious history and philosophy. Confucianism serves as the perfect witness to this long held religious position.

Felix Adler, an educator and philosopher whose family traditions were in the rabbinate and Reformed Judaism, founded the Ethical Culture movement in New York City in 1876. The centrality of ethical living for the individual and society is the organization's defining tenet. The roots of the movement in Greater Boston go back to 1904 when for a year there was, under the leadership of Morris Raphael Cohen while he was doing graduate work at Harvard University, a short-lived Harvard Ethical Society. When he left Cambridge, this first effort collapsed. In 1920 a second attempt to have an Ethical Society arose in Boston which flourished until 1933 when it was dissolved due to the Depression and the lack of a local leader. Finally, in 1952 a third attempt was made as the Ethical Society of Boston; it began first in Cambridge, then moved to Boston, and then returned to Cambridge in 1994.

The American Humanist Association was established in 1941; the Humanist Association of Massachusetts, which is located in Cambridge, is one of its 65 chapters. In the words of Linus Pauling, humanism "is a rational philosophy ... of service for the good of all humanity, of application of new ideas of scientific progress, for the benefit of all humankind."

There are also those in the city who support no present day religious institutions. There can be several reasons for not doing so, but not to support organized religion does not mean that the individual does not have his or her own private religious views. Many people do. It is part of the genius of the present time that they are free to do so unhindered by the collective laws and rules of the majority society.

A word of caution is also appropriate here. When speaking of Cambridge worship, it is quite possible that one tends to think that most of the city's inhabitants belonged to a religious organization. Certainly since the end of Puritanism—and not even then—that has not necessarily been the case. Census figures are helpful to our understanding of this point, although census listing of church members in relation to the total population ignore the fact the many people worship a given way without ever having bothered to become a member of their society. Nevertheless the figures are suggestive. For example, total church membership in Cambridge in 1890 was 29,094 out of a total population of 70,028, in 1906 45,896 out of a population of 98,544, and during the 1920's the ratio was much the same. Even allowing for census mistakes or erroneous interpretations, the figures are revealing as to the depth of the practicing religious commitment of the community.

RELIGIOUS OUTREACH AND CONCERN

During the Puritan era the church played a major role in assisting the community to care for those with special needs. It was possible then, given that the town had but the one religious institution, for that aid to be a unified one. With the rise of other Protestant churches and the coming of Roman Catholicism in the nineteenth century, that undivided response was no longer generally possible. This was in part due to the fact that the first Catholics found the Protestant community often hostile to their beliefs and worship rites. Faced with this situation, and with the poverty and many social and educational needs that their immigrant congregations had to struggle with, the Catholic Church's natural response was to try and help their own. Which they did.

A century later the Cambridge religious community—now more tolerant of each other's views and faith—had begun to move toward some form of cooperation when possible on a whole variety of social endeavors. It will never be the unified approach characteristic of the ruling Puritan days, but it will be and is a symbol of the rich heritage of freedom and understanding so deeply embedded in the spirit behind the American democratic experiment.

Evidence to support this growing religious social concern and cooperation is not difficult to discover for examples are literally everywhere. In Harvard Square

Homeless person asleep near the Common.

the area churches have divided the task of providing hot meals for the needy, each congregation being responsible for a meal one night a week. Further, University Lutheran has opened its building for the Harvard Square Homeless Shelter which has been in operation since 1983. Run by students from Harvard's oldest public service organization—Phillip Brooks House—it has since its founding provided a place to sleep for more than 1,500 guests and served more than 160,000 meals. First Church also has long supported a shelter which provides each evening food and a place to eat for fourteen to nineteen homeless men.

In Central Square the Syrian Orthodox Catholic Church of St. Mary's supports both international Orthodox social work and programs for its local community such as its food program for those who are hungry. The congregation of St. Paul's African Methodist Church has long been active in helping the community through its housing assistance activities and its biweekly food pantry. The Salvation Army, long know for its caring attitude, maintains a drop-in center for over 200 homeless people, a shelter called "our Place" for homeless children, and regularly offers 50 men beds for the night. In addition they run a meals program for those who are hungry and are one of the many churches in the city where those without garments can obtain good clothing to keep them warm and fit.

Old Cambridge Baptist Church is illustrative of another new development in the religious life of the city. It has its own active congregation but it has also opened its premises to a number of other local caring and service groups. Some of these are or have been: the Big Brother Association, the Cambridge Tenants Union, Youth Against AIDS, the Ethiopian Art Corporation, and the Naked City Coffeehouse. Other churches also do this.

Baptist responsiveness to people's needs is nothing new for them for as long ago as 1834 Baptist ministers in Cambridgeport and in East Cambridge along with several of their lay leaders were actively engaged beside their Unitarian brethren at the Harvard Divinity School in the short-lived but useful Cambridge Antislavery Society. Today under the able leadership of the Rev. Jeffery Brown, the Union Baptist Church, six hundred strong, has made community activism a cornerstone of its religious commitment. Among their many endeavors is taking part in community meals for the needy (as does the Metropolitan Baptist Church) and their efforts to help reduce violence among Cambridge's young people. Cambridgeport Baptist also has a strong commitment to the community; among its activities are a Clothes Closet and Food Pantry and monthly worship services for those in the Cambridge Jail and the Cambridge Nursing Home.

In its first century the Roman Catholic church tried to build within the Greater Boston community a whole structure of social institutions to keep out Protestant influences. But they could never fully cope with the poorer Irish, who crowded into the main charities public or private. Catholic congregations today continue their active support of social services but no longer within their more narrow original approach. St. Anthony's, for example, has food and clothing programs for the needy and St. Mary's of the Annunciation not only maintains a food pantry but makes special efforts to aid Central American immigrants. Other Cambridge Catholic sponsored institutions do the same; for example, Youville Hospital & Rehabilitation Center.

This descriptive list, of course, does not represent all of the efforts of the religious community to ameliorate the living conditions of the city's extended family, but it does give an idea of how religious organization reach out to serve.

THE RELIGIOUS IMPULSE

At its start most religious people in Cambridge were Puritans; now they are free to elect the way which gives their life and ideals its deepest meaning and significance. This growth of individual choice has brought with it, for the most part, not the discord and community disharmony that some might have been concerned about, but just the opposite state. Those who subscribe to organized religion, as well as those who do not—and people can be religious yet belong to none of the traditions discussed here—respect the ways followed by both the members of their own family and the practices of their neighbors, known or not known. In addition, whenever possible they work together to achieve social justice and to meet needs such as feeding and clothing the homeless and the hungry.

The result has been that the religious impulse associated so long with the species called *Homo sapiens* can be said to be one of the blessings of Cambridge living. But that blessing will last only as long as all the religious expressions in the city continue to respect each other. That includes both the older established religious institutions in the city and the newly forming ones. It is all too easy for faiths that become dominant to curtail the freedom and rights of minorities. This must not be allowed to happen in any community.

FURTHER READING

ABBOTT, EDWARD. *St. James's Parish Cambridge: Forty Years of Parish History, 1864–1904.* Cambridge, MA: The Vestry, 1909.

DAY, GARDINER M. *The Biography of a Church. A Brief History of Christ Church Cambridge, Massachusetts.* Cambridge, MA: Privately printed, 1951.

DERRY, CECIL THAYER. *A Brief History of the Old Cambridge Baptist Church 1844–1944.* Cambridge, MA: no publisher, 1945.

DORMAN, FRANKLIN A. "Antislavery on the Banks of the Charles," *Harvard Divinity Bulletin,* 20 (Spring 1990) 12–14, 23–24.

ECK, DIANA L. AND ELINOR J. PIERCE, ED. *World Religions in Boston: A Guide to Communities and Resources.* 3rd. edition. Cambridge, MA: Pluralism Project, 1998.

GEROULD, FLORENCE RUSSELL. "Historical Sketch of the First Church in Cambridge (Unitarian)," *Cambridge Historical Society Proceedings,* 31 (1945)62–65.

GILMAN, ARTHUR., ED. *The Cambridge of Eighteen Hundred and Ninety-six.* Cambridge, MA: Citizens' Trade Association, 1896.

The Jewish Guide to Boston and New England. Ed. by Rosie Rosenzweig. Boston: Jewish Advocate, 1995

MACNAIR, WILLIAM M. "One Hundred Years of Church Life," *Cambridge Historical Society Proceedings,* 20 (1927–1929) 62–83.

MITCHELL, RUDY AND BASS, JEFFREY, EDS. *The Boston Church Directory 1995 Update.* Boston, MA: Emmanuel Gospel Center, 1995.

MORAN, SUSAN DRINKER. *Gathered in the Spirit: Beginnings of the First Church in Cambridge.* Cleveland, Ohio: United Church Press, 1995.

O'DONNELL, FRANCES. *Vatican II and St. Paul's Parish: An Analysis of the Role of Historical Context in the Creation of Records.* (Thesis) M.A., University of Massachusetts Boston, 1995.

PAIGE, LUCIUS R. *History of Cambridge, Massachusetts. 1630–1877.* Boston: Houghton, 1877. *Supplement and Index.* Mary Isabella Gozzaldi. 1930.

St. John the Evangelist Centennial Committee. *St. John the Evangelist Church Centennial:1893–1993.* Dallas, TX: Taylor Publishing Company, 1992.

SELLECK, GEORGE A. *Quakers in Boston, 1656–1964. Three Centuries of Friends in Boston and Cambridge.* Published by Friends Meeting at Cambridge, 1976.

SMALL, BESSIE E. *A History of St. Peter's Episcopal Church, Cambridge, Massachusetts, 1842–1942.* The Parish, 1942.

WILLS, JEFFREY, ED. *The Catholics of Harvard Square.* Petersham, MA: Saint Bede's Publications, 1993.

WRIGHT, CONRAD, ED. *A Stream of Light: A Sesquicentennial History of American Unitarianism.* Boston: Unitarian Universalist Association, 1975.

Fireworks Over the Charles.

214

CHAPTER NINE

Cambridge Entertains Itself

How Cambridge entertains itself is a wonderful and surprising cornucopia. For example, some people actually enjoy attending wakes and funeral services for those they don't even know while others have fun just standing in Central or Harvard Squares people watching. Over the years Cambridge has enjoyed dances, plays, the wireless then the radio and television, coming-out parties, singing songs around the piano, bingo games, bridge, whist, loving, gambling, birding at Mt. Auburn, swimming at Magazine Beach, biking, their small private home gardens, and taking slides and showing them forever to family and friends. So there it is—entertainment.

But there is more entertainment. Cambridge jogs or strolls about Fresh Pond, goes to school dances or step dances at health clubs, reads books or rents videos, spends limitless hours as web weavers creating and editing everything and anything, blasts boom boxes or whistles at work, attends Little League games, youth hockey, or high school football games, walks dogs with scoop-it-up disposable bags, shops until it drops, and reads Dante at the Italian Cultural Center.

Beside these activities, throughout its almost four hundred years as a community, Cambridge folks have also found entertainment in observing and commenting, usually negatively, on the lives and activities of their family members and their neighbors. Cambridge people, then, like people everywhere, have devised countless ways to make their short turn at living interesting and entertaining. If the Puritans voted for frequent praying and two sermons on the Sabbath, later "puritans" have made their choices, too. So let's consider some of them.

ROW, ROW YOUR BOAT

The Charles River has often been for those who have dwelled by its banks an "entertainment center." If the business community has used it to move goods and supplies, the people have used it for swimming, fishing, ice skating, and boating. So too has it been a home for the athletes of the city's colleges and universities who have maintained over the decades boat houses along its shores.

But local citizens have also had a boat house and a boat club since 1909. It was preceded by "the casino," a private club limited to one hundred men and fifty women which had been organized in 1882. It built a boat house near Ash Street which provided its members with tennis courts, a bowling alley, and space for their boats and canoes until 1895 when the club ceased its activities. About a decade later the Cambridge Boat Club took over its site and erected its own boat house which in 1947 was relocated to Gerry's Landing. Besides boating on the Charles, the Club sponsors

Neighbors gossiping.

talks, gives boating instructions, holds teas, dinners, and dancing parties for its members and their friends.

In addition to these groups there are others using the Charles including both the public schools and some of the private schools and from time to time various companies which run vessels on the river for tourists.

A sense of what it's like to be out boating on this river is conveyed in Craig Lambert's book *Mind Over Water*. "We row," he says, "into splendor, as the setting sun fires the river with magenta and flames of gold … Some energy flow grips us like a river current, synchronizing our motion; we row as one body. Thinking disappears, leaving behind only presence and rhythm; yes, presence and rhythm are rowing this boat, using us for oars … Rushing water bubbles under our hull, as if a mountain brook buried within the Charles flows directly beneath us. I have never heard this sound before, but I know that it means *we are doing something right.*"

Boating on the Charles near the Weld Boathouse.

TWO ON THE AISLE

Among the thousand and one marvels of Cambridge is the Brattle theatre. Its curtain first rose in 1871. That January the Unitarian minister Samuel Wadsworth Longfellow and other Cantabridgians concerned that young people have proper intellectual opportunities and moral entertainment established the Cambridge Social Union.

Their programs were held initially at Lyceum Hall in Harvard Square and stressed amateur theater productions, operettas, lectures, and dancing. Lois Lilley Howe, who grew up in Cambridge during these years, remembered that it was also the place for parties for young ladies coming out in society.

Eventually the Union needed its own building and so bought in 1889 the present lot on Mt Auburn Street and built Brattle Hall. It was designed in Queen Ann style by Alexander Wadsworth Longfellow. The Hall was essentially one room with a stage, and cloak and dressing rooms in the basement. Over the years the space was remodeled to include stores and restaurants such as the popular Casablanca Restaurant. While the Hall was often rented out to various groups including the Christian Science and Lutheran churches, and the Cambridge Police which used it as a gymnasium, its chief activity was always theater productions. Paul Robeson, T. S. Eliot, and Prof. George Pierce Baker, who taught the famous 47 Workshop on playwriting at Harvard, all appeared on its stage.

In the 1940's the Veterans Theatre Workshop, started by World War II veterans at Harvard, produced their plays at the Hall. In 1948 the Union, which had changed its name in 1938 to the Cambridge Center for Adult Education and moved next door to Brattle House which they also owned, sold the Hall to the father of one of the veterans and the Workshop became the Brattle Theatre Company.

It was a stock company with a core of local professionals. To lure audiences, they hired stars from Broadway and Hollywood. Some of these were Cyril Richards, Zero Mostel, Eva LeGallienne, Sam Jaffe, Hermione Gingold, Jessica Tandy, and Hume Cronyn. The plays were by Shakespeare, Chekhov, Moliere, Shaw, Sartre, Christopher Fry, and other famous dramatists. Two of their big hits were "Billy Budd" and the first Greater Boston staging of O'Neill's "Desire Under the Elms." When the Brattle Company folded after four years, the theatre was turned into an art cinema house.

If two words could express the spirit that animated the various owners and the Brattle Theatre since 1952, and who made it one of the more interesting and innovative cinemas around, they would be Humphrey Bogart. During exam period at Harvard, the Brattle has run for decades a week of Bogart films. Is there a student of a Boston college who didn't see "Casablanca" here?

At the Brattle: "Who else but..."

The films have always had an "Arabian Nights" flavor. One night it might be W. C. Fields and Mae West in "My Little Chickadee," the next Marlene Dietrich in "The Blue Angel," the next "A Clockwork Orange" or "Rebel Without a Cause," and then a little something from Ingmar Bergman or a Gay/Lesbian offering. For

five decades, through several changes of decor and a major building renovation, the emphasis has always been quality films, American and foreign, old and new. With this kind of past, it is easy to understand why the Brattle Theatre is a Cambridge marvel.

The Brattle, of course, has not been the community's only theater outlet. The educational institutions, as well as church groups with their yearly Christmas pageants, have always promoted theater. At Harvard these efforts have gone from the fun and foolishness of the undergraduate Hasty Pudding Club, the oldest theater company in the country and the third oldest in the world, and their annual all-male musicals which have been presented since 1888 in their own clubhouse, to the various productions of the Harvard-Radcliffe Dramatic Club and to the artistic and often unique presentations of the American Repertory Theatre (ART).

Other theater opportunities in contemporary Cambridge have included smaller dramatic groups such as Theatre Redux, Inman Square's Back Alley Theatre, the Nora Theatre Company, the Little Flags Theatre, The Revels, and The Poet's Theatre, which was organized by seven poets in 1950 "to produce and present with the assistance of volunteers... experimental plays" and "to encourage poets to write for the stage and to educate them in the techniques of the theatre." In addition to these thespian outlets, the Cambridge Multicultural Arts Center in East Cambridge also sponsors live theater as one of its many community programs.

The American Repertory Theatre.

IN THE EAR AND EYE
OF THE BEHOLDER

First, singing. Not just the professional and semi-professional kind, but this: some of the young folks who worked at the Carr Fastener Company in Kendall Square in the 1920's gathering about the piano in the lunch room after they had eaten their sandwiches doing just for fun some community singing. Or the pupils of "William Hicks, Tenor of Cambridge" taking part in the annual recital of his students.

Second, painting. Not just being another Cambridge-born Winslow Homer but this: sitting in the kitchen painting by numbers, sitting in a high school French lesson drawing Donald Duck, producing public art on a bathroom stall, or helping to make a colorful mural on a brick wall like the one on Church Street.

In the 19th century the students at "the college" had established the Harvard Glee Club and the teaching of music was gradually incorporated into the curriculum of the public school system. It also became available outside of these settings; two fine twentieth century examples would be the Longy School of Music and the more recently established non-profit community-based New School of Music on Lowell Street whose purpose is "to foster a love of music and musical growth in an environment of sensitivity and mutual respect." An interesting if accidental by-product of all this was the establishment in East Cambridge of Goodrich's church organ factory in 1809, of Mason and Hamlin's melodeon and parlor organ company in 1874, and of the Ives and Pond piano company in 1881.

The Cambridge Art Association came into being in 1944 when several artists donated some of their work for an auction to help raise funds for the war-effort. The action proved most successful, and so the artists decided to organize themselves as an art group and find a gallery where they might display from time to time their creative work. Their first real gallery space required much volunteer effort to make presentable—the dirt floor needed floor boards and the walls and ceiling required new panels.

Fifty years after its establishment, the Cam-

bridge Art Association had a small executive staff, a regular newsletter, operated two galleries in the city, presented twenty-four exhibits a year run by several volunteer committees who took responsibility for the selection and mounting of the various shows, sponsored art classes for children and adults, and put on programs for those at day care centers and for those living in nursing homes. It could never have done its work without the assistance of countless volunteers; indeed, it estimated that over the first fifty years seventy-five thousand work hours were donated to its mission by its volunteers.

One of the most significant organizations in the city dealing with music, painting, and other artist efforts is the Cambridge Multicultural Arts Center. Founded in 1978, it functions as a part of the historic courthouse at Bulfinch Square in East Cambridge; its space there includes a theater, two galleries, a kitchen, and several meeting rooms. The group's purpose is, in its own words, to foster "cross-cultural understanding by producing a culturally-diversified mix of arts and humanities events designed to educate and dispel racial and ethnic stereotypes." Its activities support more than 500 visual and performing artists a year and its programming ranges from chamber music to Native American drumming and dancing, from Afro-Latin Jazz to Scottish fiddlers, to exhibitions of photography by students from Cambridge Rindge &

Latin, shows of recent works by local artists, and puppet and magic shows.

Then, lest they be forgotten, there are also many small independent Galleries in the city such as the Stebbins Gallery at the First Parish, The Sacramento Street Gallery on that street, and the funky Zeitgeist Gallery on Broadway. The latter has once a week its own Coffeehouse with an open mike for art, film, and poetry performances.

POPCORN, BUTTER, AND SALT

The big day was Saturday afternoon, October 30, 1926, at 2 o'clock; the place was the brand new University Theatre, Harvard Square; the Inaugural Program had two main features: "The Midnight Sun" with Laura La Plante and Pat O'Malley, and "Laddie" with Gene Stratton. In addition, there was an "Our Gang" short, the Pathé News, and between shows a live "top specialty act."

The University—its interior architecture was in the Italian Renaissance style from the period of Florentine art—had orchestra seats, balcony seats, boxes, and loges where you sat on wicker chairs. "Ample space" had been provided between each row so that patrons could pass those seated "without raising the occupied seats!" The theater also had an open hallway and ticket booth fronting Harvard Square, a men's smoking room, an orchestral organ, nearly 2000 seats, up-to-date electric lighting facilities, commodious dressing rooms, and a huge stage whose curtain contained an original oil painting celebrating Washington as he took Command of the Continental Army, Cambridge Common, July 3, 1775. After the show, patrons could step into the theater's next store neighbor, Garfield's, for a soda and ice cream.

Its owners called the University Theatre "A Cambridge Institution" and while it was not the first film house in Cambridge, it certainly was its most posh cinema when it opened. Furthermore, the owners promised only to show "feature pictures of superior merit selected by experts." There were three shows a day and two changes of programs each week. At its opening the Governor of the Commonwealth, Alvan T. Fuller, praised the new venture and indeed all motion pictures for their "wholesome influence" for community good. Whether films have had over the decades a wholesome influence or not, they were immediately and immensely popular with the populace. This was largely due to two facts: it cost less to see movies then to attend the theater and families/children could see them without having to leave their own neighborhood.

The University Theatre prospered under its original owners for 35 years, but then their lease came to an end and they sold out to new management, who also owned at the time the Brattle Theatre. The theater, now called after Harvard Square, was renovated and was reopened in December, 1961 as a place for both films

"Art Triumphs Over History," The stage curtain of the University Theatre: Washington takes Command of the Continental Army, Cambridge Common, 1775.

and live entertainment. The first feature was the Bolshoi Ballet's film of Prokofiev's "Cinderella," and the first live program was Sir Michael Redgrave reading stories by Hans Christian Anderson.

In 1982 the theater again changed ownership and underwent further renovations. The lobby facing the square was made into an independently run pizza parlor and a new one was opened on Church Street. The original screen was kept but two additional ones were added; eventually the individual cinemas were to be expanded to the current six. It is now known as a Loews/Sony Theatre.

Nearby was yet another motion picture house, the Janus, but its existence was rather short-lived and it was closed in 1999. A somewhat longer-running establishment and one that possessed a unique mystique was the Orson Welles on Massachusetts Avenue between Harvard and Central Squares. Conceived by two Harvard Business School graduates and named for the distinguished Hollywood actor, it was opened as a three-screen complex in 1969. It emphasized artistic and classic films and soon developed a steady loyal audience. Its showing in 1985 of Jean-Luc Goddard's film "Hail Mary" brought both pickets and the local media to its doors. Unfortunately for the community, a fire which started in its popcorn machine one May afternoon in 1986 gutted the theater. There was talk that it would be renovated and reopened, but that never happened.

Further down the "Avenue" in Central Square were additional picture houses: The Cambridge Theatre, Gordon's Cambridge Central Sq. Theatre, the Rex, and the Central Square Cinema. The old Cambridge Theatre on Western Avenue and River Street, which was torn down in 1954, was opened in 1910 as a vaudeville house; in 1913 under its new name, the Olympia Theatre, it started showing silent films. From the first one, they were immensely popular. Gordon's was another of the early vaudeville and motion picture houses in the city and included live acts as well as films. Built in 1919, it had a pipe organ, orchestra pit, and 2,100 seats. In 1921 one of its shows was "Playthings of Destiny" with Anita Stewart and Little Dickie Headricks PLUS five Big Vaudeville Acts right there on its stage.

The independently owned Central Square Cinema showed films during the 1970's (it closed in April 1980); its fare was avant-garde and revival films. As with the Orson Welles, it had its own special breed of devoted followers and fans or, as someone declared, its "diehard battalion of cineastes." They needed to be diehard because while the architecture of the theater was at best "funky," its seats were torn, its floor had vintage bubble gum everywhere, its men's room was known for its graffiti, and the entire auditorium always felt damp. Donna Maguire remembered the "dump" very clearly, and her feet sticking to its carpet, even rats running across the stage. All her memories were not negative, however, for it was here that she almost saw Elvis Presley's first movie, "Love me Tender." Almost because the theater was giving away 10 by 12 glossy photographs of Elvis at the concession stand and she spent most of the movie trying to get one. And did. Only some years later did she actually get to see the film.

North Cambridge also had for many years its own movie houses, one at Porter Square which, as so many theaters once did in the 1930's, gave its patrons a piece of dinnerware once a week (ivory colored, trimmed by 22-carat gold, and with pink flowers in the center), and the Harvard Theater (1914–1954) at 2321 Mass Ave with its ticket box out front. In the North Cambridge area of today is the multi-complex Fresh Pond Cinema, and in East Cambridge can be found the multi-complex Kendall Square Cinema. So Cambridge still entertains itself with popcorn, butter (if one is not on a diet), and salt (if one does not have heart problems).

GOLF ANYONE?

The 1932 state legislature gave Cambridge the okay to build a public golf course in the Fresh Pond area. It took almost two years to construct. The workers were supplied by the Unemployment Committee of the Cambridge Industrial Association and the material used was supplied by the city. On June 13, 1934, the new municipal golf course, known today as the Thomas P. O'Neil, Jr./Fresh Pond Golf Course, was officially opened when the Mayor, Richard M. Russell, swung and hit the first ball toward the green.

The course has nine holes and is open from early April right through to early December. At first it only had a temporary clubhouse, but in 1939 a new one, named for Edwin H. Hall, was erected as a WPA project on the site of the former practice tee. The operating expenses of the golf course are raised through membership and league fees as well as green fees. Among the various special activities that the city golf course has sponsored over the years have been company leagues, a weekly women's league, a Cambridge Rindge and Latin league, a Matignon High School league, and numerous tournaments.

The community garden on Sacramento Street.

GREEN THUMBS

During the Second World War the people of Cambridge, along with folks living in many other American cities and towns, raised vegetables in their back yards. These old fashioned "kitchen gardens" were called now Victory Gardens. In 1943 it was estimated that the city had about 5,000 of them. The City helped this good cause by turning over four large plots of land for citizens to use for planting potatoes, green beans, tomatoes, onions, and such eatables. Some 2,000 residents immediately took advantage of this opportunity to help win the war by growing and harvesting their own fresh vegetables.

Although that war is now just a memory, the city's

community gardens are not for they still exist. For example, in 1977 there were eleven of them worked by about 300 "city farmers," and at the end of the century there were just as many but now taken care of by almost 500 gardeners. Clearly there are lots of green thumbs in Cambridge.

NO COOKING, NO CLEANING UP, JUST A TIP

Barney's, Iruna's ("*Iruna*" is Basque for Pamplona), Ferdinand's, Cardell's, Frank's Steak House (Massachusetts' oldest steak house, established in 1938), Leo's Place, Georgian Cafeteria, Henri IV, Casa Mexico, Charlie's Kitchen, Hungry Persian, Oxford Grille, Young & Yee, Legal Sea Foods, Hong Kong, Cafe Pamplona, Elsie's, the Paradise Spa, The Peasant Stock, Buddy's Sirloin Pit, Alexander's, Izzy's Restaurant and Sub Shop, and over the decades tons more.

Of course, from its earliest days the community had places where it was possible to obtain liquid refreshment. Examples would be the well known Blue Anchor Tavern, the Davenport Tavern, and a century later, the several inns at Cambridgeport. But just restaurants for the average citizens to go for lunch or supper, that was another matter. Indeed, that practice, which was to grow so common for so many, awaited the arrival of another century.

Now if eating out at a restaurant or taking food out for consumption at home has become for many in the city a fairly normal practice after the Second World War, for most of the community's existence it was not the norm. Eating out was more a treat than a regular practice and often that eating out was limited to religious, fraternal, and other organizational "suppers" or "parties."

Elizabeth Woodman Wright remembered, for example, the Halloween party she and other young people from the First Parish attended in 1905 at a farm in Waltham where the menu consisted of baked beans, brown bread, rolls, sweet corn, cold chicken, apple sauce, pickles, chocolate, and apple juice. "We had," she reported later, "a most splendid supper" followed by "stunts" and a barn dance. In 1918 St. Paul's Church held another kind of party, its annual summer field festival where its five hundred church members and their friends availed themselves of home-made candy, ice cream, and soft drinks while engaging in the afternoon in such games as a potato race, a road race, and other sporting events; their evening was devoted to social dancing.

Of course, it had always been possible even in the 17th and 18th centuries for strangers to get something to eat at one of the town's public houses. If at first it might just be beer and bread, later it could be, if one had fifty cents, a nice beef-steak.

Yet it was really only during the last half of the 20th century that eating out gradually became accepted as

Matchbooks from some Cambridge restaurants, old and new.

another ingredient of the nation's fast developing leisure industry, just as baseball and hockey, movies and theater, travel and outdoor recreation, are now considered vital parts of an individual's personal leisure activities. Several factors account for the change in how Americans and those living in Cambridge now entertaine themselves. Certainly an important role must be assigned to the automobile which made transportation for a night on the town for a family, a date, or a group of friends, convenient and affordable for both middle-class and lower middle-class workers. Another was the healthy condition of the post-war economy when taken as a whole and when compared with the leisure restrictions placed on individuals and households during the last World War and especially during the Great Depression of the late 1920's and 1930's. But perhaps more significant than those two factors was the growth of modestly priced restaurants after the First World War due to the development of techniques for the mass production of food which enabled commercial caterers to be cost effective.

The contemporary fare in Cambridge restaurants includes just about anything the human palate might desire (at least once). That anything stretches from hot dogs with mustard and relish to chicken vindaloo with garlic naan to glazed seared fillet of salmon with truffled potatoes, swiss chard and wild mushrooms orange-glazed. Further, the types of available menus, as they have always been, are affected by national concerns about such things as cholesterol, proper

Sen Lee, founder of the Hong Kong.

nutrition, dietary agendas, the ever-changing food fads that come and go, food tastes, and other various economic and social issues.

America's major contributions to the restaurant business include the cafeteria (the first one was at San Francisco during the Gold Rush years) with its emphasis on self-service and a wide selection of inexpensive dishes; the small diner with its counter and stools serving the kind of foods Americans are used to getting in their homes; specialty eating places featuring but a single or sometimes two choices; coin operated vending machines; and finally fast food establishments such as the Kentucky Fried Chicken, Burger King, or McDonald's chains. Examples of all of these are to be found in present day Cambridge.

Yet that's only half the Cambridge restaurant business today for because of its centrality within the communities that make up Greater Boston, the fact that it houses two international universities, and the affluence of a good many of its citizens and visitors, especially the latter, it has a generous availability of upscale eating places. Cambridge may not have New York City's famed Rainbow Room, but it does have more than its share of brilliant and poetic eateries that satisfy the taste buds of most gourmets.

As neighbor Julia Child would say, "bon appetit."

So what will it be tonight: Tex-Mex, Chinese, French, Italian, Cambodian, Portuguese, Spanish, Near Eastern, African, Indian, Tibetan, or just plain or posh American. Remember too, there's no preparation or cooking needed, no dull cleaning up either, but most certainly unless one is very cheap a decent tip is one of the rules of eating out. And if you are too lazy to bother to go out, just call and have it delivered to your household table, for most Cambridge folks do love to eat. And eat. As the young lad says in the musical "Oliver": More please!

PLEASE GO AWAY OFTEN

Above the doorway to one of the city's travel agencies it says: Please Go Away Often. It's an appropriate sign and sentiment for post-World-War-Two Cambridge where so many in the city have both the time and the means to travel anyplace they want to in the world. Clearly the growing fashion of leisure foreign travel, below the level of that once done almost exclusively by the very well-to-do, is one of the telling characteristics of modern American recreation. Indeed, the seduction of traveling to other countries is promoted by an abundance of travel agents, the relative cheapness of air and boat fares, the year-round frequency of planes flying from Boston's airport, as well as the convenience of travelers' checks and credit cards. In previous centuries this was not the situation.

Then traveling abroad was limited to the wealthy few. Indeed, many of the city's immigrants once they departed from their homelands were fated never again to see the members of their families who did not come with them. The rich who were able to travel—usually for enjoyment and education but also for business—often did so for several months or even for several years at a time. In the Greater Boston area such travelers usually went to Europe on their trips, although some did journey as far as the Holy Land and Egypt.

While abroad, they would write long letters to the folks back home, and some when they returned reported their adventures in lectures, essays, and books. James Russell Lowell, who among his many activities taught modern literature at Harvard College and served as the editor of the *Atlantic Monthly,* wrote for example—in his best literary style—a long piece about his 1864 trip to Italy and the Mediterranean. This fairly serious essay is to be found in his often reprinted volume, *Fireside Travels.*

Not every one, of course, had access to magazine or book publication. Nevertheless, the letters they wrote to Cambridge family and friends on their trips were cherished and saved. Lois Lilley Howe in her "How Cambridge People Used to Travel" shared a series of letters written to members of her family from those on trips—to Europe but also from such American cities as Middletown, Connecticut, Pittsburgh, and Cincinnati. In addition to traveling to see relatives, some Cambridge people did so for adventure and/or to become rich. A prominent example would be Nathaniel Wyeth from the ice business at Fresh Pond.

Many of these written accounts were on the serious side. But not all. In 1869 Mark Twain visited the Continent and the Holy Land by chartered steamer. On the trip he wrote a series of witty and sly letters to an American newspaper relating what he and his fellow passengers (who he found rather ridiculous) saw and did. He entitled the book that resulted *Innocents Abroad.* So most of us remain. Still, more and more Cambridge people find it fun today to go traipsing about the planet.

FURTHER READING

Brattle Theatre at Historic Brattle Hall: 1890–1990. Cambridge, MA: The Theatre, 1990.

HOWE, LOIS LILLEY. "How Cambridge People Used to Travel," *Cambridge Historical Society Proceedings,* 24 (1936–1937) 27–48.

LAMBERT, CRAIG. *Mind Over Water: Lessons on Life from the Art of Rowing.* Boston: Houghton Mifflin, 1998.

LOWELL, JAMES RUSSELL. *Fireside Travels.* Boston: Houghton, Mifflin, 1884.

MAY, RALPH. "The Cambridge Boat Club," *Cambridge Historical Society Proceedings,* 39 (1961–1963) 125–141.

STEELE, JR., CHAUNCEY DEPEW. "A History of Inns and Hotels in Cambridge," *Cambridge Historical Society Proceedings,* 37 (1957–1958) 29–44.

TWAIN, MARK. *Innocents Abroad.* NY: Oxford, 1996.

WRIGHT, ELIZABETH WOODMAN. "Recollections of the First Parish in 1905–1906," *Cambridge Historical Society Proceedings,* 44 (1976–1979) 105–121.

The Five Major Squares of Cambridge.

CHAPTER TEN

HARVARD SQUARE

At first it was simply a typical Puritan village, a center for godly living, and the place where the new colony founded its college; later as that College matured and came to dominate the community's activity and intellectual life, it was that special place proudly called by its inhabitants Old Cambridge; today it is known as Harvard Square, and while its eye is still upon the University, it is only one of the several unique places that define this city.

It is important to remember that for many decades this "Harvard Square" had been the religious and political center of the village and the town. Its shift to its present business and recreational emphasis, in other words to shops and stores, restaurants, cinemas, and theaters, whose basic initial constituency are the students, faculty, and support staff of the college, especially those living in the immediate neighborhood, was obviously a gradual one. Once this fact became a reality of the times, however, that role and definition of the Square increased, and as Harvard became a national institution, it drew to the area people and students from communities around about the city as well as tourists from the rest of the country and eventually people from all over the world. Fortunately, those who have grown up or lived near Harvard Square have written down some of their memories of its essences over the last two centuries.

Cambridge's Neighborhoods

Such remembrances serve as verbal maps to what it has been all about.

One of the Square's earliest shops, a variety store run by Andrew Bordman until he became the college's cook and steward, was in operation by the middle of the seventeenth century. Nearby, one of his relatives, Aaron Bordman, and his descendants for more than a century repaired locks, clocks, and other machinery. Also doing business in the Square were Edmund Angier as a woolen draper who was also keen "to sell rome [rum]", William French and his successor William Barrett as tailors, John Stedman who dealt in furs and rum (his daughter Sharp was once "molested" by the court for selling rum for the "support and comfort" of her aged father), John Bunker as a saddler, Thomas Stacey as a smithy, Vashti Bradish as a baker (President Dunster was one of those who praised her bread and penny beer), and two church deacons, John Chesholm who ran an inn which sold spirits and Nathaniel Sparhawk who also sold in his tavern "wine and strong water." Perhaps the best known of these early taverns was the popular Blue Anchor which under several owners and in various locations flourished until the start of the nineteenth century. Clearly, then, from its first days the Square proved good to its business community, especially on court days and Commencement days.

This was the Square, if painted with quick brush strokes that missed some spots, before the American Revolution. By then the three-story Old College House across from the Yard, which never had shops, had just been built as a dormitory; in 1858 it was to be extended to Church Street, contain in its first level various shops, and be called by local residents College Row. In 1813 a Market-house had been placed in the center of the Square, but if its life span was short-lived, it remained a vivid presence for many. Charles Eliot Norton for one remembered that it was for his Old Cambridge its source for "country produce, especially of wood and hay, loads of which drawn by oxen were brought in almost every morning for the village supply." Here too for a period was a great elm, a watering-trough, hay scales, and a "cellar" where Zenas C. Atwood kept oysters for sale. The town, always on the alert to protect the morals of its citizens, forbid "gambling, tippling or riotous behavior to be suffered" in that cellar.

Levi Farwell, a Baptist deacon, long ran a store at the corner of Boylston Street; indeed, he operated it so long that the locals renamed the corner after him. His customers had to climb three steps to enter (the deacon installed an iron railing for them to use during the winter so that they would not slip if the steps proved to be icy), then go to the right for china and crockery or to the left for dry goods, and were waited on by either the "formidable" deacon or by the more patron-friendly Miss Stone who worked as the deacon's only other salesperson.

Next to Farwell's was the Willard Hotel where Old Cambridge gathered to catch the "Hourly" omnibus to Boston. Initially there were three coach lines into the

Harvard Square at 2000. Harvard University is seen at the left and the Old Cambridge Baptist Church in the center.

city, but by 1847 they had all been absorbed into one and the schedule improved to a coach every fifteen minutes. Charles Eliot Norton noted in his memories of Old Cambridge that if the post office had a strong daily appeal for many of the inhabitants, which it surely did, then so did, for some of them at least, the hotel or more particularly its bar-room.

On one of the side of the hotel was yet another Baptist deacon, William Brown, who kept a flourishing provision shop. Miss Hannah Tucker the dressmaker

and milliner ran her establishment in rooms over Read's store; a second dressmaking shop was run by Mrs. Experience Hyde and her sister Miss Dana. The sisters also mended clothing, taught girls how to do embroidery, and sold toys.

Drugstores, or as they were once termed, apothecaries. were kept by A. H. Ramsey, William Hill, and John H. Hubbard whose store survives today as Billings & Stover's; a furniture store was opened by Thomas Russell in 1828 and later by James Cannon

Wadsworth House, built in 1726.

who also made cabinets and repaired things for the college students; Alfred Wood and Orrin Hall, who were succeeded by Frank P. Merrill Co, ran in College Row a West Indies goods store which in spite of that unusual term was really a grocery store specializing in goods such as coffee, sugar, and molasses imported from that area; Dearing & Gooding had a provision store in the old Lyceum building; David and Thomas Brewer had a meat market on Brattle Square; and finally Ivory P. Estes had one of the Square's first hardware stores.

The Square has seen too many shops open and close to list them all as much fun as that would be. Yet, one can not ignore the bookstores as they are such an integral part of its character. The first two bookstores, that run in the Lyceum building by James Munroe and the University Book Store nearby, were also book publishers, and of course Cambridge was for decades a printing center. As George H. Kent noted in 1927, "These shops were the resort of the Literate of Cambridge, and one could hardly go to the University Book

Store in the morning without meeting some distinguished author."

Special notice should also be taken of another of the Square's long term institutions, the Edwin R. Sage Company. This grocery was started in 1898 at 21 Brattle Street by Daniel H. Dean; ten years later his clerk Edwin Rodney Sage bought him out, and still later took over another well known grocery the J. H. Wyeth Co. which had previously purchased the old George A. Wood grocery. In 1926 Sage's moved its store to its own building on the corner of Church and Brattle Streets. Later it opened a branch on Huron Avenue as well as additional outlets in Boston, Belmont, and Waltham. In June 2000, however, its long service to the Harvard Square community came to end when the Cambridge store was closed.

As the nineteenth century wound up its activities, Eleanor Parker Fiske wrote about how the Square seemed to her on an autumn evening. "The whistles have all blown for six o'clock... Bustle and confusion are everywhere; the incoming cars are loaded to the steps, and the turmoil increases as each empties its burden in front of the crowded station. Now and then a trolley slips from the wire, causing a chorus of sparks to fly out for moment... Little groups of students coming from the side streets hasten across the yard, bound for Memorial Hall, and in spite of the general din, fragments of their gay talk come clearly to the passerby. A broad band of light streams from the baker's window, and the buyers of bread and rolls for the family supper keep the door constantly in motion... John the Orangeman and his donkey clatter by homeward bound. John waves his whip at the students in the doorway, and they shout a hearty good-night after his retreating cart. The peanut man's stand has a delightfully mysterious look... Belated grocers' wagons, laden with to-morrow's dinners, rattle by... It is time to shut the ledger and put it up, to slip into one's great coat,

John the Orangeman.

lock the office door, and catch a foothold on the next outward bound car, with thoughts of a warm supper and the hearth fire ..."

On February 22, 1882, Charles Hayden Kip, a Harvard junior, held a meeting in his dorm room to find a way for students to buy their clothes, books, coal, used furniture, soap, and other necessary and useful items at lower prices than those being charged by the merchants of Harvard Square. A committee of five was formed to do something and that something was the Harvard Co-operative Society or, as it is familiarly called, the Coop. Soon a constitution and by-laws had been drawn up, officers elected, a manager selected, and an annual membership fee determined upon; within a year about forty-nine percent of the student body had joined the Society.

The plan established was to sell merchandise at five percent above cost, to require that everything be paid for in cash, and to return any profit to capital. Only later was it decided to pay a yearly dividend to the membership.

During its early struggle to survive the Coop had several homes. The store was opened as but a few shelves in a fruit store on Harvard Row, then moved to the rear area of Drury's tobacco shop for some months, and finally to Dane Hall, the old Law School building. Here it remained for the next twenty-one years at which time the Society purchased Lyceum Hall in the very heart of the Square just about where today's book department is located. In 1925 that building was torn down and replaced with the current red brick and white limestone trimmed structure.

The Coop was to have fluctuating periods of good and lean years and to alter its mission statement a number of times. One of the most important changes was made in 1887 when the directors voted to open the store to non-members which is still the policy. That decision probably kept it from an early demise. Other innovations followed including the opening of branches at MIT and the Medical School. In the 1990's, faced again with serious financial questions, the directors drastically re-oriented its business operation. Over the decades this student-originated enterprise has become an integral part of the image one has of the Harvard Square.

Of course the Square has always been more than its stores and shops for around its perimeter lived many of their customers. Towards Watertown and Belmont are the homes of those with higher incomes than most of Cambridge's inhabitants and they occupy the fine old homes associated with Brattle Street and its immediate neighborhood as well as the great homes built during the Victorian period. Many of these remain lovely single homes still. However, as times changed a number of the Victorian mansions gave way to apartment buildings such as those presently found on Mass Ave between Harvard and Porter Squares. Eventually the condos arrived, and if they did not do away with the apartment buildings, they did change the status of many rental units to owner-occupied flats.

The Coop at 2000.

Around about the Square were also two and three-decker houses more typical of other sections of the city. Dorothy Squier in her memories of growing up in Cambridge wrote charmingly about living in them. "Our back piazza ran the width of the house, a three-decker near Harvard Square in Cambridge. We were on the middle floor. Most of the houses on the street were single or two family, but now they were flanked by a curve of three-deckers on the corner of Kirkland Street. Built to house six families, this was occupied on the ground floor by Jimmie's Meat Market, Phil's Dry goods, and Hamilton's Bakery—only we always called it Hammie's … The rooming houses started on the next Street, Trowbridge." Not so many decades earlier Kirkland was known as Professor's Row.

Yet still another significant Harvard Square institution is its Kiosk. The first, the earliest entrance to the subway, was round and made of bricks. In time it came to be considered a traffic hazard and was replaced in 1927 by the present Kiosk, a smaller structure with a prominent copper vaulted roof beloved by all devotees of the Square. When the subway was extended to Alewife, a different stair configuration prevented it from being re-used, so it was relocated next to the present entrance and became the home of the Out-of-Town News. Its official address is Zero Harvard Square. A rival newsstand next to the Coop and directly across from the Kiosk is Nini's Corner which had on its staff for years a cat often to be seen asleep on one of the various piles of newspapers for sale outside the store and familiarly known to regulars as Louie.

During the First World War the Square and the College were just about taken over by the military. Indeed, even before America entered that conflict, Harvard had arranged to have its R.O.T.C unit, which soon consisted of more than twelve hundred volunteers, trained by disabled officers from the French Army. Among their accomplishments was the digging of trenches at Fresh Pond and holding there the so-called "Battle of Fresh Pond." Later many of the college buildings and the Cambridge Common were taken over by the Navy for the training and temporary housing of the men in its Radio School. Fortunately, America's participation in the war was of short duration, and Harvard and the Square soon returned to its special stuffy and quiet breed of normality.

The next ten years, however, were anything but normal for they laid the ground for radical societal changes in America and in Cambridge. Often popularly termed the Jazz Age, they did have a light-hearted heady flavor, for people felt good that they had saved the reality behind the concepts of democracy and freedom; they also felt good that money at last truly seemed to grow for just about everyone on the stock market tree. A workable image for the spirit of the Twenties is the fact that although Prohibition was the law, Harvard students and other "residents" of the Square had no problems obtaining sidecars, Alexanders (gin and chocolate ice cream), nonalcoholic Benedictine (with gin added), and other popular drinks of the times. Later when the Depression arrived, such liquid refreshments probably proved to be medicinal as well as enjoyable.

In the thirties Marian Cannon Schlesinger remembered that the Square still reverberated with the noise of streetcars and boys near the Kiosk shouting the latest news of the moment. The great student riots of that decade amounted to a few of them throwing toilet paper from the windows of the dorms facing the Square and snake dancing therein. She also recalled that "the ladies of Cambridge" armed with their shopping bags loved their daily visits to Sage's, Campbell and Sullivan, the fishmongers, Amee's, the paper store, or the post office." The college kids, however, patronized a different set of establishments. Those with limited means were attracted especially in the evening to eateries like the Waldorf on Mass Ave and Gustie's in Brattle Square while the more affluent ones enjoyed martinis, club sandwiches, and literary conversations at St. Clair's or if they were from the Law School argued the finer matters of cases over their lunches at the Brattle Inn.

After the Second World War, the Square continued to have much the same feel about it as it did before that conflict. Joan Braverman Pinck, who graduated from Radcliffe in 1950, remembered many of the same spots familiar in the 1930's: for example, St. Clair's and the Waldorf She also recalled drinking beer for 10 cents a glass at Cronin's, coffee and English muffins at Albiani's, and Baileys' ice cream parlor with its tiny tables and spindly chairs beloved by Cambridge ladies. Students did not go to Baileys as much as they did to the Hayes-Bickford (often referred to as simply the Bick) or to Hazen's. Those who thought of themselves as serious beer drinkers hung out at the Rathskeller's, and while the Wursthaus had now arrived in the Square, most students ignored it for the simple reason that to occupy one of its booths you had to order a meal as well as drink. As far as the students were concerned, booths were not for eating but for conversation and liquid refreshment.

Bookstores were still an essential part of Harvard Square. Joan Braverman Pinck is bold to proclaim that in the fifties, "it was the best place in the United States for bookstores," and sadly adds that is "an honor that has long since gone elsewhere." She cites for her statement the old Harvard Bookstore which "was a great messy space full of used books…good for hours of browsing." Also the Grolier when it was owned and managed by its founder Gordain Cairnie (he ran it for

The Grolier Poetry Book Shop, at 2000 (Est. 1927).

30 years). "A student," she adds, "hanging around— hanging around was positively encouraged—could get an entire literary education at the Grolier."

The arrival of the exciting 1960's—the Civil Rights Movement, the Women's Rights Movement, and the movement to secure the right of all persons to determine their own sexual partners, the Vietnam War and the vigorous protests to that event by both students and many members of the Cambridge community, the blossoming of Flower Children and hippies—brought changes to the Square that revised both its traditional image and its more innocent longstanding character. Before all was said and done, Harvard Square certainly became more sophisticated and for many funky.

Perhaps the most dramatic of these events were the protests conducted by a large number of people against their government's war in Vietnam. These were meant to be a positive tool to achieve the goal of stopping that war; however, they often took on negative aspects. This was due in part to the ways the protests were conducted, to the misuse of legal technicalities to obstruct free expression of ideas and speech, to the use of law enforcement forces often in brutal ways by both the government and private organizations, and to the general and repeated failures of all branches of the media to objectively cover and report news. Even today, for example, much confusion still remains over the decision of the sincere Christian president of Harvard in asking the local and state police to remove his own students from University Hall after they themselves had "forcibly" occupied it in their attempt to change certain university practices.

But the protests of that decade were not limited to the college's campus; they also boiled over into the Square. Barbara Ackerman vividly depicts the results:

"Harvard Square, poor Harvard Square,
Its light went out. Though it had been shabby
with its gents clothing and bookshops, it had
been cheerful, and safe at night. Now it was dismal and scary, smashed street lights and store windows, looted goods. Some merchants replaced the bright windows once. When they were invaded again, they put up boards, soon covered with cheap fliers and even cheaper messages in pencil and grease paint."

It was not for the Square "happy days."

Then there were the "hippies" who made for themselves a virtue of less—less work, food, warmth, clothes, water, soap, scissors, razors, but unfortunately not drugs. On the whole, however, the hippie phenomenon was a fairly harmless one and could even at times be a fine one. In the end it has proved to have been one of the forces that has made Cambridge and many another American community more tolerant of the real and good differences that exist among people. Also on the lighter side of the sixties were the arrival to the Square of the street musicians—pipers, singers, guitarists, banjo players, clowns, jugglers, and magicians. For all their music and magic, they caused some legitimate problems for the Square's year by year merchants who had to pay then and still do very high rents and related expenses to conduct their businesses in this locality. If their concern was not always fully resolved by the city authorities, there came to be a working accord between the groups, and street performers are still very much an ingredient of Harvard Square's "mystique."

Robert Campbell, a practicing architect in the city,

wrote in 1958 that "Harvard Square may be the most vital little downtown in America. In its few blocks it packs more life than most urban cities: 17 bookstores, 50 restaurants, and just about everything else!" Pinck in her comparison of today's square with the way it was a generation before declared that if it is "prettier now, cleaner, and more fashionable," it is also a place where "you can spend a lot of money in its franchised shops and boutiques." She added, "as I visit it these days, it seems to me that in acquiring some good looks and affluence it may have lost its character." Lynda Morgenroth, a Cambridge resident, writing in the *Globe* would strongly agree. "Once upon a time, Harvard Square was an urban village, a quirky, hip enclave with one-of-a-kind galleries and shops, tiny chef-owned restaurants and enough appealing oddities to delight the urban wanderer. The feeling was festive and neighborly, the buildings small scale, and there was nary a chain store

Cambridge Common at 2000.

in sight." For her the good older stores are Bob Slate's and Cardullo's; the suspicious ones are HMV, The Gap, Tower records, and Starbucks. But she quickly added that there was no need for Cambridge to despair for the "Harvard Square of yesteryear exists today in a new incarnation, north of the Cambridge Common along Mass. Ave. up to Porter Square."

So it may be, but if Harvard Square has been around since 1630 it has certainly also been around as a series of Squares and not just the one. Its character has always been marked by development and changes. In all of that, what has probably defined its reason to be more than anything else was the decision made by the Puritans to plant in this spot their college.

PORTER SQUARE

Through a special dispensation from Dr. Lucius Paige, Porter Square here includes all of North Cambridge. And why not, for when the boundaries of the "newe towne" were drawn up, the area north of the village was considered as a single unit. Its backbone is Massachusetts Avenue which has been in existence since 1635. Over the years, however, it has had several names such as The Greate Country Road, the Road to Menotomy, the Road by Davenport's Tavern, the Road by Porter's Tavern, and North Avenue. If these early names for Mass Ave seem delightful, a journey on it

was not, for in summer it was dusty and in winter muddy and filled with ruts.

As necessary, the Avenue developed lanes to the right and left which in time shed their colorful first names when they became streets and avenues. So Poor House Lane became Harvey Street, Kidder's Lane became Rindge Avenue and Cedar Street, and the old path to the fish weirs at Alewife Brook became Tannery Street. Around the main highway and lanes up through the Revolutionary War were a series of farm houses with gambrel roofs and outbuildings; an example of these houses which still remains is the Cooper-Frost-Austin house on Linnaean Street.

The overall story of old North Cambridge has three significant focuses: the Porter Square area, the clay pits and brick making business, and the influx of its nineteenth century immigrant community, especially those of Irish and French background. The immigrants also brought with them their supportive Roman Catholic heritage and traditions which gave to the area its sense of being and its purpose. Even today there remains in the memories and the story telling of many a feeling of pride for the lives of those who lived and worked in North Cambridge. For those who made it their home it was true what Tip O'Neill claimed it was—a "special place"—which has appropriately been recognized in David Judelson's sculpture of the brickman which stands in Rindge Field.

After the West Boston Bridge was constructed in 1792 a toll road using it was built from Boston to our

Porter Square at 2000.

present city of Lowell; fortunately for Cambridge the road ran through Porter Square and right by John Davenport's tavern which stood on the corner of Massachusetts Avenue and our Beech Street. The road was known for some years as simply The Turnpike, then as Hampshire Street, and now as Beacon Street. In 1841 the Charlestown Branch Railroad was authorized by the state and when it was built it connected Swett's Wharf in Charlestown with Fresh Pond. Its route was similar to that of the line now traveling through the community and running under Massachusetts Avenue in Porter Square. By this time Porter's Tavern and The Cattle Market had arrived.

Today's meatpacking and production stems from colony times when the then seasonal trade was carried on by farmer-butchers and local slaughterhouses. Nothing changed much in the trade until after the Civil War when the new transcontinental railways, refrigeration technology, and the emergence of midwestern entrepreneurs laid the foundation of the present livestock and meatpacking industry. Here in Massachusetts as topsoil lost its ability to produce worthwhile harvests, more and more farmers turned to raising sheep and cows as a means to provide for the needs of their families. Therefore, both the creation of the Brighton meat market which provided Bostonians with red meat and later of the Cambridge cattle market were natural and necessary economic developments.

In 1830 Davenport's Inn and Tavern was sold to Sylvester Edson who passed it along to a bank which sold it to Zachariah B. Porter and two associates. Porter, who was from Brighton and had run a tavern in that town near its cattle market, hoped to repeat his success there in Cambridge. What he got for his purchase was seventeen and a half acres stretching from Creighen Street down to Upland Road plus the buildings they contained. The site of his tavern was near Upland Road, and of course it faced what we call Porter Square and was near the stables and slaughterhouses of the market.

In Cambridge the market day was held on Wednesdays. The cattle that had previously been shipped in packed cars via the Fitchburg Railroad and stored by the drovers in the many pens between its tracks, the pasturage grounds, and Porter's tavern, were sold to satisfy "human voracity" as the reporter for *Ballou's Pictorial Drawing Room Companion* aptly phrased it. It was always a lively spot, what with the buyers, the speculators, the butchers, the lounging on-lookers, young boys shouting and running up and down, the bellowing of the cows and oxen, the grunting of the pigs, and the bleating of the sheep.

Before long Porter's and the developing cattle business became almost synonymous, and its famous Porterhouse steaks and flip are still spoken of with delight by those who have tasted neither. Thomas Wentworth Higginson writing of this period justly pointed out that "North Cambridge as yet was not, though Porter's Tavern was." No wonder that Zachariah Porter's name was given to this Square.

There were several other taverns about the cattle sheds and stables; some of these were the Elm House on Frank Street, the Telegraph House on Hudson Street, and of course the always popular Fresh Pond Hotel (even though it was a long way from the Square.) As wonderful as these taverns and hotels were, and Porter's was said to have seen many "gay and brilliant affairs, attended by fashionably dressed men and women" while the Fresh Pond Hotel was noted for its fine wines and meals as well as for its winter trapping and skating and summer swimming and fishing, they certainly never offered the comforts and conveniences demanded by later generations.

As Chauncey Depew Steel, Jr. reminds us, staying at one was fairly primitive. "Even for their age," he wrote, "they were crude in furnishings and equipment…Poor construction permitted gusts of rain, wind, sleet, and snow to penetrate the walls. To get to their sparsely furnished rooms, guests had to go up steep and creaking staircases…Light was provided

The cattle market.

mainly by candles. Some hotels also used kerosene and gas lamps, though the former tended to be smoky and the latter smelly. Rooms were heated, probably inadequately, by inefficient coal furnaces. Washing and bathing was done in a bowl on the washstand, with water from a pitcher. In the midst of winter, formation of ice on top of the water was not at all unusual. To bathe in a tub, guests had to wait for hours to get into the common lavatory." Even the beds, tables, and chairs in the rooms were plain, practical, and utilitarian.

Porter and the others to help finance their enterprises, especially the cattle market, established in 1851 the Cambridge Market Bank and erected its building close by Porter's tavern. It existed but sixteen years and was used really only for market business, and when that came to an end so did the bank. Also closely related to the market and taverns was Trotting Park, a race track which was situated between Harvey, Cedar, Clifton Streets and Rindge Avenue. The Park ran in addition to its horses its own tavern, the Park House. By 1855 the owners of the track seeing the future direction of the area closed it down and moved into the booming real estate business. Others had done so as early as ten years before. Soon where the horses had run appeared streets and two family houses and North Cambridge moved with all deliberate speed into the era of brick making.

There was still yet another landmark associated with North Cambridge that deserves to be celebrated, and that was the estate of Benjamin Rand, a carriage maker, which was roughly located where today's shopping center is in Porter Square. His first house which was built in 1813 faced Mass Ave directly; his second which had been constructed in 1855 faced Elm Street. This was possible because in 1821 he had purchased the two

acres that connected the two byways. The second house, which was much larger and fancier than the first one, Benjamin gave to his son Henry Clay who when he died passed it to his son Harry and Harry's wife Mabel. Contemporary photographs capture the estate's lovely lawns, footpaths, garden, and trees. In addition to its wonderful grounds, the estate kept cows and horses.

Mabel Rand, the last of the family to own the land, tried to find before her death some way the property

The Rand Estate.

might be preserved as it was but that proved impossible although at one time the Catholic Archdiocese of Boston had expressed an interest in obtaining it as a church site. In 1950 Mabel died and two years later the estate along with several nearby homes were purchased and replaced by one of the conveniences of the twentieth century, a shopping mall.

As important as a source for jobs and livelihood as was the brick business, there were other opportunities for workers to earn a pay check. One very key one was connected with the railroads that came through North Cambridge and, by the end of the nineteenth century, with the electric streetcars and trolleys. From 1841 the trains which ran between Fitchburg and Boston regularly stopped at the depot in Porter Square, and after the Boston & Maine assumed control of that system they built a brand new depot here. Electric trolleys were fully operational by the 1890's.

As a result there was a demand for workers to do such things as dig ditches, lay and maintain tracks, serve as gate keepers, ticket takers, motormen, and conductors. Some of these jobs as their titles indicate involved hard, physical work, and all of them were low-paying if steady positions.

Clearly, too, the rewards of honest labor in North Cambridge were far different than that for most of those living in Old Cambridge. A vivid illustration of this was the effects of the 1929 depression on all too many North Cambridge families. Emily Broussard who lived with her family on Harvey Street put it this way:

"We had a rough time during the Depression. We had no money at all. My father and brothers weren't working. Then my oldest brother found a job for $20 a week and he gave my mother $10 a week … Our neighbor's couldn't help us; they weren't working. So we did the best we could. We had to move in with my grandparents. If you had a home, and it was paid for, like my grandfather's, the taxes took care of it. But the people who were still paying mortgages lost their homes."

A third major work force supporting North Cambridge life were those involved in providing the inhabitants with their meat and potatoes, eggs and milk, mittens and shoes, ice and heat, and all the other everyday items so necessary to living. In those days it was not just the family doctor who made house calls but also the butcher, the milk man, the ice man, the fruit and vegetable man, and many others. Your local merchant was almost a member of your family and as familiar as the priests and sisters of Saint John the Evangelist and Notre Dame de Pitié.

As these two memories of growing up in North Cambridge illustrate. Dan Huntington Fenn recalled that Murphy's Variety Store in Porter Square was the place neighborhood kids "bought our pens, pencils, erasers, notebooks, or what not, and also some toys. Murphy's had tops, jump ropes, kites, marbles—the dime-a-dozen doggies of clay, exciting glassies, and, if you had saved enough money from your allowance, a precious aggie."

Another local business landmark is the Porter

Square Cafe. Eileen McNamara has written about it as "a place as dark and mysterious as any religious sanctuary, its beery smell as exotic as incense and its wooden booths worn as smooth as church pews by the visits of so many penitents. For a bar, it was an oddly quiet place, claimed by men in search of a few moments' peace between the noisy demands of their bosses and the pressing needs of their families. On the few occasions I slipped inside as a child, I recall the men exchanging only whispered remarks, maybe a nod of the head. Nothing like animated conversation happened there." Many more such memories of the way things were are contained in the wonderful book *In Our Own Words: Stories of North Cambridge 1900–1960* which was put together by Sarah Boyer.

Constant change, however, is one of the keys which unlock what people are fond of calling the mystery of human life. North Cambridge has not escaped this process and Tip O'Neill's special place is becoming a new special place. The forces that operated on the old Harvard Square have also altered the old Porter Square. "In the past 20 years," Eileen McNamara wrote in the Boston *Globe,* "it has sometimes seemed that the neighborhood was racing to keep up with its yupped-up self. The white-steepled Congregational church [really the Cornerstone Baptist Church] came down and condominiums went up in its place; the Abraham Lincoln School closed its doors to students and reopened them to condo owners; CVS came in and Stollers' Drugstore went out; the Henderson Carriage

Building was renovated and the Ford dealership on the ground floor gave way to tony restaurants and specialty shops; the storefronts that once housed Nilson's bakery became home to the Cambridge School of Culinary Arts. Also good Sears became the Porter Exchange."

But enough, enough. Let us step into Andy's Diner with its tables and booths, with its counter and stools, for a good home-cooked meal, and this being a Thursday that would be his New England boiled dinner like Ma use to make it, plus a cup of just plain old fashioned coffee (with refills), and be thankful for what was and hopefully for what will be.

Andy's Diner at 2000 (opened, 1958). Try the codfish cakes and beans made just like one of their waitress's grandmother made it.

Kendall Square at 2000.

KENDALL SQUARE

Riding the T to the courthouse for jury duty you hear over the loud speaker system "Entering Kendall—MIT", so get off, climb the stairs to ground level, and exit to mud flats, a low tide, salt marshes, swamps, and a glacial drumlin or Graves' Neck as it was called by its first white "owner" Thomas Graves. Between it and Harvard Square are some more drumlins, Miller's River (also called Gibbons' or Willis Creek), Rabbit Island, and lots more salt marshes.

As Sophia Shuttleworth Simpson put it in 1859, "The lands in the easterly part of Cambridge were chiefly valued for the abundance of hay and forage which the salt marshes furnished. These marshes extended far out from the banks of the river. The situation was very uninviting. The grounds lay low, and it was a sort of insulated tract, detached from every other. There were no roads; access could be obtained to Boston, only by boats, or by the circuitous route of Roxbury or Charlestown. In the course of the year, very few persons passed down into the neck, or isthmus, as it was called, unless for farming purposes, or fishing and fowling."

So it is quite natural for you to stand here blinking, perhaps even unbelieving your eyes, for what you see is essentially Kendall—MIT and the area about it as it appeared during the 17th and 18th centuries. Before exploring this lonely landscape, therefore, I think it might be a good idea for you and I to have a draught or two of Mr. Porter's famous flip.

Now with our batteries thus charged we set out for a walk about this very different East Cambridge. No sooner have we started than we bump into wily old Andrew Craigie, the early 19th- century land speculator, who pulled out of his mind, wallet, and greed, the second reincarnation of East Cambridge. Mr. Craigie was sort of a magician who with what seemed like a mere wave of his wand produced the Canal Bridge he wanted built between Charlestown and Lechmere Point, moved the proposed location of the new Charles Bulfinch courthouse from Old Cambridge to East Cambridge, and finally who built against much opposition a highway (Cambridge Street) which stretched from the town's common to his growing settlement in East Cambridge. Fortunately for Mr. Craigie his Lechmere Point Corporation (he held most of its shares)

largely owned East Cambridge at this time. In the game of land acquisition Andrew Craigie was an early Harvard University and Massachusetts Institute of Technology.

While the business, political, and social story behind the creation of 19th century East Cambridge was more complicated and slower to develop than this overview suggests, the shape it was to take was given precision by Craigie, by the Lechmere Point Corporation whose board of proprietors included beside him a number of other wealth Boston investors, and later after Craigie's death by the Canal Bridge Corporation. It was they who hired Peter Tufts, Jr. to survey the area and draw the street grid arrangement of how the new community should look, and it was their plans which established here commercial and local business endeavors, had house lots developed and sold, and it was these actions which attracted the immigrants the community needed to be viable and to work in its many factories. Indeed, its industrial base during the last decades of 19th century and the first two of the 20th century was amazing, and for a while it rivaled that of the much larger city of Worcester.

The next reincarnation for East Cambridge and Kendall Square, and one which is still in process, owes its primary genius to two related events: the arrival here in the opening decades of the 20th century of MIT and the rapid and radical technological advances provided by scientists, especially those connected to MIT as teachers and graduates. Their first demand was to

Second Street houses which go back to the 1840's.

meet the government's military needs in fighting and winning two world wars and then the demands that came to face the country when it assumed leadership for both the free world and the emerging global business economy.

The development of Kendall Square and East Cambridge was succinctly summarized by Robert Campbell this way: "It went from houses to factories and then, after World War II, fell into disrepair. Since 1979, it has been gradually redeveloped, with new uses including a hotel, office space, research labs, and small retail stores."

The actual unfolding of these events was much more complicated than any summary could possible indicate, for the thrust to "improve" the area had to travel over a goodly number of potholes and speed bumps. In other words, there were beside the remaining flats to be filled in lots of ideas and preliminary plans that addressed the "how" of the area's development. Among the voices offering and urging solutions were those of the Cambridge Improvement Company, the Cambridge Park Commissioners who had hired in 1892 the landscape architectural firm of Olmsted, Olmsted & Eliot to design a park system for the city which would include also the Charles riverbank, and various business concerns. Influential too in the way East Cambridge was to be shaped was the creation of the Charles River Basin and Dam and the opening of the Cambridge Parkway in 1928 between the dam and the West Boston Bridge.

A second major renewal of the area, often referred to as the Kendall Square Urban Renewal Project and the Lechmere Triangle project, took place in the decades after the end of World War II. These projects were distinctly different and were carried out by different agencies, one in the 1960s and one in the 1980s. Kendall was classic urban renewal: a public agency declares an area blighted, condemns the properties, clears the buildings, and sells the land to a private developer at a price subsidized by the Federal government. At Lechmere, there was no land taking, just publication of a plan and a huge public investment in infrastructure.

The Kendall Square Urban Renewal Project was under the supervision of the Cambridge Redevelopment Authority (CRA); it was they who reviewed all the proposed architectural designs and who had initial title to the land although they employed Boston Prop-

erties as the firm that had charge of developing the new buildings. The CRA were given also the responsibility for the required parks, streets, and landscaping. So Cambridge Center and Technology Square with its massive structures began to replace the older buildings, the vacant factories, the blighted tenements, the demolished houses. At one point the National Aeronautical Space Administration (NASA) had one of its facilities here but that was phased out in 1969 to be replaced by the U.S. Department of Transportation Systems Center. Private investors were also involved but outside the urban renewal area itself; examples of their structures are the Cambridge Gateway, the Riverfront Office Park, and the One Memorial Drive office building.

The *East Cambridge Riverfront Plan,* a study done by the Community Development Department for the city's Planning Board, came out in 1978; it recommended that East Cambridge, which was now bereft of its once flourishing businesses and factories, needed a thoughtful renovation of existing structures along with new ones and as well as appropriate open spaces so that the result would be an East Cambridge with houses, retail stores, and office units. While much of the funding for this would come from the private sector, the city's role was to rebuild many of the area's streets and to create public parks and pathways.

The most distinguishing feature of the various parks would be Lechmere Canal Park and its rebuilt canal with the huge fountain it its center. The City Council

Technology Square.

approved the report and the Lechmere Triangle has gradually come into being at a cost totalling more than $600 millon. As Susan E. Maycock has appropriately stated in her new edition to the Cambridge Historical Commission's original architectural survey on East Cambridge, "The public improvements associated with the Lechmere Triangle project are unprecedented in Cambridge for their rich design."

The older 19th and early 20th century Kendall Square and East Cambridge area, however, was more than just a collection of factories. It was also a living, breathing community with its own rich culture and traditions. At first and for several decades it was the Americans-to-be from Ireland that gave this region during this period its cultural and religious shape but by 1920 the new folks from Italy and Portugal had become large enough to add their traditions to the community's mix. To these dominant groups must be added those who had arrived from Germany, Canada, Russia, and Poland. Woods and Kennedy's *The Zone of Emergence,* which is a study of this marvelous community between 1905–1914, rightly observed that "the most interesting thing of all about East Cambridge is the fact that it embodies in miniature all the aspects of

Lechmere Canal Park.

the larger industrial world." It did so then but it also does so today, and that embodiment has as we know both its negative and positive aspects.

It seems right to celebrate one of these positive and joyous aspects: The Feast and Festivities honoring the Saints of Gaeta, Italy (one of Cambridge's sister cities), Saints Cosmas and Damian, the Healing Saints, the Patron Saints of doctors and pharmacists. By the end of the 20th century after the festival had been going on here for over seventy years the special two-day occasion was attracting anywhere from 10,000 to 40,000 each year.

The people come for the religious candlelight procession where the honored Saints are carried through the streets of the neighborhood; they come to be with their priest as he celebrates Mass; they come for the big Sunday afternoon parade with its marching bands and gaily decorated floats; they come for sausages, peppers, pasta, eggplant parmesan, fried calamari and cherry-stone clams; they come also for the amusement rides and games; but mostly they come in the words of a resident because "It's a block party" where you get to see all your old friends, your cousins and aunts and uncles, and almost just anybody who ever lived in this unique friendly Cambridge area or in the adjoining East Somerville neighborhood." The Feast is not just for those with an Italian background. Far from it. It's an open house party for all the area's neighbors: Portuguese, Irish, Polish, oldtimers, newcomers, and for all those who love Italian culture and cuisine.

You are riding the T, hear over the loud speaker system "Entering Kendall—MIT", so get off, climb the stairs to ground level, and exit to late 20th century Kendall Square. What you see about you is a far cry, even as the crow flies time, from Thomas Grave's first house on the neck and from the Boiler Factory operated here in the 1860's by good Deacon Edward Kendall for whom the square was named.

Roughly the area which starts at the intersection of Main Street and Broadway runs from MIT to the skyscraper which is Middlesex Court House, and from the Charles River and luxury condos to a series of two and three-decker house. In between these boundaries are parking lots, business firms which are mostly in buildings of fairly recent constructions such as architect Moshe Safdie's One Cambridge Center, the Federal government's Volpe Transportation Center, the CambridgeSide Mall, two hotels, and various shops and restaurants that supply the needs of those who work here but mostly live elsewhere. That last phrase is in large measure the key image of the current Kendall Square. So be it, but the Square is not without its own special loveliness just as the functional and monumental buildings designed during the 20th century by Le Corbusier and the unconventional and original music written by John Cage can charm those willing to experience the surprises in "a thing of beauty." Today's Kendall Square is such a surprise. And a nice one.

CambridgeSide Mall.

INMAN SQUARE

On December 3, 1998 a Harvard student decided to walk from Kendall Square back to the University to see what could be seen. His journey took him to Broadway to Hampshire Street to the Columbia market on the corner of Columbia and Harvard Streets and finally to the restaurant "Atasca." This is some of what he saw.

Houses that are "brightly-colored two-story affairs with wood fences around a backyard just big enough for a clothesline and a lawnchair." Many of them had been converted to apartments. "A street with a sandbox and jungle gym on the side and rows of laundry flapping in the breeze." The houses on Hampshire Street were "a sleepy row of dusty bright colors. One, with lemon yellow wood siding and the tiniest of gardens, has a brick staircase with a wrought-iron railing leading up to a '70s cream-tiled facade with an iconic painting of `Santo Antonio' holding Baby Jesus over the door. There are three mailboxes; they bear the names of Garcia, Kwon, and Thirukkonda."

Now on Broadway he finds himself walking by Caribbean grocers, drugstores, the Spanish Church of God, the "Le-Bon Samaritan Barber Shop", and the Portuguese restaurant Atasca with its racks of wine bottles, pine walls, overhead fan. Then he sees the Zeitgeist Gallery and stops to inspect the paintings in the window. Back in his dorm room he decides that Inman Square and East Cambridge possess all the ingredients for many walks "this lovely."

Inman Square today is truly a quiet and lovely section of the city. Robert Campbell, one of its residents at the close of the 20th century, called it "one of those villages-in-the-city more often imagined than actually found." The Square was named for Ralph Inman, a Cambridge citizen and Boston merchant who owned 180 acres here just prior to the Revolutionary War. In 1766 he had built for his family on land that is today 15 Inman Street a luxurious three-story home, with paneled rooms, a semicircular driveway, that had a magnificent view of Boston across the Charles. Fond of parties, everything would have come up roses for him in the years ahead except in the upcoming revolution he chose the wrong side. Normally this would have meant the loss of his "Tory" property, but thanks to his wife's influence that specter was banished. In 1792 it was sold to Leonard Jarvis who soon was developing building lots on the property. Unfortunately for Leonard, he had big ideas but a small economic pocket and he ended up bankrupt.

Then that old rascal of 18th century Cambridge, friend Andrew Craigie, eventually ended up with the Inman estate, indeed with almost all the area from Inman Square to the Lechmere Point. Of course he continued the process of breaking it down into house lots. The "Square" itself is where that street intersects with Hampshire Street close to the city's border with Somerville which was also an early toll road as was

Inman Square at 2000.

Cambridge Street leading to Boston. In time the convenience these roads made possible helped to turn the area into one of the early "bedrooms" for the capital city of the state.

The first Portuguese immigrants to the city settled generally in East Cambridge and more particularly in the area of Inman Square. Before too long they got involved in their own neighborhood life and opened

The Inman Estate, built in 1766.

markets and bakeries, various kinds of stores and eating places, saw to the establishment of their own Portuguese church of St. Anthony, and created their own social clubs such as the Faialense Sport Clube, the Santo Cristo Center, and the Clube Recreio Madeirense. The heritage they laid down continues to be one of the dominant and stable influences in this part of Cambridge. Indeed, a 1972 study of the Portuguese community made for the city's Department of Planning and Development reported that even then "along Cambridge Street it is possible to work, play, worship, and die without speaking a single word of English ... In short, it is possible to satisfy one's needs in this world and the next in the Portuguese language."

These Americans of Portuguese descent come primarily from the archipelago of Azores, especially from the island of Sao Miguel, and from Madeira rather than from "Metropolitan Portugal." While some of the immigrants had arrived before the American Civil War, the great bulk of them came after that bloody conflict.

The chief reason for their coming was economic and their first jobs were unskilled ones as factory workers in the various industrial enterprises then available in East Cambridge. Some however had enough skills to get employment as cabinetmakers. A 1970 listing of "foreign stock" population of the city lists a total for Portugal of 2,630 of which 1,100 were native-born and 1,530 were foreign-born. This made the Portuguese component of the city's population "the second-largest foreign-born group."

So they came, and like so many others who have journeyed here and planted their roots, they have flourished. An example would be the adventures of Manuel Rogers, Sr. whose parents left their original homeland in the Azores for the banks of the Charles. As a youngster "Manny" as he was popularly called lived at the corner of Charles and Fourth Streets and from 1927 to 1942 owned and operated at 352 Cambridge Street the beloved almost legendary Paradise Spa with its back room where the younger generation filled the booths, played the jukebox, and enjoyed perhaps a tulip sundae or a banana skyscraper and cold Coca-Cola. Later in his life he opened and ran the Rogers Funeral Home also on "the street."

Religion, the old country, one's home and family, are still important for Americans with a Portuguese heritage. The annual spring celebration by St. Anthony's Church of the Feast of Santo Cristo who was reported

Manuel 'Manny' Rogers, Sr. and his Paradise Spa..

to have made miracles happen is a feast unique to the Azores.

The Feast begins in the evening with the ringing of the church's bells. Then the doors of St. Anthony's open, and a solemn meditative procession with silver lanterns held high emerges: first the men in their red vestments and carrying "a devotional canopy—-a plaster cast of Jesus Christ surrounded by red and gold draperies, studded with red and pink roses"; then the altar boys and the clergy in their white robes; and finally the members of the congregation. The sacred procession halts the traffic as it marches through the streets of East Cambridge before it finally ends up back at the church. It is but one of several such feasts celebrated by Cambridge's Portuguese community, for as

Manny Roger's wife Mary explained, "Feasts are part of being Portuguese, the life you've had since you were born."

Inman Square is more than its Portuguese community. Just remember that it is also the home of the widely-known and widely-praised S & S Deli, as American as a deli can get, and of the Alfred E. Vellucci Plaza, and of the block party held every spring since 1977 by the

Get your chickens in Inman Square *(left photo)*.
"Ma" Eldelstein, the founder in 1919, of the S & S Deli. The S & S —"*Es und es*"—is a Yiddish expression for "eat and eat." Try their "Inman Omelette"*(right photo)*.

people who live in the seventy-six houses that astride Antrim Street. If Inman Square has any distinctive characteristic it is the simple truth that over all these decades it has retained a small-town atmosphere. It has problems, of course, but it has also multigenerational family and longtime friends, *caracol* and the Squirrel Brand Co.'s warehouse, "The Flower Pot" and the Ferandez Fish Market, the House of Sarah and Roosevelt Towers. As Ernest J. Taylor, a veteran of the Second World War and of Cambridge living, put it one day in Inman Square: "You never really know what good things are going to happen in life." Inman Square is a good thing.

CENTRAL SQUARE

If the image for a city, indeed for all cities and towns, is change—and this is the correct image—nowhere in Cambridge as the year 2000 starts is the image more appropriate than for Central Square. The other four squares and neighborhoods have passed through their latest change and for the moment give the appearance of standing still, but Central Square is in the midst of leaving a longtime beloved stage and moving into a new one whose physical qualities and personality is not yet, as they say, written in stone. But before describing this evolving change,let us go back to the beginning of the Central Square story.

The first change of this tidal marsh and swamp land was the transformation that resulted with the unexpected (and no doubt unwanted) arrival of the lighter skinned *Homo sapiens* from the continent of Europe. They came in their ships and claimed for themselves the land frequented by generations of Native Americans. There is no contemporary record that they ever apologized for what they did. The area now known as Central Square was but one bead on the necklace worn without shame by the Puritans.

The next significant change was the town's decision in 1656 to spend two hundred dollars for the construction of a bridge between Cambridge and Boston. Opened in 1662 and grandiosely called "The Great Bridge" it made it possible for waggons from the various country towns to travel more directly and quickly to the chief port of the colony. This proved helpful, but as the decades went by and commercial Boston steadily developed its local supremacy, there was a growing demand for an even more efficient route to Boston. After much agitation the Charles River Bridge was built in 1786 by Charlestown and in 1793 the West Bridge by Cambridge. This latter bridge was one of the foundation stones which permitted the emergence of Cambridgeport and later modern Central Square.

As we have seen, the attempts to make the area a shipping port and to secure its own railroad terminal facilities both failed. What did materialize instead was the twofold development of the community as both a residential and industrial/commercial suburb of

Central Square at 2000. In the center is the First Baptist Church which was built in 1881.

Boston. The social and business aspect of the area has already been discussed, and if in contemporary Central Square the industrial facilities have been replaced by a new business technology, its historical reputation as a place to live for people who work hard but whose incomes never match the efforts they put into that work has not. This factor along with its broad immigration heritage is still basic to its character and spirit.

Now this may already be changing as a result of the demise of a housing policy which sought to keep the city open to all participants of the American pie.

Sheila Choi in her 1993 thesis "Public Space in Central Square" states that by the 1920's the area had become "saturated both residentially and commercial-ly." She then notes that from the 1930's onward "a large scale effort is made to unify the public, low-income scale housing." Her reference is to New Town Court, Washington Elms, Roosevelt Towers, Putnam Gardens, Woodrow Wilson Court with all their hopes and disappointments. Nonetheless, they changed along with

The famous Bread & Circus Whole Foods Market.

other developments here the older "urban fabric." Yet the Central Square area retained its cultural mix and its lively heritage. "There seems to be a durability to Cambridgeport," she concluded, and rightly so, "a toughness that is exuberant…In addition, there has developed a unique atmosphere because of the various activities and the different types of people who use Central Square."

Mark D. Levine in his *Working It Out: Crimewatch, Democracy, and Community Reconstruction in Cambridgeport* spells out very plainly the people's exuberant toughness: "The Cambridgeport/Central Square neighborhood, studied by Fellmen and Brandt in the 1960's was a traditional working class neighborhood in lifestyle. Residents lived near their jobs; many walked or took public transportation to work. Most were pleased with the local public and parochial schools. About two thirds attended church, about one-third Roman Catholic; half attended church at least once a month. They shopped locally and 44% walked to their doctor's and dentist's offices. Almost half had extended family within walking distance, one fourth on the same block or in the same buildings; and one third visited extended family members almost every day, one half at least once a week. One quarter contacted nearby friends every day; 61 percent got together with nearby friends at least once a week. While many did not know their neighbors well, in the words of one woman, they 'spend time talking while we garden, and of course, in emergencies.' Another said, 'The neighborhood is friendly without prying into your affairs. They're ready to help you when needed; people don't go into each others' houses, but talk outside.'"

If African Americans have been a part of Cambridge living since Colonial times, and they have, Central Square, the lower Port, and Kendall Square have been for generations a place they have been pleased to call home. Census figures clearly demonstrate the consistent black presence here. The earliest colonial figures show that in 1754 there were 56 blacks in Cambridge and in 1765 their numbers had increased to 90. After the Revolutionary War the figure dropped by a third, remaining at that level until 1850 when it just about doubled to 141. From this period the figures consistently rose so that Cambridge by the Civil War had 371 black citizens which made it the second largest African American community in Greater Boston; only the capital city of the state had more (2572). By 1910 the total black population for the Commonwealth had grown to 4707 with Boston and then Cambridge still the favorite place for African Americans to live.

In addition, Cambridge blacks had started, if in small numbers, to contribute to the political, educational, and religious culture of the city. Several examples of individuals who served their larger community are Milton S. Clarke who was the first African American elected to the Cambridge Common Council in 1870 (he was also reelected for a second two-year term); Clement G. Morgan who was elected to both the Common Council and the Board of Aldermen;

Patrick H. Raymond, Fire Chief, 1871–1878.

William H. Lewis who also served both on the Common Council and as a State legislator; Patrick H. Raymond who was the city's Fire Chief from 1871 through 1878 and was also editor of the *Cambridge Press* (1869-1890); Emery T. Morris who held for some years the position of deputy sealer of weights and measures; the Reverend J. Henry Duckrey who was appointed by Mayor McNamara a trustee of the Cambridge Public Library; and Maria Baldwin who taught and then served as head of the Agassiz Grammar School from 1882 to 1922. These people who represented but a single era of Cambridge's history are but

suggestions of the many other women and men who have served their city and continue to do so.

These fine individuals and their accomplishments cannot allow us to ignore the prejudice that most all African Americans have been subject to throughout the American experiment in democracy. For example, the harsh fact is that most African Americans in Cambridge were employed at menial work tasks. In 1900 they earned less than their white counterparts in the working class. Women, of course, almost always earned less than males in the 19th century (a situation still largely characteristic of the contemporary Cambridge work force.) Further, the types of jobs usually available to Cambridge African Americans were these: waiter, janitor, cook, laundress, carpenter, and clerk. Once again there was not that much of a dramatic improvement offered to the average working man and women during much of the 20th century.

A second major population group who have found a welcoming home in this section are the community's Hispanics. While the Spanish language is their familiar tongue, many also have become fluent in English. For the most part, and exclusive of the Spanish-speaking students at the city's various colleges, these Spanish speaking immigrants represent a new mix to Cambridge's population heritage.

In the 1970's they consisted of about 4,500 individuals, the majority of them having come from Puerto Rico and Cuba. While some hold white-collar positions, most are employed as blue-collar workers

Peter Podobry, one of the city's many street musicians and performers.

especially in factories. When surveyed by Susan E. Brown in 1973, most stated that they had come to Cambridge for three reasons: 1) The availability of jobs for those with few job skills at the time of their arrival, 2) the fact that they already had family and friends living here, and 3) because the city offered its citizens "a relatively quiet and peaceful environment in which to live." The Hispanic community has added an important and vital element to this area of the city, a place regarded for decades by many as the true center of Cambridge. Indeed, the Central Square area is where

over 40% of those who live in Cambridge dwell. Furthermore but not exclusively, it is here that they city's most recent immigrants—Haitians, Indians, West Indians—have come to find their first Cambridge home.

As the twentieth century ended, Central Square was in the midst of evolving changes once again. The city government is in favor of "improvements" to the area, developers have ready funds and have done a good share of work on preliminary plans towards these "improvements", and, finally, neighborhood groups and associations have been active in voicing concerns and offering suggestions regarding these "improvements." The final shape of the Square and what living there will mean, however, has not yet fully emerged.

Clearly one of the basic traits of Central Square for several generations has been the fact that it has been a family-oriented neighborhood. As Francis H. Duehay, a city councilor for 28 years put it: "I think that it is a place which is very representative of the entire city. The city is very diverse in terms of people who use the Square. There are many people there in low and moderate means, there is a commitment by the YMCA and the YWCA to affordable housing and they have built additions to their facilities so that people of low and moderate income will be able to live in or near Central Square. Central Square is attractive because of its ethnic restaurants, there is a homeless shelter for people who are alcoholic. There is, I think, a vitality to Central Square that is very representative of the urban, multicultural population." The people living here clearly like their reality of the Square and do not want to lose that characteristic in what ever changes eventually come. As one individual expressed it: "I hope it doesn't become yuppified, is what I hope. I hope it doesn't become slick, and that there are slick stores that come in and that all the nice little places and the family owned businesses leave. I hope that what happened to Harvard Square doesn't happen to Central Square. I hope big chains don't come in is what I hope. I would hope that we could make sure that there's a real good balance of that. And I wouldn't want to out price the market; I wouldn't want to make it so that people couldn't afford to be here."

It is at this stage that the chronicler must leave it—for now. The egg has cracked, something new and yet something old is about-to-be. As one of the Square's elder residents has said, "This was quite a square in its day!" We can only hope that one hundred years from now some other elder resident can also exclaim, "This was quite a Square in its day!"

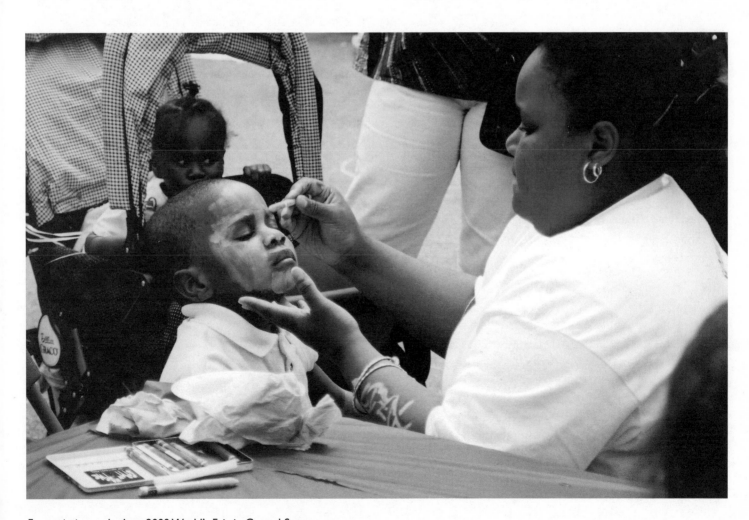

Face painting at the June 2000 World's Fair in Central Square.

FURTHER READING

BOYER, SARAH. *Crossroads: Stories of Central Square.* Cambridge Historical Commission, 2001.

BRIGHAM, COURTNEY CLAIRE. "Feast Celebrates Italian Culture," *The Cambridge Tab* (September 9–15, 1997) 11.

BROWN, SUSAN E. *The Hispano Population of Cambridge: a Research Report.* Brown, 1973.

BULFINCH, ELLEN SUSAN. "The Tudor House at Fresh Pond," *Cambridge Historical Society Proceeding,* 3 (1908) 100–109.

[Cambridge Black Citzens. Short Biographies of Twenty Famous Blacks Who Lived in Cambridge.] No publisher, no date. Available from the Visitor Information Booth, Harvard Square.

CAMPBELL ROBERT. *Cityscapes of Boston: An American City Through Time.* Photographs by Peter Vanderwarker. Boston: Houghton Mifflin, 1992.

CHOI, SHEILA. (1993). *Public Space in Central Square.* Unpublished thesis, Graduate School of Design, Harvard University, Cambridge, MA, 1993.

DANIELS, JOHN. *In Freedom's Birthplace.* NY: Arno Press and The New York Times, 1969.

DAUGHTERS OF THE AMERICAN REVOLUTION. *An Historic Guide to Cambridge.* Cambridge, MA: Hannah Winthrop Chapter, National Society, Daughters of the American Revolution, 1907.

DORMAN, FRANKLIN A. "Antislavery on the Banks of the Charles," *Harvard Divinity Bulletin,* 20 (Spring 1990) 12–14, 23–24.

———. *Twenty Families of Color in Massachusetts: 1742–1998.* Boston, MA: New England Historic Genealogical Society, 1998.

EDELMAN, JOSH. "December 3: Kendall's Other Side," *The Harvard Independent,* 29, (December 3, 1998) 5.

Ethnic Minorities in Cambridge, vol. one, *The Portuguese,* Dept of Planning and Development, City of Cambridge, 1972.

GLAZER, NATHAN. "The New Harvard Square—There's No Square There," *The Boston Sunday Globe* (April 17, 1988) B2.

GOODE, DAVID R. *The Quota Question.* Thesis for the Master of Arts in Urban and Environmental Policy, Tufts University, 1994.

GRAS, N. S. B. *Harvard Co-operative Society Past and Present 1882–1942.* Cambridge, MA: Harvard University Press, 1942.

HACHIKIAN, KEN. "Harvard Square Looking Backward," *The Havard Independent,* 31 (October 28, 2000) 11.

HARRIS, JOHN. *The Boston Globe Historic Walks in Cambridge.* Chester, CT: The Globe Pequot Press, 1986.

HOWE, LOIS LILLEY, "Memories of Nineteenth-Century Cambridge," *Cambridge Historical Society Proceedings,* 34 (1951–1952) 59–76.

In Our Own Words: Stories of North Cambridge, Massachusetts, 1900–1960 / as told to Sarah Boyer. City of Cambridge and the North Cambridge Stabilization Committee, 1997.

KENT, GEORGE H. "Merchants of Old Cambridge in the Early Days," *Cambridge Historical Society Proceedings* 8 (1913) 30–40.

LILLIE, RUPERT B. "The Gardens and Homes of the Loyalists," *Cambridge Historical Society Proceedings,* 26 (1940) 49–62.

McFADDEN, JAMES P. "Cambridge Street: Memorial to City's Past," *The Harvard Crimson,* 208 (May 6, 1998) 1, 5.

MAGUIRE, KEN. "Healing Saints Enliven Streets in Italian Festival," *The Cambridge Chronicle* (September 17, 1998) 7.

MAYCOCK, SUSAN E. *East Cambridge.* Cambridge, MA: MIT Press, 1988.

MERRILL, ESTELLE M. H., ED. *Cambridge Sketches by Cambridge Authors.* Cambridge, MA: Cambridge Young Women's Christian Association, 1896.

MORGENROTH, LYNDA. "The Feasts of East Cambridge," *Yankee,* 58 (May 1994) 72–83, 131–133.

———. "What Happened to the Old Harvard Square?" *The Boston Globe Calendar,* 23 (December 18, 1997) 8–11.

O'MALLEY, THOMAS F. "Old North Cambridge," *Cambridge Historical Society Proceedings,* 20 (1927–1929) 125–135.

PINCK, JOAN BRAVERMAN. "College in a Square," *The Harvard Gazette* (June 1, 1990) 8.

PLECK, ELIZABETH HAFKIN. *Black Migration and Poverty: Boston 1865–1900.* NY: Academic Press, 1979.

RETTIG, ROBERT BELL. *Guide to Cambridge Architecture: Ten Walking Tours.* Cambridge, MA: MIT, 1969.

RODGERS, PATRICIA AND CHARLES SULLIVAN AND THE STAFF OF THE CAMBRIDGE HISTORICAL COMMISSION. *A Photographic History of Cambridge.* Cambridge, MA: MIT, 1984.

ROSENBLATT, ROGER. *Coming Apart: A Memoir of the Harvard Wars of 1969.* Boston: Little, Brown, 1997.

SAMMARCO, ANTHONY MITCHELL. *Images of America: Cambridge.* Charleston, SC: Arcadia, 1999.

Voices of Central Square. The Central Square Project, Isabel and Susan's Class, 5th/6th Grade, Fayerweather Street School, June 1996.

WOOD, JOHN W. "Cambridgeport, A Brief History," *Cambridge Historical Society Proceedings,* 35 (1953–1954) 79–89.

———. "Some Aspects of the East Cambridge Story," *Cambridge Historical Society Proceedings,* 36 (1955–1956) 93–105.

WOODS, ROBERT A. AND ALBERT J. KENNEDY. *The Zone of Emergence: Observations of the Lower Middle and Upper Middle Working Class Communities of Boston, 1905–1914.* Second Edition. Cambridge, MA: M.I.T., 1969.

The Cooper-Frost-Austin House, the oldest "complete" house in Cambridge. The right half was built about 1690; the left half about 1720.

CHAPTER ELEVEN

Montage of Cambridge Living

THE SEVENTEENTH CENTURY

It is February 23, 1641 and the Reverend Thomas Shepard is writing in his journal "At night after lecture I saw my vileness and saw I was not to seek myself in prayer, and hence the Lord made me to see nothing but shame to belong to me. And hence praying for the church I asked my soul if those prayers should be heard, and I found an answer: the Lord will hear the prayers of the humble, will not despise their cry—which sweetly cheered my heart..."

A small white dove pigeon crashes against the window of Old Harvard Hall... two students take it cooing and bristling to their chamber for the night... in the morning they give it freedom...

A winter Sabbath at Fresh Pond... two boys skating happily... then the ice cracks... Death takes them...

Faith killing the snake.

Mr. Shepard, the Church's pastor, instructing his flock "that the visible church of God on earth, especially in the times of the gospel, is the kingdom of heaven upon earth. For look upon the face of the whole earth; there you may see the kingdoms of men, and the kingdom of Satan, sin, and death, which the apostle saith (Rom. v.) reigneth over all men; here is only the kingdom of heaven upon earth, viz., in the visible church" which shall "by little and little, beat down all other kingdoms of the world"…

On a winter's fast day Samuel Gibson and his gang enjoy a delicious turkey supper after having first filched the poor turkey from a neighbor's farm…

It's September 15, 1648 and the first sermon of the third session of the Synod that is to produce the Cambridge Platform. Suddenly a snake slips into the pulpit which results in mad commotion until "a man of much faith" pins it with his foot and staff and kills it dead…

While helping to build the "new" College John Francis has his right leg broken above the ankle by a "peece" falling upon him…

Goodwives are reading The Tenth Muse OR Severall Poems, compiled with great variety of Wit and Learning, full of delight… by a Gentlewoman in these parts.

A Godly Puritan using his chamber-pot in bed discovers that its bottom has come out and that all the water is running upon him…

And there was the Charles, the Charles, always moving by it…

THE EIGHTEENTH CENTURY

The *Boston News Letter,* February 25, 1716–7: "Besides several snows, we had a great one on Monday the 18th current, and on Wednesday the 20th, it began to snow about noon and continued snowing till Friday the 22nd, so that the snow lies in some parts of the streets about six foot high." People call it an "extraordinary" snow storm …

"We implore Thee, O King of kings," the Reverend East Apthorp is praying on Thursday, October 15, 1761, at the dedication of Christ Church, "to crown with the blessings of heaven and earth our most Gracious Sovereign Lord, George the Third, by Thy grace King of Great Britain and Ireland and of all the dominions thereunto belonging" …

Richard Lechmere's slave Joseph with financial help from his friends sues The Master for keeping him in slavery …

From the Orderly Book of General John Glover: "The General does not mean to Discourage the Practice of bathing while the weather is warm enough to continue it. But he expressly forbids any Person doing it at or near the Bridge in Cambridge, where it has been observed and complained of that many men lost to all sense of Decency and Common Modesty are Running about Naked upon the bridge while Passengers and even ladies of the First Fashion in the Neighborhood are passing over it as if they meant to glory in their Shame" …

"O Lord our Heavenly Father, high and mighty, King of kings," Colonel Palfrey is praying on Sunday, December 31, 1775, at the New Year's Eve Service at Christ Church for General and Mrs. Washington, "we beseech Thee to look down with mercy upon his Majesty George the Third. Open his eyes and enlighten his understanding … that he may purse the true interest of the people … We also pray Thee to bless our provincial assemblies, magistrates, and all in subordinate places of power and trust. Be with thy servant the Commander-in-chief of the American forces. Afford him thy presence in all his undertakings" …

Timothy Fuller, Jr. is writing in his diary for November 5, 1798: "The day appointed by law for choosing a member of Congress. The contest between Federalists and Jacobins is violent. In Cambridge the candidates are Timothy Bigelow of Groton, Federal, and J. B. Varnum, Jacobin. The former had 85 votes, the latter 119. As soon as that issue was announced, a number of students who were present expressed their disapprobation by a general hiss! The infatuated dupes of Jacobinic fraud bawled aloud to drive all students, without distinction, from the house. Pierce and myself, who had neither hissed nor made the least disturbance, were shouldered out with the rest" …

A wintry night and good Doctor Holmes, the Rev. Abiel Holmes, goes to his study's frosty window, draws some stars on its surface and then writes "Per Aspera ad Astra"…

And there was the Charles, the Charles, always moving by it…

Rev. Abiel Holmes drawing stars.

THE NINETEENTH CENTURY

As the sun rises Concord farmers and with their sons atop wagons loaded with potatoes, eggs, and butter ride past the College on their way to market…

Old Cambridge, October 25, 1827: "Stayed at home all the morning quietly sewing, and for a wonder without visitors. Thursday, Nov. 27. I am still deeply engaged in Scott's 'Life of Bonaparte'—I have got my hero out of Russia after the fatal and wicked campaign—and most truly do I agree with Mr. Channing's excellent review of his character—a cold-hearted, self wretch, sacrificing everything dear and precious to his vain and unprincipled ambition. I can have no sympathy with such a monster… Thursday, Dec. 27.—A snowstorm which disappointed the three Ladies of going into town. This morning Anna made some apple pyes for the first time—we have not been very agreeable to-day. I have had a cold and been rather cross… Anna desires me to tell you she has got a new gown, and expects to look sublime in it. It is a red striped calico morning gown"…

The first day of 1828. Frederic Tudor and a friend walk to Fresh Pond, skate for an hour, and then lunch at the Fresh Pond House on delicious pickerel. As they eat they watch several men fishing through the ice…

The sport of Winter Punging… five or six kids riding and shouting on the sideboards of the horse drawn sleighs of S. S. Pierce and Sawin's Express…

Mrs. Lyman describes Fresh Pond in 1865: "The visit was on a lovely Autumn day. The trees were just changing color. The grass was still green and fresh. The pond was as blue as ever and as beautiful, and the natural repose of the place was over all"…

Small Cambridge boys and small Charlestown boys shouting "Pointer" "Port Chuck" "Charlestown Pig"…

The lamp-lighter coming up the street with his ladder on his shoulder, stopping at the first post, putting the ladder against it, climbing it to light the lamp…

"Stubby" Child on a June day in the 1860's saunters over to the home of his next door neighbor, the Peabodys, and gives the lady of the house a bud from his beloved rose-garden…

See! There stroll some of the worthies… Henry Wadsworth Longfellow, Richard Henry Dana, William Dean Howells, Margaret Fuller, Thomas W. Higginson, William James…

In winter the conductors put straw for warmth between the two rows of facing bench seats on the Brattle Street horse cars… kids cuddling there… a lucky one finds a penny in the hay…

Harvard's President Charles William Eliot and his wife Grace regularly bicycling up Brattle Street during the breakfast hour…

Smiling from her throne… its the Queen of the May… with frizzed hair and a crown of daisies…

Sign: Try and Hit the Spittoon Please…

A tiresome Saturday morning chore: cleaning the kerosene oil lamp. One has to see that it has plenty of

Try and Hit the Spittoon Please.

oil, one has to trim the wick, and finally one has to clean the chimney which tends to cloud up from the smoke…

Plus… every once in a while shoveling out the accumulation beneath the seat of the outhouse…

Frank Kennedy's cookies in gaudy red cans with pictures of his very pretty daughters painted on them…

Some Cambridge birds: Green Heron, Black-crowned Night Heron, Yellow-billed Cuckoo, Northern Flicker, Chimney Swift, Ruby-throated Hummingbird,

A two-seater Necessary.

Least Flycatcher, Blue Jay, Bobolink, Cowbird, Baltimore Oriole, Purple Finch, American Goldfinch, Chipping, Song, Tree, and Barn Swallows, Indigo Bunting, Cedar Waxwing, Red-eyed, Warbling, and Yellow-throated Vireos, Yellow Warbler, Catbird, House Wren, American Robin, Bluebird…

From the journal of Charles Lane Hanson, Harvard undergraduate: "I think the custom of running up North Avenue in squads must be disagreeable to many of the citizens of quiet, civilized Cambridge. I don't imagine it is particularly pleasant for women to be on the lookout for twenty athletes running along in a body as if they meant to turn out for nothing or nobody.

Then there is another point that causes some unfavorable criticism. I mean the habit the boys have of wearing almost nothing. Besides being too meager for this climate, some of the costumes are hardly decent"…

At first by horse and wagon, then by truck, the iceman cometh…he sees the card in the window asking for 25 or 75 pounds of ice…with the cake of ice over his shoulder he goes to the kitchen and the oak ice box…outside, at the back of the wagon, the neighborhood kids wait his return, wait for ice chips to suck…

It's October 9, 1876 and Alexander Graham Bell in his Boston garret and Thomas A. Watson in an office of the Walworth Manufacturing Company in Cambridge are having the world's first telephone conversation…and so are born Ma Bell and the baby Bells, crank calls, telephones resembling Mickey Mouse…

The friendly horsecar conductor who knows you and is always happy to stop at your front door…

William H. Lewis, a graduate of Amherst College, and a student at the Harvard Law School, goes to a barber shop for a hair cut and is refused one because his skin is not white…

Going to Billings & Stover for a sarsaparilla soda…

William Brewster writing in his journal on May 9, 1893: "I stepped out into the garden. For the first half hour I heard only a Yellow Warbler, a Chippy, and Robins singing. But a little before 9 a.m. I added three birds to my list, an Oriole fluting in the horse chestnut

Some Cambridge birds near William Brewster's Observatory.

The Misses Palfrey's tricycle.

at the corner of Sparks Street, a Red-start singing in Mr. Hubbard's grounds, and a Lincoln's Finch in the garden"…

The tricycles of the Misses Palfrey which had flounces about their wheels so that no one might ever see their ankles…

And there was the Charles, the Charles, always moving by it…

Wearing his tall silk hat and carrying his rods and brushes Oenschlager, the chimney sweep, is walking up Sparks Street…

The reliable factory whistle of the Boston Woven Hose and Rubber Company blowing the fire alarms, signaling no school on wintry days, and the 9:30 nightly curfew...

Walking at Norton's Woods on Christmas Eve and seeing every window of Professor Norton's large white mansion sparkling with a flaming candle...

Standing next to a coal stove and dressing on winter mornings...

Nude boys diving into the Broad Canal for a summer swim...

Fly-catchers, sticky coiled strips hanging from the ceiling...

The children's Mass at St. Paul's on Christmas Day... pennies from Papa for the poor box... gazing at the creche in wonder...

Children running to see the soldiers marching down Harvey Street to the trains...

The first cat registered to vote in the city was Oliver Peirce, Independent...

Walking around in dark room with hands in the air groping for a pull chain... finally found... light...

Plucking chickens for two cents a chicken at Welch's chicken farm...

Hide 'n seek, red light, jack knives, leap frog, and statues...

Sledding on double-runners at Shady Hill...

A very young Tip O'Neill and the Barry's Corner gang liked to sit on the Barry family's front steps chatting on warm spring and summer evenings in the 1920's... when they stayed too late or made to much noise and didn't move after one warning from Old Man Barry, he'd fill a bucket with water...

A winter's delight... standing on a hot-air register with the coal and coke furnace going full blast...

Pigeons following Dick Canavan's horse drawn fish wagon along Kirkland Street and some scallywag shouting, "Hey, Dick, your fish stink!" and Dick shouting, "So does me arse!"...

Sitting on the curb waiting for the "hoky poky" man to clean the gutter...

Central Square... Wimpy's Hamburger with its 12 cent hamburger... Coolidge Cleansers, the Honey Bee Restaurant, Hunt's Drug, the B & D wallpaper store, Bunk's stationary store run by the two ladies, the Manhattan Supermarket with its lunch room and where a clerk waited on each customer, Kilfoy's Barroom and the Irish Whip... Central Square where every barbershop had a singing canary...

On the afternoon of July 1, 1921 at 3:10 the 240 foot high chimney of the old New England Glass Company

Swimming in Broad Canal.

topples to the ground. Those watching cheer and then run to get one of its 1,055,754 bricks as a souvenir ...

It's 1927, June, the Harvard Commencement, and the grads in white linen suits are laughing and talking while drinking illegal champagne, illegal because it is the Age of Prohibition: not far away a teenager from North Cambridge being paid 17 cents an hour by the University for cutting its grass and trimming its hedges feels his Irish temper boiling ... "Who the hell do these people think they are that the law means nothing to them?" ...

It's the great hurricane of 1938 ... twelve trees in the Common tip over, fall to the ground ... others lose limbs and branches ...

Brickyard Charlie chasing the kids swimming in the clay pit … frappes from Zahka's and penny candy from Bumgardners …

During the Second World War 14,237 citizens serve in the Armed Forces: 401 gave up their life for what they believed in and for what they hoped would be a better way for all of America's children …

At home their family and friends collect for the war effort 20,000 pounds of metal and scrap, 50,000 pounds of waste paper and magazines, 800,000 pounds of fats and grease, 800,000 pounds of old rubber and tires, 500,000 pounds of tin cans, and 15,000 pounds of silk stockings …

Books requested by Coop customers: *Stud in Love Again* (Stud Lonigan), *Brothers Carry Me Off* (Brothers Karamazov), *Scarlet Mouse* (Scaramouche), and *Away with the Breeze* (Gone with the Wind) …

Horses, lions, and elephants riding the train of "The Greatest Show on Earth" on its way to Boston Garden stopping for a bit near the brickyards of North Cambridge … and out come kids and grown ups for a look at these beautiful circus stars …

"May Party, May Party, rah, rah, rah" at Rindge Park with decorated bikes, carts, doll carriages, games, and eating lunch on the grass … the baseball rivalry between Rindge Park and Raymond Park … the "Twilight League" featuring such teams as the Cambridge Red Sox, the North Cambridge Knights of Columbus, and the Notre Dame A. A. … where the rule was that a long fly ball to left-center that bounced through one of the windows of Mrs. Bumgardner's house was an automatic home run …

Magazine Beach before it had its swimming pool … learning to swim summers in the Charles with

Two strikes and then a …

help from the Red Cross folks…and in winters learning how to ice skate on the Charles after the Metropolitan Police declare the ice safe…

"What's a Cambridge intellectual? It's somebody who sits on the floor drinking black coffee when there's a chair and cream in the room"…

At eighteen Joan Baez…with bare feet, bangs, guitar, and a good soprano voice singing folk songs about love and heartbreak at Club Mt. Auburn 47…later putting out with her friends her first record *Folksingers 'Round Harvard Square*…

The car you parked on Green Street gets stolen with the alarm on…

Little kids in May on an extra warm spring day and little kids in July on a very hot and humid summer day, some in just their underwear and some in just their skin, running with shouts of joy in and out of the spray of mist hidden in the garden of rocks before Harvard's Science Center…

And the big kids at MIT playing pranks: an MIT weather balloon suddenly inflating on the 46th yard line during a Harvard-Yale game…an MIT police vehicle with its lights flashing balanced majestically atop the Great Dome…

Oaks, sycamores, Japanese maples, elms…Harvard is home to 3,340 trees…and the City of Cambridge has 11,116 street trees…and then there are the trees in private yards and those at the Mt. Auburn Cemetery…

Cambridge living in novels and mysteries: Helen Howe's *We Happy Few;* Erich Segal's *Love Story;* John Kenneth Galbraith's *A Tenured Professor;* Alan Dershowitz's *The Advocate's Devil;* Irene Allen's *Quaker Silence;* Michael Blumenthal's *Weinstock Among the Dying;* Jane Harvard's *The Student Body;* George Weller's *Not to Eat, Not for Love;* Jane Langton's *The Memorial Hall Murder;* Pamela Thomas-Graham's *A Darker Shade of Crimson;* Susan Conant's *Bloodlines;* Alfred Alcorn's *Murder in the Museum of Man;* Emily Hiestand's *Angela the Upside-Down Girl;* and George Packer's *Central Square*…

Summer Sundays along the stretch of Memorial Drive closed to cars, strolling, roller blading, lazily biking…perhaps sitting with the family reading the paper, having a picnic, gabbing, debating politics, arguing the chances for the Red Sox to win two games in a row…maybe just being alone thinking or listening to music…maybe just being with someone special holding hands, laughing, kissing…but no matter why one is there certainly enjoying the sunlight on the Charles, the boats drifting along, the breeze in the leaves, the fresh air…

He sits at a table outside Au Bon Pain in Harvard Square waiting. On his head an old wide brimmed straw hat; between his teeth and lips a cigar; on the table a sign: Play the Chess Master. $2.00…

THE PIT!   THE PIT!   THE PIT!
THE PIT!   THE PIT!
THE BOOT!   THE BOOT!   THE BOOT!
THE BOOT!   THE BOOT!

It's the 1369 Coffee House where your 10th cup of "House Brew" is free and it's Rosie's Bakery for a Boom-Boom, a Chocolate Orgasm or a Snow Queen …

Your Ma calls as you're walking on Magazine street and tells you to get some milk for supper …

The third story window on the round building facing Harvard Square between J F Kennedy and Brattle Streets: Dewey, Cheetham & Howe …

The Political Window on Hilliard Street that pulls no punches: Republican Congress Record: 1) Killed Health Bill 2) Killed Campaign Finance Reform 3) Named DC Airport After Ronald Reagan …

Can you spare twenty-five cents?… Spare any change Sir, Ma'am?… Hel-lo Young Lady, You Look Gorgeous Today, how about helping the homeless by buying a copy of *Spare Change?*…

Pooh's house … at Harvard …

This is a test. Question: Using the sidewalk marks on the Massachusetts Avenue Bridge for your measuring unit, how many "smoots" are there between Boston and MIT?… Okay, a clue: & an ear!…

Music, Music, Music … and Singing … amplified and with loudspeakers … almost always on the inbound to Boston platform of the Harvard Square T

Enjoying a cappuccino at the 1369.

stop … sometimes just a violin, guitar, flute, or a sax, and sometimes a combo—a trumpet and accordion, an electric organ and a trombone … rock, folk, classical, jazz, original compositions …

Donuts, coffee, and gossip with the regulars at Verna's …

Riding the 69 bus along Cambridge Street to the courthouse … a phone starts ringing …

Women police, women fire fighters, women T drivers, women taxi drivers …

Recycling programs, non-smoking areas in restaurants, no smoking in public buildings, bike paths in the streets, jogging, aerobics …

A siren wails as a police car speeds through Central Square, then Harvard Square, and up Mass Ave … It stops abruptly, its doors fly open, its officers burst out … on the sidewalk another officer struggles with an older man … after the three have subdued him they find his gun in the gutter …

Art object on Massachusetts Ave with this sign: Paul Richard, Untitled 1998, Steel and Paint, 16 x 16 x 87, Special Thanks to the City of Cambridge …

Summer Sundays … at Central Square and at the Charles Square … Farmer's Markets … corn, tomatoes, organic vegetables, baked goods … Come visit and support your local farmers …

Festivals: The River Festival with its reggae, jazz, big-band, Caribbean, African, Latin, traditional, and Gospel music, and its folk, dance, children's stages … The Festival of Saints Cosmas and Damian, begun in 1926 by immigrants from Gaeta, Italy with its healing service, carnival, games, ethnic foods, and its grand parade of the saints winding through the streets of East Cambridge … Oktoberfest at Harvard Square when 200 merchants and artisans take their wares and crafts to the streets along with music and musicians, children's rides, a beer garden, and a Puppet Piazza … The Head of the Charles Regatta which attracts about 5,000 women and men from 250 clubs, colleges, and universities from many countries to row the Charles each autumn …

Brother Blue and his wife Ruth …

The Festival of Saints Cosmas and Damian.

Fresh Pond: yesterday and today.

On the back of T shirts worn by employees of Tealuxe: The Only Legal Pot in Harvard Square...

Standing in the hubbub of Central Square and the phone rings...

It's a Shrove Tuesday evening at Christ Church and after the meal of pancakes, sausages, and apple sauce they are burning palms for Ash Wednesday... suddenly the smoke sets off the fire alarm... when the fire fighters arrive all they have to do is eat some of the freshly made apple sauce. Says one of them, "No problem. We were all a little bored anyway"...

Out of nowhere it seemed to come... a red granite bench, two feet wide and two feet deep and weighing 400 pounds... here on the shores of Fresh pond... with a chiseled inscription from *Orlando* by Virginia Woolf saying "I should lie at peace here with only the sky above"... So come, sit, rest on this bench... and meditate on Cambridge, her people, their history...

And there is the Charles, the Charles, always moving by it...

FURTHER READINGS

ABBOTT, ELEANOR HALLOWELL. *Being Little in Cambridge, When Everyone Else Was Big.* NY: Appleton-Century, 1936.

EMERTON, EPHRAIM. "Recollections of Sixty Years in Cambridge," *Cambridge Historical Society Proceedings,* 20 (1927–1929) 53–59.

FENN, DAN HUNTINGTON. "Let us Remember: A Cambridge Boyhood," *Cambridge Historical Society Proceedings,* 44 (1976–1979,) 9–27.

HOWE, LOIS LILLEY. "Memories of Nineteenth-Century Cambridge," *Cambridge Historical Society Proceedings,* 34 (1951–1952) 59–76.

In Our Own Words: Stories of North Cambridge, Massachusetts, 1900–1960 / as told to Sarah Boyer. City of Cambridge and the North Cambridge Stabilization Committee, 1997.

NORTON, CHARLES ELIOT. "Reminiscences of Old Cambridge," *Cambridge Historical Society Proceedings,* 1 (1906) 11–23.

O'NEILL, TIP. *Man of the House: the Life and Political Memoirs of Speaker Tip O'Neill.* With William Novak. NY: Random House, 1987.

SCHLESINGER, MARIAN CANNON. *Snatched from Oblivion: A Cambridge Memoir.* Boston: Little, Brown, 1979.

SQUIER, DOROTHY. *Treasured Memories of Cambridge.* Cambridge, Ma.: Cambridge Public Library, 1993.

Voices of Central Square. The Central Square Project, Isabel and Susan's Class, 5th/6th Grade, Fayerweather Street School, June 1996.

Index